Educational Audiology:
Hearing and Speech Management

Frederick S. Berg, Ph.D.

Department of Communicative Disorders
Utah State University
Logan, Utah

GRUNE & STRATTON
A Subsidiary of Harcourt Brace Jovanovich, Publishers
New York   San Francisco   London

Library of Congress Cataloging in Publication Data

Berg, Frederick S
    Educational audiology.

    Bibliography: p.
    Includes index.
    1. Deaf—Means of communication. 2. Deaf—Education.
3. Children, Deaf.   I. Title. [DNLM: 1. Hearing
disorders—In infancy and childhood.   2. Hearing disorders—Rehabilitation.   3. Speech therapy—In infancy
and childhood.   4. Education, Special.   WV270 B493e]
HV2471.B46   362.4'2   76-43011
ISBN 0-8089-0973-8

©1976 by Grune & Stratton, Inc.

Grune & Stratton, Inc.
111 Fifth Avenue
New York, New York 10003

Distributed in the United Kingdom by
Academic Press, Inc. (London) Ltd.
24/28 Oval Road, London NW1

Library of Congress Catalog Number 76-43011
International Standard Book Number 0-8089-0973-8
Printed in the United States of America

Contents

Preface

Since 1966 the United States Office of Education has supported the development of an educational audiology curriculum through the Department of Communicative Disorders at Utah State University in Logan. This prototype curriculum has been designed to fill a major gap in the clinical and educational management of the hard-of-hearing child. Such children may be defined as those with hearing impairments who can be trained through audition to identify most if not all of the prosodic and phonetic features of speech, at least under good listening conditions. Audiometrically, the hard-of-hearing child might have a mild to profound bilateral hearing loss. Perhaps fewer than 20 percent of such children have been receiving adequate supportive services in either schools for the deaf or the regular classes in which most are enrolled. Other groups of hard-of-hearing children include youngsters with slight bilateral hearing losses or varying degrees of unilateral hearing loss, both conditions being communicative handicaps.

This book is organized around a major educational audiology model of *areas affected by hearing loss*. This model encompasses the total characteristics and needs of the hard-of-hearing child, including basic, communication, and end-product variables. The factors of speech and listening or speech perception are located at the focal point of these variables. Listening is defined as the perception of speech by use of audition, vision, and/or a combination of auditory and visual clues. Every child with a unilateral or bilateral hearing loss has a listening problem under one or more communication situations. Children with moderate, severe, and profound bilateral losses characteristically also have defective speech. The book focuses mainly upon children with both listening and speech problems, whether enrolled in special classes for the hearing impaired or in regular classrooms of the nation's school systems. However its contents also give attention to groups of hard-of-hearing children with less serious communicative handicaps.

This book incorporates eight chapters of practical information, which initially focus on basic considerations and thereafter on hearing and speech management and on models of delivery of services at infant and preschool, elementary and secondary, and university levels of programming. The first chapter defines the hard-of-hearing child and details the educational audiology curriculum. In the second chapter, audiometry, sound spectrography, and the methods of communication used in the management of the hearing impaired are related to the educational audiological approach. These two chapters include important sections on the audiogram, the auditory area and speech signal, vocal tract phenomena including prosodic and phonetic features, listening considerations and conditions, and visual communication technology. The third chapter describes types of auditory trainers and hearing aids, with major emphasis on wireless systems of amplification and comparative analysis. The process of amplification, common problems with hearing aids, trouble shooting, and the selection of aids for children are also discussed.

Chapters 4 and 5 describe audiological and communication programming for infants and preschoolers and for school-age children respectively. Sections of these chapters deal with early identification of hearing loss, differential diagnosis, and the early Swedish and American contributions to infant programming. They also encompass types of school programs, comparison of communication methods, prosodic and phonetic notations, and features and guidelines related to progressive programs of auditory training, speech instruction, and visual communication training. Drawings of scenes and dialogues of exemplary auditory training demonstrations are included.

Chapters 6 and 7 document many of the technological developments in speech instruction and listening training. In chapter 6, speech evaluation, perceptual learning of sensory clues, shaping and refinement of utterances, and transfer and generalization of corrected productions are described. A major section of this chapter also reviews many of the promising electrovisual speech aids, including the Video Articulator and an innovative speech program developed by the author. Other related topics include serial and paired associate learning, precision teaching and the daily behavior chart, target formats, criteria for termination of training, and clinical research studies. The listening technology of chapter 7 is girded by descriptions of operant conditioning, behavior engineering, and instructional media. An examination of the early studies of auditory training is followed by a look at some significant contributions to programming made during the last decade, including an auditory training program developed by the author.

The eighth chapter concentrates on supportive services for the hard of hearing. It describes national goals and commitments, professional organizational input, exemplary models of delivery of services, mainstreaming and cascading innovations, aural rehabilitation roles in the regular schools, and implications of impedance audiometry. The tasks and responsibilities of the school audiologist and the hearing clinician are described, as are guidelines for aural–oral programs for the hearing impaired.

The book provides extensive text material for basic and advanced courses in communicative disorders. It should be a valuable guidebook for the audiologist, speech pathologist, or educator of the hearing impaired. It also provides useful reference information to the related disciplines of special education, otology and pediatrics, psychology, and elementary and secondary education. It is anticipated that this volume will contribute to a needed acceleration of audiological and educational services for hard-of-hearing children in special and in regular classes.

The following publishers, copyright holders, organizations, and agencies have kindly given permission to use quoted materials, tables, figures, scripts, and programs: Acta Oto-Laryngologica, Alexander Graham Bell Association for the Deaf, Amera Incorporated, American Electromedics Corporation, Arizona State University, Basic Education Computers Incorporated, Bill Wilkerson Hearing and Speech Center, Bell Helicopter Company, Bell Telephone Laboratories, Central Institute for the Deaf, Clarke School for the Deaf, Colorado State University, Ekstein Brothers, Electronic Futures Incorporated, Federal City College, Fontbonne College, Gallaudet College, H.C. Electronics, Institute of Logopedics, Mayo Clinic, Oregon School for the Deaf, Porter Memorial Hospital, Quan Tech Industries, Royal Institute of Technology, San Diego State University, St. Joseph Institute for the Deaf, The Columbia Dispatch, University of Alabama of Birmingham, University of Arizona, University of Illinois at Urbanna-Champaign, University of Indiana Medical Center, University of Iowa, University of Minnesota, Unitron Industries LTD, Utah State University, Voice Identification Incorporated, Western Pennsylvania School for the Deaf, and Willie Ross School for the Deaf.

Dr. Gordon Holloway of Minot State College and Dr. Mark Ross of the University of Connecticut have assisted the author with the preparation and editing of the book: Dr. Ross has been kind enough to write the forward to the book. Deep appreciation is offered to my family for their support throughout this major undertaking.

Foreword

The recent emphasis in mainstreaming the "special child" has been bringing into focus the plight of the hard of hearing child. Neither "deaf" nor "hearing", this child has often been conceptualized and educationally treated as one or the other, to his detriment in both instances. Our recent concern for the hard of hearing child, both in his own right, and as part of a larger group of "special children", has been anticipated by Dr. Berg for many years. His previous book, "The Hard of Hearing Child", exemplifies his long-standing professional commitment to these children. In the very title of the present book, "Educational Audiology", Dr. Berg has again shown that he has anticipated and helped stimulate the major therapeutic focus appropriate for the hard of hearing child. Indeed, one can hardly use the term "educational audiology" without acknowledging his many professional contributions to the field.

In addition to a comprehensive survey of the literature, Dr. Berg has included in this book much of his own work never before published. He presents his own carefully organized methods of collecting therapeutic data, particularly in regards to speech and listening training. In this, to my knowledge, he has no competitiors; no one else has been looking at the communication skills of the hard of hearing child in the same careful manner. No one else is providing us with a longitudinally organized sequence of clinical and research endeavors in the area. As one surveys the literature on the hard of hearing child, and observes the fragmented, unsystematic, uncoordinated and unsequenced pot-pouri of clinical reports and studies, one can appreciate and put in perspective Dr. Berg's many contributions.

One of the points made by Dr. Berg deserves special emphasis, and that is the number of potentially hard of hearing children now found in schools for the deaf. The intent is not in any way to demean, belittle, or express any negative feelings toward "deaf" children, their needs, and their right to secure the best therapeutic services we can offer them. He is simply expressing the view that we owe our hearing-impaired children the obligation to exploit residual hearing to its maximum. In doing this, we *will* find that many of them can develop speech and language primarily through an auditory mode, and that they will be able to deal with the larger society as hard of hearing rather than deaf individuals. Is this beneficial? Does functioning as a hard of hearing rather than a deaf person offer any significant advantages to the hearing-impaired person (with this latter term being used in a generic sense)? I think it does; Dr. Berg thinks it does.

The evidence on the relative speech, language, academic and socioeconomic status of hard of hearing and deaf individuals supports our mutual beliefs. The information in this book will assist the "educational audiologist" to increase the number of hearing-impaired people who can function as hard of hearing and will help them raise their communicative performance to higher levels. Dr. Berg is to be commended for his efforts in their behalf.

Mark Ross, Ph. D.

Professor-Audiology
Department of Speech
University of Connecticut

1

Hearing Impairment, the Hard-of-Hearing Child, and Educational Audiology

PREVALENCE AND DEFINITION

The prevalence of hard-of-hearing and deaf children and youths in the United States may be derived from data of a recent national survey (Willeford, 1971) and from a demographic study from Gallaudet College (1971). In the former study careful audiometric testing in specially constructed mobile units was conducted in the regular schools of this country. Table 1 presents pertinent data on the 38,568 sample of males and females in grades 1 through 12. It may be noted that 170+/1000 had unilateral (one ear) hearing loss and 41/1000 bilateral (two ears) impairment.

In all, 211+/1000 or about one in every five children suffers a hearing loss in one or both ears that is at least medically significant. Seven children per thousand have bilateral auditory insensitivity of mild to profound loss; they constitute the population usually referred to as those having educationally or socially significant losses. However a recent study in Elgin, Illinois, by Quigley and Thomure (1968) revealed that verbal and educational retardation exists among elementary and secondary school children with even slight bilateral auditory insensitivity. (See Table 5.)

A study by Giolas and Wark (1967) has shown that even children with unilateral hearing loss misunderstand speech more often than normally and suffer consequent feelings of embarrassment, annoyance,

1

Table 1
Number of School-Age Hard-of-Hearing
Children per 1000 Youngsters with Varying
Unilateral and Bilateral Hearing Impairment
in the United States

dB Loss	Unilateral	Bilateral	
11–25 (slight)	154+	34	
26–45 (mild)	13+	5	
46–100 (moderate- severe-profound)	3+	2	$\left. \begin{array}{c} \\ \\ \end{array} \right\} = 7/1000$

inadequacy, and helplessness. In the final analysis each child with any
degree of hearing loss might well be individually evaluated for auditory,
communicational, and educational deficit or skill, when such factors
can be isolated, in order to determine the impact of hearing loss upon
performance.

A Gallaudet demographic study indicated that an additional 42,000
hearing impaired individuals were enrolled in the special schools and
classes for the deaf and hard of hearing throughout the United States
(Demographic Study, 1971). Table 2 provides a breakdown by degree
of loss in the better of two impaired ears and by percentage of persons.
The data were available from an estimated 80 percent of these students.

It may be noted that 39.8 percent of these hearing impaired students had a loss of less than 85 dB. Looked at dimensionally, almost
40 percent of the youngsters in special programs for the hearing impaired has slight, mild, moderate, and severe losses, whereas the other
60 percent has more severe, profound, and total acoustic deficits.
Davis (1970) of the Central Institute for the Deaf suggests that 92 dB is
an appropriate statistical referent for a hypothetical dividing point
between the hard of hearing and the deaf. Suggestions by Bitter and

Table 2
Percentages of Children with Varying Degrees of
Hearing Loss among 33,542 Pupils Enrolled
in the Schools and Classes for the Hearing Impaired
in the United States during 1969–1970

DB Loss	Under 25	25–44	45–64	65–84	85–98	99+
Percentage	3.1	6.4	10.7	19.6	19.1	41.0

Mears (1973) that 56 dB, and by Vernon (1972) that even 45 dB be that referent are entirely out of line with audiological findings and auditory training data obtained during the past 20 years. As a consequence of longitudinal studies of auditory training with many preschool children with severe and profound hearing losses, Wedenberg (1967) concluded that as many as 80 percent of children in schools for the deaf in Sweden could have been educated as hard-of-hearing children.

Another criterion for differentiating the hard-of-hearing child from the deaf youngster is the manner in which each learns language (DiCarlo, 1968).[1] The hard-of-hearing child learns language in the usual way, that is, through the auditory processes, and in time he or she approximates normality in linguistic and academic competence provided that guidance, differential educational attention, stimulation, and tutoring are utilized from the very early years of life. The deaf child, in contrast, acquires language through nonauditory processes and may characteristically fall short of linguistic and academic normality, even when the same amount of time and effort is exerted.

The definition of the hard-of-hearing child may be clarified by comparing the oral communication and the language competencies of such youngsters with those of the normal-hearing child and the deaf youngster (Berg, 1973).

The normal-hearing child is a youngster who often can hear the entirety of speech, if it is not too faint or too far away. Figure 1 reveals this complete perception as a banana-shaped speech signal that is completely "packaged" into the large auditory or gray area which comprises the physical dimensions of normal hearing. Because the normal-hearing child often hears the entirety of what others say and what he himself says, at an early age he develops a refined skill in producing speech as well as basic mastery of the language.

The hard-of-hearing child hears varying amounts of the distinguishing features of speech. What he hears and perceives at a given moment depends upon a combination of one or more of the following factors: hearing insensitivity, faintness of sound, distance between speaker and listener, noise background, language deficiency, past experience, environmental unawareness, and corresponding lack of compensatory adjustments. Because the hard-of-hearing child often hears imperfectly or inconsistently, he characteristically speaks defectively,

---

[1] DiCarlo's statement was based in part upon his own study of 15 hard-of-hearing teenagers and young adults. By 15 years and 2 months to 19 years and 5 months, all of these children had achieved linguistic competence that was normal for their age levels. However their speech was typically defective. In a report of this investigation DiCarlo presented three audiograms: a composite of the group, an abrupt high tone loss averaging 80 dB in the better ear, and a gradual high tone loss averaging 87 dB in the better ear.

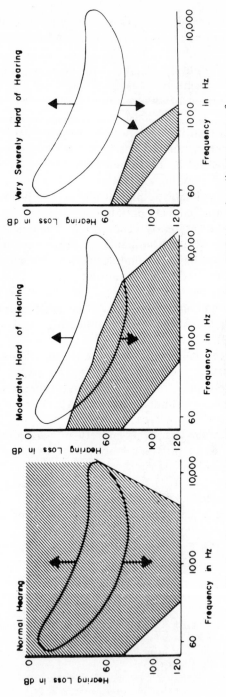

Fig. 1. Conversational speech signal (modified from Fant, 1959b) and auditory areas of a normal-hearing child and two hard-of-hearing children with bilateral impairment, one with a moderate loss and the other with a very severe loss.

misunderstands others, and learns vocabulary and sentence structure more slowly or to a lesser extent than does the normal-hearing child. Figure 1 illustrates the auditory areas of two hard-of-hearing children with bilateral impairment, one with moderate loss and the other with very severe loss. Before the availability of newer design and delivery concepts in hearing aids and techniques for evaluation, both of these children might have been classified as deaf, particularly the youngster with the very severe loss (Fellendorf, 1966). Now, the child with the moderate and severe loss, and even in many instances the youngster with very severe loss, functions to varying extents as a hard-of-hearing youngster (McConnell, 1968).

The deaf child typically has profound or total loss of auditory sensitivity and very little or no auditory perception. Under the most ideal listening and hearing aid conditions, he either does not hear the speech signal or perceives so little of it that audition may not serve as the primary sensory modality for the acquisition of spoken language or for the monitoring of speech.

Figure 2 shows three auditory areas of children who might be audiometrically classified as deaf. One area shows no response to amplified auditory stimuli at the extent of the audiometer. The other two auditory areas are those of children with very severe losses, the one relatively flat across the frequency range, and the other with no response at the mid and high speech frequencies (Wedenberg, 1954). The latter two auditory areas are even more restricted than that of the very severely hard-of-hearing child shown in Figure 1.

Two procedures are valuable in indicating whether or not a child with very severely impaired hearing can function as a hard-of-hearing child. One is to fit the child experimentally with a hearing aid, monitor its adjustment and use, and carefully stimulate the youngster with meaningful language learning situations over a period of three months. An accompanying initiation or increase in vocalization or verbalization under such a condition usually indicates the presence of functional residual hearing.

The second procedure becomes appropriate once the hearing-impaired child is about three years of age or can articulate several of the sounds of speech or some short words. The specialist then requires that the child repeat these sounds or words without looking but while wearing the hearing aid. The child who can consistently echo even some of these items can usually learn language and speech through hearing. The items should be chosen to be representative of the population of phonemes. Berg (1972) described such an experiment with a 22-year-old man who was functionally deaf but potentially hard of hearing.

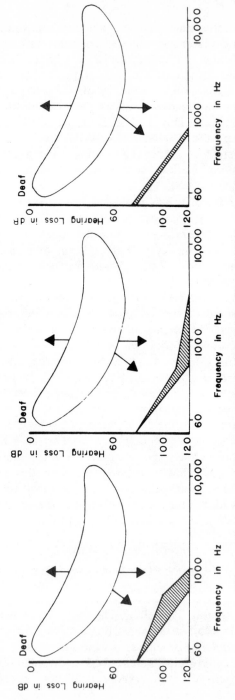

Fig. 2. Conversational speech signal (modified from Fant, 1959b) and auditory areas of three children who might be classified as audiometrically deaf.

Children who cannot perceive amplified speech at all or who perceive it insignificantly should be called deaf. All other hearing-impaired youngsters should now be called hard of hearing, notwithstanding whether they happen to be enrolled in a school for the deaf or in a regular classroom. All too often our use of the term *deaf* has led to dichotomous or polarized thinking, and the consequences in areas of diagnosis, planning, placement, and expectations have been unfortunate (Ross and Calvert, 1967). In other words this polarization of thought which we have mistakenly fostered has acted as a self-fulfilling prophecy. Through tradition, confused thinking, and bias we have called a child deaf who is hard of hearing, have often treated him as if he were deaf, have frequently expected him to function as a deaf child, and have looked the other way at his lack of achievement and adjustment (Fellendorf, 1966).

RELEVANCE OF HEARING

Hearing is perhaps our most versatile and valuable sense. Uniquely designed as a high fidelity stereo system, it personalizes or decodes much of the world in which we live. It reaches behind, under, above, around corners, through walls, and over hills, bringing in the crackling of a distant campfire, the bubbling of a nearby stream, the closing of a door, the message of a voice, the myriad of sound which identifies much of our experience.

Hearing (decoding) the sounds of his environment enables an individual to spin a web of language during his early childhood. At this time sensations from events and from word and sentence patterns become associated in a person's brain. The language web or code, as it is often called, provides a means for the individual to express ongoing experience and his ideas and feelings toward it. Note the two remarks made by one precocious preschooler (Berg, 1970b).

> My tummy hurts so much it's going to cry its heart out. He's a househopper. If he was on the pavement, he'd be called a pavementhopper. If he was on the grass, he'd be called a grasshopper like he usually is.

The child also learns to communicate verbally with other people. Interpersonal communication requires not only use of a common language and competence in decoding experience by use of hearing; it also depends on speaking ability. Fortunately, hearing also makes speech possible.

During the child's development, hearing provides him with a way of comparing how he is saying words with the way people around him say these same words. For example, the child may try to say *candy,* which he hears another family member say, and hear himself say *ay, dany, tandy,* and finally *candy,* as his speech improves over a span of years. After teaching him to articulate *candy* correctly, hearing informs the child whether or not he is continuing to say it correctly, and does so into and throughout adulthood.

It is only when the basics of language and speech are acquired by the child that he can go ahead and learn to read and write. The acquisition of skills in reading and writing is a process of transferring language meaning utilized in listening and speaking into written or printed symbols. The beginning years in school are designed in large part to aid the child in making this transfer so that he can communicate meanings by use of cursive and manuscript markings as well as by employing speech sounds.

Hearing also contributes to the manner in which a child plans his life, copes with problems, and organizes experience. It has a pervasive influence that affects personal adjustment, social competence, and vocational fulfillment. Hearing causes a child to perceive the world, conceptualize experience, describe events, and anticipate the future in a manner different from the way he would if hearing were absent or not utilized (Allen, 1969).

Hearing is possible because buried within each side of the head is a masterpiece of creation called the ear. The human ear, or hearing mechanism as it is sometimes called, is delicately arranged so that almost infinitesimally small amounts of sound can be faithfully received and recorded in the brain. It also has a built-in system to protect itself somewhat from unusually loud and unwanted stimuli.

MEDICINE AND SURGERY

Like other structures of the body, the ear is amenable to medical and/or surgical help. The family doctor or pediatrician, for example, can stop an earache and eliminate infection of the middle ear. The otolaryngologist can repair an eardrum that has burst and even rebuild a middle ear wasted away by prolonged infection. The preventive contribution of the public health nurse in innoculating against disease and teaching ear hygiene should also be recognized. In the process of these medical or health endeavors, certain cases of hearing impairment may be prevented, others reversed, and still others at least lessened in degree. Examples of cases of ear pathology and hearing loss and corresponding medical and surgical assistance are described in Table 3

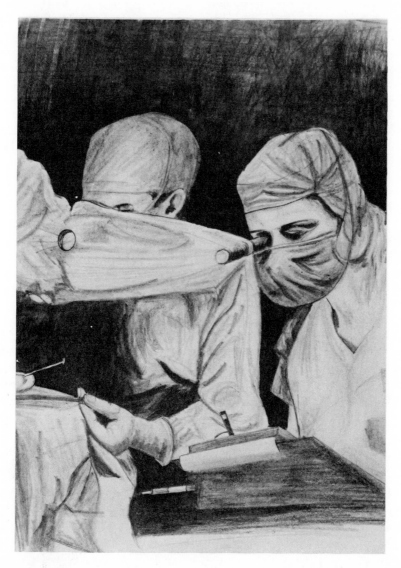

Fig. 3. Microsurgery being performed to restore partial or complete functioning to the human ear. (With permission of the Columbus Dispatch, Columbus, Ohio.)

Table 3
Possible Interrelationships Between Etiological, Pathological, Medical–Surgical, and Restorative Conditions of the Ear

Etiology	Condition or Pathology	Treatment	Range of Improvement in dB
Wax is secreted or object is inserted into ear canal.	Ear canal becomes plugged, impeding passage of air-conducted sound.	Specialist removes wax or obstruction.	20 dB loss originally; normal hearing afterwards.
Enlarged adenoids and allergies obstruct eustachian tube preventing ventilation of middle ear.	Middle ear becomes filled with fluid, impeding passage of air-conducted sound.	Specialist removes adenoids, lances eardrum, inserts tube to drain middle ear, prescribes a decongestant drug, and later repairs drum.	40 dB loss originally; possibly normal hearing afterwards.
Previously untreated condition progresses to become chronic infection of middle ear.	Ossicles erode and closteatomas (skaly growths) occur in middle ear, impeding passage of air conducted sound and threatening brain.	Specialist uses microsurgery to rebuild the middle ear ossicular system.	60 dB loss originally; possibly normal hearing afterwards.

Rubella occurs during first trimester of pregnancy.	Child is born with fragmented atrophy of cochlear structures with resulting interference in transfer of most sound energies into nerve impulses.	Specialist cannot help; innoculation of mother against rubella beforehand probably would have prevented embryological damage.	75 dB loss originally and permanently.
Dominant characteristic of hearing loss is transmitted genetically to child.	Child is born without high frequency cochlear structures and nerve fibers with resulting interference in transfer of many sound energies into nerve impulses.	Specialist cannot help; genetic counseling beforehand might have prevented conception of child.	85 dB loss originally and permanently.

11

(Hart, 1967). Etiology (cause), condition, treatment, and change in hearing loss when it occurs are considered.

It should be noted that medical and surgical repair of the hearing mechanism is limited to the outer and middle ear and can alleviate, to varying degrees, only conductive-type hearing loss. Inner ear and cochlear nerve problems are currently irreversible. The variety of pathological conditions associated with impairment of the delicate hearing mechanism far exceeds those exemplified above. Among other etiologies are blows to the head, unwise use of certain drugs, loud noise exposure, tumors, and diseases and genetic factors other than those referred to in the table. By far the most common types of hearing impairment are middle ear infections and associated complications. Permanent damage to the cochlea and cochlear nerve structures, with associated perceptive hearing loss, also occurs in many instances.

BASIC AUDIOLOGICAL CONSIDERATIONS

Normal hearing occurs when both ears are functioning well. For example, the child apparently perceives spaciousness and direction because of the following phenomena.

1. Sound travels from its source at a fixed speed and with continually decreasing intensity. It thus arrives at one ear earlier in time and with different intensity than it arrives at the other ear, provided that the two ears are at different distances from the sound source.
2. Nerve impulses similarly travel at a constant speed from the cochleas to the brain. Therefore the time and intensity differences of sound arriving at the ears are conveyed to the brain, where they are perceived as being different.
3. "Sound shadows" for certain energies (high frequencies) are created by the presence of the flaps of the outer ears. Thus sound coming from the front of the listener is localized from sound coming from the rear.
4. Small sound differences in high frequency energies seem to occur because of ridges and folds inside the ear flaps. Thus the listener can judge the height from which sound is coming.
5. Additional spatial and directional clues seem to be provided by small movements of the head.

This explanation of stereophonic (binaural) hearing is based on a combination of certainty, incomplete knowledge, and speculation.

The capabilities of hearing often are expressed by two terms: Hertz (Hz) and the decibel (dB). Hz refers to the frequency or vibration rate of a sound. A child with normal hearing, for example, can detect sound frequencies from an extremely low-pitched tone of 20 Hz to a very high-pitched tone of 15,000 Hz. By way of reference, telephone transmission ranges from only 500 to 4,000 Hz, and the piano keyboard from 27.5 to 4186 Hz. It should be remembered that a given sound, other than one produced electronically, includes a great many frequencies or vibration rates because sound sources, including the human vocal apparatus, produce complex rather than simple energy patterns.

Displacements occur at various positions along the length of the basilar membrane within the ear corresponding to the frequencies of an incoming sound. These displacements cannot be visualized directly. They may be similar to Fant's (1959a) spectrograms of synthetically produced vowels, illustrated in Figure 4. The energies (intensities) for a given speech sound can be seen to be concentrated in certain distinctive frequency regions. Both frequency (Hz) and intensity (dB) for each of many sounds is presented.

The decibel expresses a ratio between the intensity of loudness of a sound and that of a theoretical standard tone that is extremely faint. DB estimates of some nonspeech and speech stimuli are presented below (Berg, 1970c, p 288).

Sound	Intensity in dB
Watch tick	0–20
Pencil writing	20–30
Distant speech	30–40
Sink water	40–60
Nearby speech	60–80
Door slamming	80–100
Jet aircraft	100–160

An incoming speech signal of 60 dB, for example, is 1,000 times more intense than the standard faint tone. This relationship is figured on the basis of 10 times being equal to 20 dB.

Unfortunately, the ear is not always healthy or functioning correctly. It may not be working well within one or more of the outer, middle, inner, or nerve parts. Either a temporary or permanent hearing loss can be present. The hearing loss is definitely handicapping when both ears are impaired to a sufficient degree. Figure 5 clarifies the nature of a typical moderate hearing loss and its impact upon speech reception (Berg, 1971). Again the terms Hz and dB are applicable.

Curves A and B indicate thresholds of normal and reduced hearing sensitivity respectively. They show hearing sensitivity (dB) for each of seven test frequencies. Curve A reveals normal hearing and lies in the vicinity of 0 dB for each frequency. Curve B indicates that a 20 dB

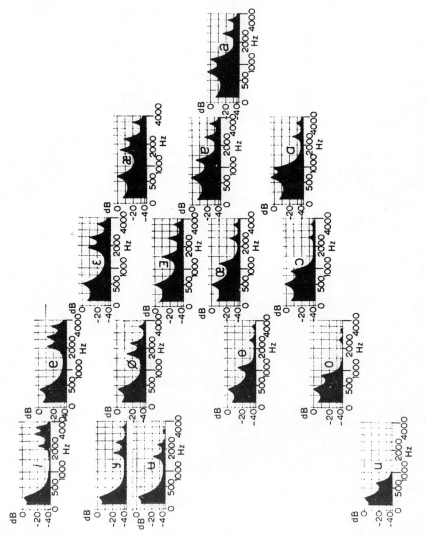

Fig. 4. Spectrograms of synthetically produced Swedish vowels (from Fant, 1959a).

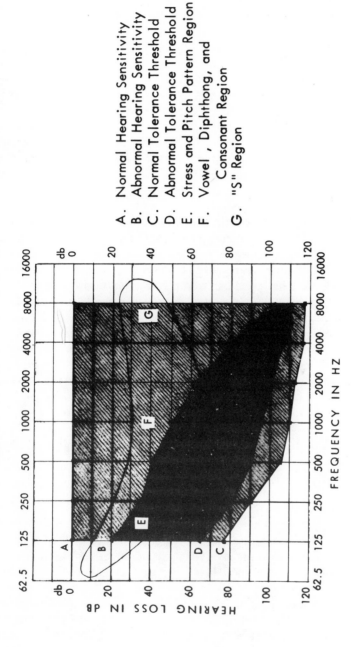

Fig. 5. Speech signal at conversational level and auditory area of an individual with a moderate hearing loss (modified from Fant, 1959b).

A. Normal Hearing Sensitivity
B. Abnormal Hearing Sensitivity
C. Normal Tolerance Threshold
D. Abnormal Tolerance Threshold
E. Stress and Pitch Pattern Region
F. Vowel, Diphthong, and
     Consonant Region
G. "S" Region

15

loss occurs at 125 Hz, 35 at 250, 40 at 500, 50 at 1,000, 65 at 2,000, 80 at 4,000, and 100 at 8,000. The average hearing loss, 53 dB, is obtained by adding auditory insensitivity values at 500, 1,000, and 2,000 Hz and then dividing by 3.

Curves C and D are thresholds of discomfort for these same ears. They correspond to intensity levels beyond which sound becomes intolerably loud to the listener. It can be seen that the threshold of discomfort for the normal ear above is 110 dB and for the abnormal ear 95 dB; both figures were arrived at by the averaging procedure described above.

The term *auditory area* is used to describe the region between the threshold of hearing sensitivity (floor) and the threshold of discomfort (lid). Curves A and C encompass a broad auditory area typical of normal hearing. Correspondingly, curves B and D include a restricted auditory area characteristic of hearing loss.

The banana-shaped insert divided into parts E, F, and G depicts frequency and intensity dimensions of the entire group of speech sounds. Area E shows energies conveying stress and pitch patterns, area F vowel, diphthong, and consonant regions, and area G the high frequency *s* region. The insert can be moved up and down with respect to curves A, B, C, and D depending on the overall intensity of incoming speech. Its current vertical position in the figure represents conversational level of speech at a typical listening distance (Fant, 1959b).

Bilateral hearing loss of the degree and slope shown by curve B permits input of much but not all of the speech signal. The situation improves as the speech source becomes louder (speaker raises voice level) or as the distance between speaker and listener becomes less. Typically, however, the restricted ear is receiving the incoming speech signal as shown in the figure. Consequently, the child characteristically is hard of hearing in that he does not perceive all of the distinguishing features of speech.

BASIC VARIABLES OF HEARING LOSS

The nature of hearing loss can be better understood by considering four variables: auditory insensitivity, intolerance for sudden loud sounds, auditory discrimination loss, and spatial and directional loss (Berg, 1971).

Auditory insensitivity (curve B above) means that sound is inaudible or less audible than desirable. For example, conversation may be completely or partially missed, or a doorbell may be unheard or barely

heard. Auditory insensitivity in just one ear is not nearly as handicapping as when both ears are involved. Sound on the side of the good ear
is at least being received and transmitted to both the right auditory cortex and the left auditory cortex of the brain for recognition and storage.
Auditory insensitivity occurs with hearing impairment in any one or
more parts of the ear.

Intolerance for sudden loud sounds (curve D above) is often characteristic of hearing loss, particularly of bilateral inner ear impairment.
This problem has led some hard-of-hearing children to reject the use of
a hearing aid or to adjust the volume control so that incoming sound is
faint.

Auditory discrimination loss (falling slope of curve B) is also
characteristic of bilateral inner ear impairment and of cochlear nerve
lesions as well. Under this condition environmental sounds or speech
stimuli are heard in a distorted or incomplete way. In mild form, when
the listener is untrained, phonetically similar words such as *track* and
trap sound alike. In its severe state, words as dissimilar as *pig* and *doll*
cannot be differentiated without training, nor can similar environmental
sounds like a doorbell and a telephone bell. This discrimination problem occurs because certain cochlear and/or retrocochlear (nerve) structures, especially those necessary for perception of vowels, diphthongs,
and consonants, are not functioning well.

Spatial and directional loss of hearing concerns inability or reduced
ability to perceive sound in depth (stereophonically) or to locate the
source of sound. It is characteristic of unilateral hearing impairment
(one ear "good," the other ear "poor") or of bilateral hearing loss
(both ears "poor") in which one ear is still "better" than the other.
Such a hearing impairment may be exemplified by the following types
of circumstances: (1) difficulty in tuning out the voice of one speaker
while trying to listen to that of another when both are competing for
attention; (2) perception of sound in a typical reverberant classroom as
sheer confusion; and (3) inability to recognize where in the house a rug
is being vacuumed, although a vacuuming sound is heard.

Instances of difficulty in localizing sound occur quite often among
individuals with unilateral hearing loss. An example from Giolas and
Wark (1967) follows.

> I came into the house, which was relatively quiet, and called to a
> friend, who said, "Yes." I said, "Where are you?" My friend re-
> plied, "Right here." I still could not locate her.

Such localization difficulty occurs most often in relatively noisy situations.

COMMUNICATION AND ADJUSTMENT DISORDERS

Hearing impairment among children is characterized by varying amounts and combinations of communicative and adjustment disorders. Immediately evident are language restriction, speech misunderstanding, and perhaps defective speech. Later on academic, social, and vocational restrictions also become apparent.

Language and Reading

Restricted language has its basis in deficiency in the oral understanding and use of words and sentences. This problem occurs because hearing loss deleteriously affects language learning opportunities during the formative years of life beginning with infancy. Environmental referents ordinarily seen or heard, or concomitant verbal descriptions, or both, become missed or misidentified. Both the event of a glass shattering and the comment "A glass fell and broke," for example, or *either* the shattering or the comment may not be sensed or perceived, and thus they will not be associated for language learning.

The severity of spoken language deficit is related characteristically to the seriousness of the auditory impairment. Examples of this deficit among six-year-old hard-of-hearing children with bilateral impairment are provided in Table 4.

Depending on the degree and type of hearing impairment, the hard-of-hearing child also may neither understand nor use figurative language patterns to the extent that his normal hearing peers do. These patterns include idioms, metaphors, similes, and personification, which are based on or make use of expressions that do not represent the literal or explicit meaning of the word or words. For example, the expressions "Don't shoot off your mouth" and "He's a ball of fire" may not be understood or used (Berg, 1970b).

Research substantiates the association between hearing loss and oral language restriction. Goetzinger (1962) noted that mild perceptive hearing impairment among 16 young children of Kansas City, Kansas, had slowed down their spoken language development up to one year. A Tennessee study by Young and McConnell (1957) revealed that each of 20 hard-of-hearing children was retarded in receptive spoken vocabulary in comparison with an individually matched normal-hearing child. These hard-of-hearing children were 8 to 14 years of age and had dB losses of 42 to 85.

Restricted oral language becomes restricted written or printed language as soon as the hard-of-hearing child faces the task of learning to write and read. For example, the child with a moderate or severe

Table 4

Expected Relationship Between Degree of Hearing Loss and
Language, Particularly Vocabulary, Development

Hearing Loss for Better Ear in dB	Characteristic Language Problem
26–40 (mild)	Only 1800–2100 of the 2500 normally spoken words are uttered. For example, the hard-of-hearing child may not say the word *binocular*, which is typically in the spoken vocabulary of the first grader.
41–70 (moderate and moderate-to-severe)	Only 1200–1800 of the above 2500 words are spoken by the hard of hearing child. For example, the *s* plural and possessive endings are also omitted, i.e., the child says "The boy hat" instead of "The boy's hat."
71–90 (severe)	Only 200–1200 of the 2500 words are spoken, and the plural and possessive form *s* is not used. In addition, unstressed words may be omitted. For example the hard-of-hearing first grader may say "Finished went home" instead of "When he was finished, he went home."

hearing impairment may simply have neither the vocabulary nor the morpho-syntactical structures to write at his grade level (Berg, 1970b). His compositions may tend to be characterized by a lack of generative, creative, and expansive forms with corresponding dearth of ideas and originality. Reading may also be subnormal at each of the stages of instruction described below (Pauls, 1958).

During the readiness period of preschool and kindergarten, the hard-of-hearing child typically lacks language facility in sharing experiences with others. Therefore he may not be advanced into first grade work on schedule.

At the first through third grade level, the hard-of-hearing child may evidence limitations in learning a sight vocabulary and in acquiring a phonetic word attack. In other words he may be retarded in becoming a reflexive and independent reader. In many instances, therefore, the hard-of-hearing child spends more than one year in the third grade.

Grades four through six frequently find the hard-of-hearing child frustrated in reading activities expected of intermediate-level youngsters. This is ordinarily a time for rapid expansion of reading vocabulary and forms, but the deprived spoken vocabulary of the child with hearing difficulties provides an unsuitable learning reference. The hard-of-hearing youngster therefore typically cannot cope well with the

Table 5
Difference Between Expected Performance and Actual Performance of
Hard-of-Hearing Children on Various Subtests of the Stanford Achievement Test

Hearing Threshold Level (Better Ear)	Number	IQ	Word Meaning	Paragraph Meaning	Language	Subtest Average
Less than 15 dB	59	105.14	-1.04	-0.47	-0.78	-0.73
15–26 dB	37	100.81	-1.40	-0.86	-1.16	-1.11
27–40 dB	6	103.50	-3.40	-1.78	-1.95	-2.31
41–55 dB	9	97.89	-3.84	-2.54	-2.93	-3.08
56–70 dB	5	92.40	-2.78	-2.20	-3.52	-2.78
Total Group	116	102.56	-1.66	-0.90	-1.30	-1.25

From Quigley and Thomure, 1968, p 12.

expanding subject matter of the interemediate grades. In other words he does not have the power and efficiency in all reading skills typical of the normal-hearing child of this grade level.

During the seventh through twelfth grades, the refinement period of reading, the hard-of-hearing child is often a frustrated youngster. His vocabulary deficit alone, for example, slows reflective and interpretive reading. He may find both informational and literary reading difficult. Socially promoted, he may fall continually further behind his normal-hearing peers.

A study in Elgin, Illinois, by Quigley and Thomure (1968) has substantiated the finding that reading deficit is widespread among hard-of-hearing children. Their data, shown in Table 5, reveal that verbal retardation exists among elementary and secondary school children with even slight auditory insensitivity.

The extreme in reading deficit based upon language retardation may be noted in the surveys of Boatner (1965) and McClure (1966), which encompassed 93 percent of students in schools for the deaf who were 16 years or older. Thirty percent of these students were functionally illiterate. Sixty percent read at grade level 5.3 or below. Only 5 percent read at a 10th grade level or better, and most of these hearing-impaired students either had normal hearing during oral language development or were hard of hearing. It should be mentioned that the minority of all children in schools for the deaf are functionally hard of hearing. The majority function as deaf children.

Speech Perception and Production Problems

Two other deficiencies arising from hearing impairment are speech misunderstanding and defective speech. A reason for grouping these difficulties together is that they are the receptive and expressive forms of what is called speech communication. In addition, they are often reciprocally related because deficiency in one is often accompanied by limitation in the other. However speech misunderstanding occurs more often than does defective speech, perhaps because a person can hear (monitor) his own speech from close by, whereas he must understand the speech of another person from a distance.

Speech misunderstanding occurs in some cases because the hard-of-hearing child is unfamiliar with the meaning of words or sentence forms being used by the speaker. Or the child may not be oriented to events or ideas being referred to in the message. Speech misunderstanding, however, need not stem from a linguistic or informational deficiency. It is often primarily a matter of just not hearing or auditorially perceiving the speaker well enough.

Speech misunderstanding happens particularly often in noisy speaker–listener situations and in instances in which the child is trying to "follow" group or classroom communications. In the former instance auditory clues are covered up; in the latter lipreading clues for decoding the message are difficult to obtain. The hard-of-hearing child simply cannot visually focus on one speaker after another quickly enough as the conversation shifts around. In addition, he is not familiar with the distinguishing lip positions and movements of all speakers.

The degree of speech misunderstanding exhibited by a particular hard-of-hearing child depends upon the amount of auditory insensitivity and upon auditory discrimination loss. With profound cochlear impairment, speech misunderstanding may be virtually complete unless lipreading clues are available to the child. Usually, however, speech misunderstanding amounts to missing only parts of conversation, prompting the child to ask "What did you say?"

Sometimes speech misunderstanding is so subtle that neither the child, his parents, nor his teacher realizes he has a hearing deficiency. This situation may result because the child may have never perceived auditorially any better than he does now. Or he may have forgotten what it was like to hear normally. Then again, he may realize he has the problem but not want others to know about it.

Speech misunderstanding is also more often than normal among children with unilateral hearing loss. Situations in which the speaker's gestures and face and/or lip movements cannot be clearly seen tend to be most handicapping. The following example is typical of misunderstanding in a quiet situation that involves distant listening.

> I was sitting on the porch and a woman drove up and stopped her car 10 to 15 yards away. She asked where my mother was and I could not understand her (Giolas and Wark, 1967).

In a classroom characterized by reverberation and background noise, speech misunderstanding among children with unilateral hearing loss is particularly distressing. A child might not even be able to understand another child immediately in front of him. The "head shadow" phenomenon associated with unilateral loss apparently precludes the squelching of these disturbances, an advantage of a binaural or stereophonic system.

Defective speech usually occurs among hard-of-hearing children with perceptive hearing loss. Mastery of speech articulation ordinarily occurs by eight years of age (Berg, 1970b). At this time a normal-hearing child can produce the 40 to 43 consonants, vowels, and diphthongs in words and sentences of everyday use.

Articulation problems are commonly found among hard-of-hearing children with auditory discrimination (perceptive) losses of varying degrees. The underlying inner ear or cochlear impairment prevents the child from accurately hearing the speech model provided by other people in his environment.

When a child hears imperfectly, he characteristically speaks defectively or inarticulately. For example, he may not hear the /s/ or perceive accurately the /ʃ/ and /tʃ/ sounds. Therefore he may omit the /s/ and distort the /ʃ/ and /tʃ/ in his own speech. In addition, he may not distinguish the subtle indications of nasalizing (producing through the nose) the /m/, /n/, and /ŋ/ or of not nasalizing (producing essentially through the mouth) the other 37 to 40 speech sounds. Correspondingly, he may misarticulate this important distinction in varying instances.

Table 6 summarizes the percentages of 15 types of speech errors exhibited by 15 hard-of-hearing teenagers (DiCarlo, 1968). Misarticulation of consonant blends (e.g. *str* in *string*) and of arresting consonants (e.g. /d/ in *red*) as well as nasalization of vowels occurred most often. The mean auditory insensitivity in the better ear for the group was 60 dB. The mean auditory discrimination loss for speech under quiet conditions was 34 percent. Remediation from early age had enabled these hard-of-hearing youngsters to develop normal sentence skills.

Table 6
Percentages of 15 Types of Speech Errors among
15 Hard-of-Hearing Teenagers

Type of Error	Percentage of Occurrence
1. Consonant omission	2.5
2. Regular consonant substitution	8.3
3. Breath–voice consonant substitution	7.9
4. Consonant blend	20.8
5. Abutting consonant	3.1
6. Releasing consonant	3.0
7. Arresting consonant	24.1
8. Nasalization of consonant	1.6
9. Substitution of vowel	9.0
10. Diphthong fractionization	8.3
11. Diphthongization of vowel	2.2
12. Neutralization of vowel	0.4
13. Nasalization of vowel	34.4
14. Abnormal rhythm (prosody)	8.0
15. Arythmic sentence	1.3

From Berg, 1970c, p 302.

The severity of defective speech seems to be closely correlated with the degree of hearing impairment (Berg, 1970c). Near the lower end of a continuum of defective speech might be children with auditory thresholds between 30 and 45 dB and associated perceptive hearing losses. At the upper end of this continuum might be children with auditory thresholds beyond 100 dB and with little or no speech perception. The number of speech errors uttered by a child with minimal hearing loss might be very few compared to the number typically employed by an individual with profound to total acoustic impairment. A review of some of the important findings from speech investigations among children in schools for the deaf may clarify this situation.

Hudgins and Numbers (1942) conducted a classical investigation of the speech of 8- to 20-year-old children in two oral schools for the deaf. They analyzed ten sentences orally read by each student to determine the frequency and types of errors made and their relationship to speech intelligibility. These children made a great many more errors of the types referred to in Table 6 than did hard-of-hearing children. They consistently misarticulated consonants and vowels and distorted stress and melodic patterns. Correspondingly, many of the sentences uttered were unintelligible to listeners. In addition, the voice quality of the deaf was generally breathy and harsh and was also often nasal.

Nickerson (1975) has extensively reviewed studies of the characteristics of deaf speech. He has classified the speech errors into five general categories: timing and rhythm, pitch and intonation, velar control or nasality, articulation, and voice quality. The speech errors specifically included abnormally slow rate of utterance, insufficient distinctions between durations of stressed and unstressed syllables, use of more pauses and pauses of longer duration, poor rhythm, inadequate breath control, excessive duration in producing certain types of sounds; inappropriate average pitch, improper intonation; tendency to nasalize sounds that should not be nasalized; failure to develop certain sounds and to differentiate between others, substitution of one sound for another, use of the neutral schwa /ə/ as a general purpose vowel, distortion in articulating sounds, malarticulation of compound and abutting consonants, difficulties in executing smooth transitions between speech sounds such as consonant-vowel combinations; throaty, flat, breathy, and harsh voice quality, too soft or too loud voicing, and erratic variation in volume.

Additional Problems

Language and communication deficits in and of themselves do not complete the typical profile of a hard-of-hearing child. As suggested previously, academic retardation, social and personal maladjustment, and vocational restriction are often present also.

Academic retardation understandably occurs much more often among hard-of-hearing children than among normal-hearing children. Educational achievement testing by Kodman (1963) of 100 hard-of-hearing children in Kentucky revealed an average deficit of 2.24 years. These children also had repeated 57 grades. They were 7 to 17 years of age and had a mean IQ of 92.3, auditory insensitivity of 50 dB in the better ear, and, similarly, auditory discrimination loss of 19 percent.

The academic gap between the hard-of-hearing child and normal-hearing youngster characteristically increases with age. A one-year retardation in the fourth grade, for example, might become a two-year deficit in the eighth grade, and a three-year gap by the twelfth grade. At college age the academic deficiency may be so severe that the likelihood of successful adjustment to a university study program is low.

The social position of hard-of-hearing children in the elementary schools of rural Tennessee was studied by Elser (1959). As a group these youngsters did not score as high in friendship and reputation and were not as well accepted as their normal-hearing peers. Individually, there was of course a wide range of acceptance. These hard-of-hearing children were 9 to 12 years of age and had auditory insensitivity exceeding 45 dB.

One director of special education in Illinois searched the school files and located 121 children with auditory insensitivity in excess of 40 dB. The teachers of these children rated their performance on a questionnaire. Only 11 of the 121 were rated as normally participating class members. Of the other 110, 28 had failed one or more grades, 43 were underachievers, 28 were socially introverted, and 17 were considered social problems (Bothwell, 1967).

The hard-of-hearing child enrolled in unspecialized schools is often labeled as uncooperative, mentally defective, or emotionally disturbed. He is typically enrolled in the regular classroom but gradually loses out in competition with his fellows (O'Neill, 1964).

Alerting and scanning for sound are also defective among these children. For example, a conversation referred to in the next room or a marching band a block away may be inaudible to even a mildly hard-of-hearing child. The missing of environmental background sounds contributes to social isolation and disorientation.

The youngster with moderate to severe bilateral hearing loss is often characterized by feelings of isolation, inadequacy, and helplessness. He may also be bitter and resentful. In addition, he tends to be more on guard than usual. Or he may become depressed and apathetic (Wright, 1960).

The child with a unilateral hearing impairment also experiences negative feelings, including embarrassment, annoyance, confusion, and helplessness associated with difficulties in understanding speech and in localizing sound. These negative feelings occur most frequently in situations in which other persons present are unaware of the individual's hearing loss (Giolas and Wark, 1967).

In many instances the hard-of-hearing child will experience more rejection than is warranted from both adults and peers. This rejection stems from his failure to hear requests made of him and/or from his attempts to bluff his way through social situations (Wright, 1960).

One 18-year-old hard-of-hearing girl, for example, pretended that she heard in instances when she did not. She refused to wear a hearing aid even though her moderate conductive hearing loss made her a prime candidate for one. She had graduated from high school but was unusually academically retarded. Toward the end of her high school days she scored 123 on the performance battery for the Weschler Adult Intelligence Scale but only 77 on the verbal battery (Berg, 1970a).

The clinical psychologist Vernon (1970) has observed that many hard-of-hearing children have become masters of the neutral response, smiling, saying yes, and periodically nodding their heads affirmatively. He has also noted that they often keep quiet or try to dominate conversation to avoid having to understand that which is unclear. Unawareness of these behaviors, and the basic underlying language and communication problems, can result in gross psychodiagnostic errors with tragic consequences.

The hard-of-hearing youngster must also look ahead to the rigors of the workaday world, which are demanding even for a normal-hearing person. The job task of a salesman or secretary, for example, requires rapid and accurate listening and speaking skills; and that of a teacher or manager requires advanced reading and writing competencies as well. A great many hard-of-hearing persons simply do not function well at these positions, notwithstanding their mental capabilities and vocational interests and aptitudes. In addition, the deficiencies arising from their hearing impairment stand in the way of their obtaining advanced training. Consequently, the hard-of-hearing person is in danger of becoming "frozen" in jobs requiring a lower level of communication and interpersonal skills, with little or no opportunities for vocational advancement.

Model

Based upon his conceptualization of the profile of the hard-of-hearing child, Berg (1973) developed a model of "areas affected by impairment of hearing," which is shown in Figure 6.

The basic underlying factors include utilization of residual hearing and/or vision, conceptualization of the problem, and commitment to alleviate it. The communication or second-level variables are spoken lan-

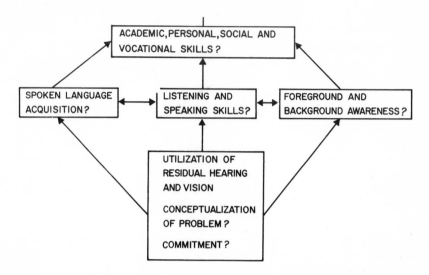

Fig. 6.   Areas affected by impairment of hearing.

guage acquisition, "listening" and speaking skills, and foreground and background awareness. The end product or third level of the model encompasses the academic or experiential, personal, social, and vocational performance of the hard-of-hearing individual. The arrows between levels and among factors of Figure 6 indicate many of the interactions and primary directions of effects. Table 7 clarifies this multiparametric model in a comparison of hard-of-hearing, normal-hearing and deaf populations of children and youth.

EDUCATIONAL AUDIOLOGY

During the last decade the term *educational audiology* has become prominent in the practice of the habilitative management of the hearing-impaired child. Defined specifically in different ways by various professionals (Alpiner, 1974; Berg, 1974; O'Neill, 1974), the term generally suggests increased utilization of residual hearing in the educational management of the hard-of-hearing youngster. Currently, increasing numbers of communicative disorders specialists are calling themselves *educational audiologists* or are being called by that name.

As a general profession, audiology emerged during World War II. The emergence of audiology came from a war effort to help men and women with service-incurred hearing loss and from similar Veterans Administration programs after the war. Within this professional devel-

Table 7
Hypothetically Typical Values or Expected Degrees of Achievement or Adjustment Associated with Being Normally Hearing, Hard of Hearing, or Deaf at each of Three Levels of Interaction and Within 13 Categories and Selected Subcategories of a Multiparametric Model (Figure 6)

Level	Component		Normally hearing	Hard of Hearing	Deaf
Basic	A1.	Audition			
		a. Bilateral sensitivity	0–10 dB	40–92 dB	92+dB
		b. Recognition (cochlear integrity)	Complete	Somewhat to nearly complete	Absent or nearly incomplete
		c. Discomfort	110 dB	Variable	Absent or variable
		d. Localization	Multidirectional	Unidirectional or somewhat multi-directional	Unidirectional
	A2.	Vision	Sensitive, perceptive, binocular, but undirectional for all three populations		
	A3–4.	Conceptualization and commitment related to expectations (too low, realistic, too high) and achievements for all three populations			
Communication	B1.	Spoken language acquisition	Achieved rapidly and completely	Achieved more slowly or incompletely	Achieved very slowly or incompletely
	B2.	Speech acquisition	Achieved rapidly and completely	Achieved more slowly or defectively, but intelligible	Achieved very slowly or unintelligible

B3. "Listening" or speech understanding (see A1, A2)	Nearly all situations	Many situations (see A1, A2, B1)	Few situations
B4. Environmental awareness (see A1, A2) (with B3 determines B1)	Can attend to great numbers of auditory and visual stimuli of foreground and background (see A1, d)	Can attend to selected auditory and visual stimuli of foreground and to visual stimuli of background (see A1, d)	Can attend to selected visual stimuli of foreground and background (see A1, d)
End Product			
C1. Academic (by age 18 years)	12th grade	10th grade	8th grade
C2. Personal (self-confidence)	Most	Less	Least
C3. Social (interaction with hearing)	Most	Less	Least
C4. Vocational (options)	Many	Fewer	Fewest

This table encompasses some 200,000 children with 40–92 dB bilateral hearing loss who are enrolled in the regular schools and regular classes of normal-hearing children and in the special schools and special classes of deaf youngsters. Hard-of-hearing children with varying degrees of unilateral auditory insensitivity and those with slight (11–25 dB) and somewhat mild (26–39 dB) bilateral impairment are not considered in this table.

opment, Newby (1958) defined *audiology* as the science of hearing and the evaluation and habilitation of individuals with hearing disorders. By 1965 perhaps 100 universities were engaged in the professional preparation of audiologists.

With maturation the profession of audiology crumbled the monolithic conception that a child either could hear or was deaf. In an article entitled "The Semantics of Deafness," Ross and Calvert (1967) scored professional and laymen alike for applying a dichotomy rather than a continuum to the concept of hearing loss. As a result, they also laid the groundwork for conceptualizing the hard of hearing child as apart from both the deaf youngster and the normal hearing child.

Definition and Curriculum

In 1966 the United States Office of Education began to support the development of a professional specialization at Utah State University (USU) that was specifically called educational audiology and focused on the hard-of-hearing child. Soon afterwards Fletcher and Berg of USU advanced a definition of educational audiology.

> Educational audiology seeks to isolate the parameters of hearing impairment, to identify the deficiencies rising from hearing disability, to relate these to the unique characteristics of individuals, and to develop educational programs specifically for hard of hearing children (Berg, 1970c).

As specialists at USU moved toward the development of a model curriculum it became evident that the professional preparation of an audiologist should encompass behavioral competencies in evaluation, design, and training across a broad spectrum of areas of concern. The conventional model of the audiologist who tested and of the teacher of the hearing impaired who taught communication and academic skills became outmoded for at least five reasons.

First, current audiologists and teachers of the hearing impaired seldom assisted each other because they could not understand the relevance of the separate competencies each could bring to the management task.

Second, the evaluative workups of the audiologist generally were limited to audiometric tests and hearing aid evaluations.

Third, the teacher of the hearing impaired often designed educational programming based upon insufficient audiological data.

Fourth, the teacher of the hearing impaired characteristically had been prepared to manage a special classroom of deaf children rather than to function also as a resource specialist for hard-of-hearing young-sters enrolled in regular classrooms.

And finally, many school district administrators were unwilling to hire two specialists to serve one child, for example, a speech (and hear-ing) clinician and an audiologist, or an audiologist and a teacher of the hearing impaired.

The USU curriculum design was unique in seven respects.

It encompassed the total characteristics and needs of the hard-of-hearing child (Berg and Fletcher, 1967).

It sought to isolate the parameters of hearing impairment, to iden-tify the deficiencies rising from hearing disability, to relate these to the unique characteristics of individuals, and to develop educational pro-grams designed for hard-of-hearing children.

It acknowledged that a coordination of skills of varied profession-als and adjustments of various laymen were needed to help the child to the utmost, although the model gave greater management responsibility to one specialist than had theretofore been the case.

It recognized that the newer developments in education—in-creasing reliance on behavioral engineering, sensory aids, and instruc-tional technology—were critically relevant to the educational manage-ment of the hard-of-hearing person.

It was designed to prepare specialists to meet the certification and coming licensing requirements in both audiology and education of the hearing impaired with a focus upon the hard-of-hearing child in regular school settings.

The model was called an audiology specialty, but it could be dif-ferentiated from the great majority of programs in audiology that were limited in the clinical and educational management of the hard-of-hearing child (Requirements for the Certificate of Clinical Competence, 1973).

The model could be differentiated from almost all programs de-signed for the professional preparation of the educator of the deaf or hearing impaired. Earlier training programs generally lacked audiologi-cal emphasis (Standards for the Certification of Teachers of the Hear-ing Impaired, 1972).

The longitudinal design of the audiology curriculum at USU is incorporated within a five-year university curriculum leading to the Master's degree. As noted in Figure 7, the curriculum includes (1) gen-eral education preparation, (2) learning and communication under-pinning, (3) observation and analysis of behavior, (4) management background, and (5) management applications. The plan calls for a con-tinuing upgrading of verbal and performance competencies through courses, apprenticeship, internship, and externship experiences.

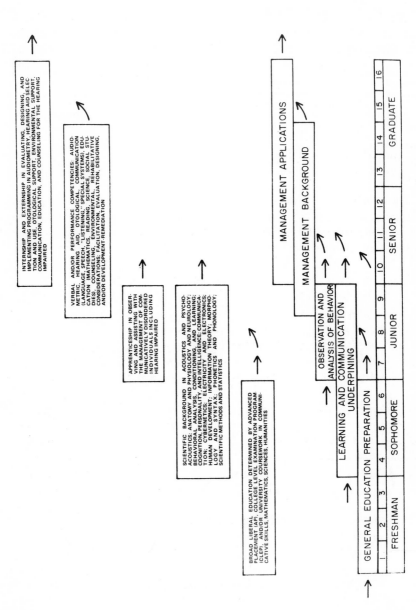

Fig. 7. Longitudinal design of the USU audiology curriculum.

INTERNSHIP AND EXTERNSHIP IN EVALUATING, DESIGNING, AND IMPLEMENTING PROGRAMMING IN AUDIOMETRY HEARING AID SELECTION AND USE. OTOLOGICAL SUPPORT, ENVIRONMENTAL SUPPORT, COMMUNICATION, EDUCATION, AND COUNSELING FOR THE HEARING IMPAIRED

VERBAL AND/OR PERFORMANCE COMPETENCIES: AUDIOMETRIC, HEARING AID, OTOLOGICAL, COMMUNICATION (LANGUAGE, SPEECH, "LISTENING," SPECIAL SYSTEMS); EDUCATION (MATHEMATICS, READING, SCIENCE, SOCIAL STUDIES) COUNSELING, ENVIRONMENTAL, REHABILITATIVE CONSIDERATIONS, FACILITATION, EVALUATION, DESIGNING, AND/OR DEVELOPMENT-REMEDIATION

APPRENTICESHIP IN OBSERVING AND ASSISTING WITH THE MANAGEMENT OF COMMUNICATIVELY DISORDERED INDIVIDUALS INCLUDING HEARING IMPAIRED

SCIENTIFIC BACKGROUND IN ACOUSTICS AND PSYCHOACOUSTICS; ANATOMY AND PHYSIOLOGY AND NEUROLOGY; BEHAVIORAL ANALYSIS, CONDITIONING, AND LEARNING; COGNITION, PERSONALITY, AND INTELLIGENCE; COMMUNICATION; CYBERNETICS; ELECTRICITY AND ELECTRONICS; HUMAN DEVELOPMENT; INFORMATION THEORY; MORPHOLOGY AND SYNTAX; PHONETICS AND PHONOLOGY; SCIENTIFIC METHODS AND STATISTICS

BROAD LIBERAL EDUCATION DETERMINED BY ADVANCED PLACEMENT (AP), COLLEGE LEVEL EXAMINATION PROGRAM (CLEP), AND/OR UNIVERSITY COURSEWORK IN COMMUNICATIVE SKILLS, MATHEMATICS, SCIENCES, HUMANITIES

MANAGEMENT APPLICATIONS

MANAGEMENT BACKGROUND

OBSERVATION AND ANALYSIS OF BEHAVIOR

LEARNING AND COMMUNICATION UNDERPINING

GENERAL EDUCATION PREPARATION

1	2	3	4	5	6	7	8	9	10	11	12	13	14	15	16
FRESHMAN			SOPHOMORE			JUNIOR			SENIOR			GRADUATE			

Field Analysis, Competencies, and Home Study

During 1970–1971 a field analysis of the audiology curriculum was made. Operational objectives within courses and practicum experiences were formulated, rating scales developed, and respondents selected from school districts, state offices, and universities. Data from respondents revealed widespread support for all areas of the USU curriculum (Crookston, 1971).

Figure 8 identifies the verbal and/or performance competencies needed by the audiologist in the management of the hard-of-hearing child (Berg, 1973). The job task of the audiologist, whose major responsibility is to coordinate the clinical and educational management of the hard of hearing child, may be described under six categories.

1. Audiometry is the measurement, evaluation, and recommendations related to auditory awareness, sensitivity, discomfort, localization, recognition, and site of lesion.
2. Otology includes referral to the medical ear specialist for possible

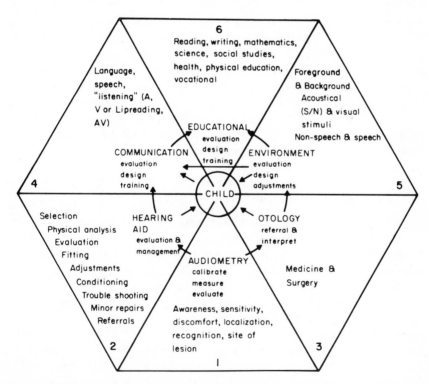

Fig. 8. Verbal and/or performance competencies needed in the clinical and educational management of the hard-of-hearing child.

medical and/or surgical alleviation of hearing loss and ear pathology, as well as interpretation of medical and surgical reports related to problems of the ear.

3. Hearing aid evaluation and management encompasses selection, physical analysis, personal evaluation, fitting, adjustments, conditioning, troubleshooting, minor repairs, and referrals.

4. Communication evaluation, design, and training concern the development and/or remediation of spoken language, speech, and "listening" (auditory only, visual only or lipreading, and auditory–visual combined).

5. Environment evaluation, design, and adjustments deal with home, school, and community considerations related to nonspeech and speech, with primarily acoustical and visual foreground and background stimuli, and with signal/noise identification and modification.

6. Education evaluation, design, and training in written language and basic substantive areas concern development and/or remediation in reading, writing, mathematics, science, and social studies.

The interactions of these six areas of management is illustrated in part by the arrows of Figure 8. For example, it may be noted that (1) audiometry contributes to otology and hearing aid evaluation; (2) otological treatment and the hearing aid facilitate environmental input, communication, and education; and (3) communication training and environmental adjustment contribute to educational achievement. Whereas the audiologist has worked particularly within areas of audiometry, the hearing aid, and interaction with the otologist, he must also encompass areas of communication, the environment, and even education to complete the scope of the job task.

Differentiation between a verbal competency and a performance competency can be based on the following tripartite scheme.

1. The *general objective* is to differentiate between normal-hearing, hard-of-hearing, and deaf children.

2. In the area of *verbal competency,* the aim is to isolate the parameters that contribute to the differentiation between normal-hearing, hard-of-hearing, and deaf children with particular focus on the speech signal, auditory area, auditory recognition, speech performance, and language performance.

3. In the area of *performance competency,* the aim is to conduct, tabulate data from, and interpret results of mini-speech, mini-"listening," and mini-language tests with three children—one with normal hearing, one with moderate or severe loss, and one with profound or total impairment.

Since the field analysis of the USU curriculum, Berg (1975a, 1975b, 1976) has been developing home study course work in educational audiology through the Independent Study Division of Utah State University. Up to 12 quarter (8 semester) hours of university credits can now be earned through enrollment in one or more of the courses: phonetics, hearing and speech management, and educational audiology. The combined course content provides competencies in phonemic identification, motor and acoustic phonetics, evaluation and development of speech, evaluation and training in listening, hearing aids, and auditory trainers, and models of service delivery. Contributions from audiology, education of the hearing impaired, electronics, instructional technology, and speech pathology are integrated into a series of 43 course modules for which videotape demonstrations and audio cassette and video photograph materials have been obtained and developed. Individuals or groups may register.

The home study course work in educational audiology is also being incorporated into subsidized projects designed to upgrade the competencies of communicative disorders specialists in listening and speech training for hard-of-hearing children and adults. Currently, a pilot project entitled "Home Study in Listening and Speech Training" is being conducted in the HEW Region VIII states of Colorado, the Dakotas, Montana, Utah, and Wyoming. This project is being funded by the Kellogg Foundation and by the Rehabilitation Services Administration. Further funding is being sought from the U. S. Office of Education, Bureau of Education for the Handicapped, in order to extend the project to all states between 1976 and 1979. The goal during this period would be to train many audiologists, educators of the hearing impaired, and speech pathologists to conduct effective listening and speech training for the hard-of-hearing child. These communicative disorders specialists would in turn provide listening and speech training for many children from 1976 to 1979 as well as conduct in-service training for additional personnel. Additional goals include mobilization of state office personnel, rehabilitation counselors, and local school personnel to support continuing programming for hard-of-hearing children and adults. Also, the specialist and client materials and procedures will be incorporated into an instructional system.

REFERENCES

Allen D: Modality Aspects of Mediation in Children with Normal and with Impaired Hearing. OE-7-0837, Detroit, Wayne State University, 1969
Alpiner J: Educational audiology. J Acad Reh Aud 7:50–54, 1974

Berg F: The locus of the education of the hard of hearing child, in Berg F and Fletcher S (eds): The Hard of Hearing Child. New York and London, Grune & Stratton, 1970a, pp 13–26

Berg F: Language development, in Berg F and Fletcher S (eds): The Hard of Hearing Child. New York and London, Grune & Stratton, 1970b, pp 111–124

Berg F: Educational audiology, in Berg F and Fletcher S (eds): The Hard of Hearing Child. New York and London, Grune & Stratton, 1970c, pp 275–318

Berg F: Breakthrough for the Hard of Hearing Child. Smithfield, Utah, Ear Publication, 1971

Berg F: Sensory Aids in Speech Remediation for the Hearing Impaired. Logan, Utah State University, 1972

Berg F: Educational Audiology, Hard of Hearing. OEG-0-71-3681 (603). Logan, Utah State University, 1973

Berg F: Educational audiology at Utah state university. J Acad Reh Aud 7:40–49, 1974

Berg F: Home study coursework in educational audiology. Vol Rev 77:461, 1975a

Berg F: Educational audiology. Aud Hear Educ 1:No. 2, 1975b

Berg F: Educational audiology, in Bradford (ed): Audiology. An Audio Journal for Continuing Education. New York, Grune & Stratton, 1:7, 1976

Berg F, Fletcher S: The hard of hearing child and educational audiology. Proceedings of International Conference on Oral Education of the Deaf. Washington, DC, The Alexander Graham Bell Association for the Deaf, 1967, pp 874–885

Bitter G, Mears E: Facilitating the integration of hearing impaired children into regular public school classes. Vol Rev 75:13–22, 1973

Boatner E: The need of a realistic approach to the education of the deaf. Presented to the joint convention of the California Association of Parents of Deaf and Hard of Hearing Children, California Association of Teachers of the Deaf and Hard of Hearing, and the California Association of the Deaf, Los Angeles, November 6, 1965

Bothwell H: Developing a Comprehensive Program for Hearing Impaired Children on a Statewide (Illinois) Basis. Institute on Characteristics and Needs of the Hard of Hearing Child. Logan, Utah State University, 1967

Crookston G: Field Analysis in Educational Audiology Curriculum. MS Thesis. Logan, Utah State University, 1971

Davis H: Abnormal hearing and deafness, in Davis H and Silverman SR (eds): Hearing and Deafness. New York, Rinehart and Winston, 1970, pp 83–139

Demographic Study. Audiological Examinations of Hearing Impaired Students, United States, 1969–70. Washington, DC, Gallaudet College, 1971

DiCarlo L: Speech, language, and cognitive abilities of the hard of hearing. Proceedings of the Institute on Aural Rehabilitation. SRS 212-T-68. Denver, University of Denver, 1968, pp 45–66

Elser R: The social position of hearing handicapped children in the regular grades. Except Child 25:305–309, 1959

Fant G: The acoustics of speech. Proc 3rd ICA, Vol. 1. Stuttgart, 1959a

Fant G: Acoutic analysis and synthesis of speech with applications to Swedish. Erics Techn 15:98, 1959b

Fellendorf G: Statement before the Maryland Commission to Study Educational Needs of Handicapped Children. Washington, DC, Alexander Graham Bell Association for the Deaf, 1966, p 10

Giolas T, Wark D: Communication problems associated with unilateral hearing loss. J Speech Hear Disord 32:336–343, 1967

Goetzinger C: Effects of small perceptive losses on language and on speech discrimination. Vol Rev 64:408–414, 1962

Hart D: Medical and Surgical Procedures for Hearing Problems. Institute on Characteristics and Needs of the Hard of Hearing Child. Logan, Utah State University, 1967

Hudgins C, Numbers F: An investigation of the intelligibility of the speech of the deaf. Genet Psychol Monogr 25:289–392, 1942

Kodman F: Education status of hard of hearing children in the classroom. J Speech Hear Disord 28:297–299, 1963

McClure W: Current problems and trends in the education of the deaf. Deaf Amer 31:8–14, 1966

McConnell F: Proceedings of the Conference on Current Practices in the Management of Deaf Infants. Nashville, The Bill Wilkerson Hearing and Speech Center, 1968

Newby H: Audiology: Principles and Practices. New York, Appleton-Century-Crofts, 1958

Nickerson R: Characteristics of the speech of deaf persons. Vol Rev 77:342–362, 1975

O'Neill J: The Hard of Hearing. Englewood Cliffs, New Jersey, Prentice Hall, 1964

O'Neill J: The school educational audiologist. J Acad Reh Aud 7:31–39, 1974

Pauls M: Language development through reading. Vol Rev 60:105–107, 142, 1958

Quigley S, Thomure F: Some Effects of Hearing Impairment Upon School Performance. Springfield, Illinois, Division of Special Education Services, 1968

Requirements for the certificate of clinical competence. ASHA 15:77–80, 1973

Ross M, Calvert D: The semantics of deafness. Vol Rev 69:644–649, 1967

Standards for the Certification of Teachers of the Hearing Impaired. Council on Education of the Deaf. Rochester, New York, Polychrome Press, 1972

Vernon M: The psychological examination, in Berg F and Fletcher S (eds): The Hard of Hearing Child. New York and London, Grune & Stratton, 1970, pp 217–231

Vernon M: Mind over mouth: A rationale for *total communication*. Vol Rev 74:529–538, 1972

Wedenberg E: Auditory training of severely hard of hearing preschool children. Act Otolaryngol [Suppl] (Stockh) 94:1–129, 1954

Wedenberg E: The Status of Hard of Hearing Students in Sweden. Institute on the Characteristics and Needs of the Hard of Hearing Child. Logan, Utah State University, 1967

Willeford J: Personal Communication, Fort Collins, Colorado State University, January 25, 1971

Wright B: Physical Disability. A Psychological Approach. New York, Harper & Row, 1960

Young D, McConnell F: Retardation of vocabulary development in hard of hearing children. Except Child 23:368–370, 1957

2

Audiology, Spectrography, and Communication

THE AUDIOGRAM

The most utilized measure of hearing or hearing loss is the *threshold of sensitivity* for pure tones. Expressed as the *audiogram,* this measure is actually a series of thresholds for up to seven or more frequencies. Pure tones or single frequencies serving as auditory stimuli can be generated by an audiometer at 125, 250, 500, 1000, 2000, 4000, and 8000 Hz. An audiogram for both ears is determined by measuring the point or narrow region of uncertainty at each of these frequencies. In each instance this region is the area in which the person cannot tell consistently whether he can hear a given tone or not.

The audiogram for one ear is not identical in location or configuration to the audiogram for the other ear. Hearing loss or threshold of sensitivity is usually figured as the average (mean) of sensitivity at 500, 1000, and 2000 Hz in the better or more sensitive ear.

The audiograms of Figure 9 are illustrative. The configurations of the two audiograms are highly similar, but the degree of loss for the right ear is not quite as great as that for the left ear. The mean hearing loss for the right and left ears are 80 and 87 dB respectively. These are computed as 75 + 80 + 85 divided by 3 = 80, and 85 + 85 + 90 divided by 3 = 87.

A series of audiograms for the better ears of nine hypothetical clients are depicted in Figure 10 to clarify the term, *degree of hearing loss.*

The distance between a given audiogram and a 120 dB loss base-

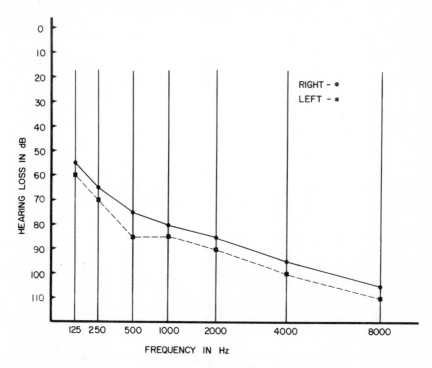

Fig. 9. Audiogram for the left ear and the right ear of a hypothetical hearing-impaired child.

line gives an optimistic estimate of the vertical dimension of the extent of a given child's hearing. For example, the child with a slight to mild loss has a 95 dB dimension (120–25), but the youngster with a profound to total loss has only a 15 dB dimension. These results are based on the assumption that each of these children does not find a 120 dB sound pressure level to be excessively intense. While the extent of the audiometer output is 110 dB, many hearing aids and auditory trainers will deliver even greater sound pressure levels. It is of interest that the level of loud speech from within an inch of an ear *(ad concham),* without electro-acoustic amplification, is nearly 110 dB.

AUDITORY PERCEPTION OF SPEECH

As noted in the previous chapter, the terms *deaf* and *hard of hearing* can be defined. Rather than base these definitions on the audiogram, however, we should tie them to the variable of auditory per-

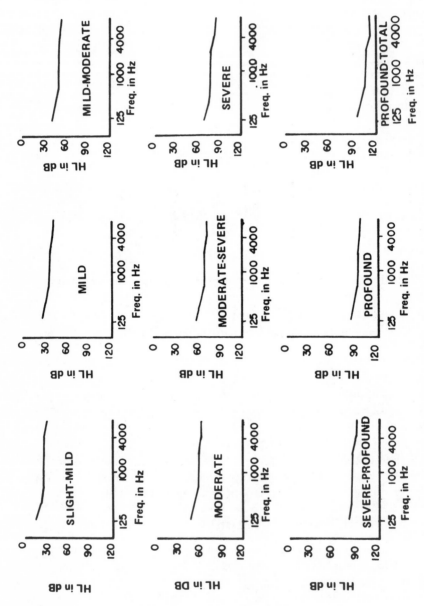

Fig. 10. Series of hypothetical audiograms for the more sensitive ears of nine clients with varying degrees of auditory impairment.

ception. In other words the consideration should not be thresholds of sensitivity for sounds but the extent to which incoming sounds can be identified or perceived.

The auditory discrimination of a young child may be more difficult to measure than auditory sensitivity. Ordinarily, a three-year-old youngster will respond to fainter and fainter sounds, indicating when he hears and when he does not. The same child may not, however, respond so that his perception of sounds can be assessed easily. The child with a hearing loss may simply not be familiar with the words or sentences used as auditory stimuli. After developing a basic receptive and expressive vocabulary, this same youngster, now older, can provide a measure of auditory discrimination or speech perception.

If a hearing-impaired child has been taught to speak by use of sensory clues other than exclusively auditory clues, he may express a vocabulary that he cannot perceive by audition only. It then becomes necessary to train him to identify these same words auditorially or without the aid of other clues. After such auditory training or perceptual learning the clinician can arrive at a measure of the child's auditory discrimination.

The auditory discrimination of the child indicates his competence in acquiring spoken language, intelligible speech, and homeostasis with his sound environment. In other words, if the child can auditorily perceive phonetic and prosodic features of speech, he will acquire language or the linguistic code of his environment unless other abnormal complications exist. Furthermore, with a combination of auditory discrimination and linguistic competence, the youngster will be able to listen and thereby function academically and socially.

The child's auditory discrimination will also determine the extent to which he or she can utilize residual hearing to acquire intelligible or natural, if not normal, speech. It only makes sense that hearing adequate enough to permit language to develop will allow prosodic and phonetic speech to emerge. Furthermore it is speech that provides the medium for reception and expression of the linguistic code.

The integration of speech and language acquisition may be clarified by use of the terms *phonetic* and *prosodic*, and *segmental* and *suprasegmental phonemes*. Phonetic and prosodic are speech terms, and the latter are language terms. Phonetic is to prosodic as segmental phonemes are to suprasegmental phonemes. Phonetics refers to articulatory features, and prosodic refers to stress (loudness–duration) and intonation characteristics. When the phonetic and prosodic phenomena of speech become classified, they become part of the linguistic code. For example, when a front *k* and a back *k* become identified as simply *k,* they are internalized as belonging together and referred to as allophones of the segmental phoneme /k/. These two *k* productions are more than just speech phenomena. They are also a part of the emerging phonological subsystem of the language of the child.

SPECTROGRAPHIC CONSIDERATIONS

Each of the phonemes, with the exception of the sibilant sounds, includes acoustic energies or features in low frequency regions. Figure 11 shows, for example, that first (F_1) formants or concentrations of energies for both English and Swedish male vowels are located below 700 Hz. In addition, the second formants (F_2) for these same sounds are positioned below 2300 Hz, and the third formants (F_3) below 3000 Hz. Corresponding formants for vowels produced by female voices or by children are only slightly higher.

Study of the spectrogram of each phoneme is made convenient by reference to the ABC's of Visible Speech in the book by Potter, Kopp and Green (1966). Further information on acoustic correlates of phonetic and prosodic information may be found in Fant (1968), Fletcher (1970), and Fry (1968). In the first three references it can be noted that voiced consonants also have formants distributed across the same frequency range as the vowels. In connected speech, transitions of acoustic energies from phoneme to phoneme make it apparent that the voiceless consonants have locations of formant energies equivalent to those of their voiced cognates, although when produced in isolation the formants of voiceless speech sounds tend to be masked by frictional energies.

Acoustic features of a representative sample of the phonemes of English speech are included by Fletcher (1970) in Figure 12. Although energies for many sounds reach up to and above 7500 Hz, the first three formants that make speech perception possible in and of themselves are located at 3000 Hz or below. Actually, even perception of the first two formants is sufficient for decoding connected speech, once spoken language has been developed. It is interesting that many profoundly hearing-impaired individuals have residual hearing that permits them to hear or sense at least the first two formants of English phonemes.

The audiogram of Staffan Wedenberg in Figure 13 illustrates the possibilities for perception of speech even by an individual whose sensitivity for sound extends only up to about 1600 Hz. With training, Staffan learned to perceive and pronounce the vowels, diphthongs, and voiced consonants. He was also able to perceive stress patterns after training, although his pitch discrimination did not permit him to decode

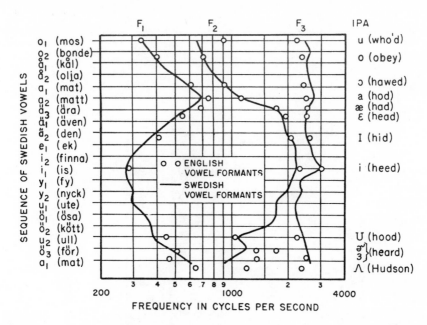

Fig. 11. Locations of first, second, and third formants of Swedish and American English vowels. From Wedenberg, 1970, p. 321.

the detail of intonation of speech. He was unable to perceive pitch changes unless they were at least 50 Hz apart. Nevertheless the significant features of speech that he was able to learn to perceive enabled him to acquire spoken language by utilizing residual hearing. Later a combination of speech training, reading instruction, and apparent transposition of high frequency sibilant energies into low frequency sounds through a coding amplifier (Johansson, 1961) enabled him to perceive acoustic features of speech even better.

Each of the segmental phonemes—consonants, vowels, and diphthongs—has a unique distributions of acoustical energies. The spectrogram of the /ɵ/ phoneme, for example, looks very different from that of the /o/ phoneme and somewhat different from the similar sounding /f/ phoneme.

An individual with a hearing loss does not auditorily differentiate between speech sounds as if normal hearing were present. However he still can make or learn to make auditory discriminations among similar sounding consonants, vowels, and diphthongs. Such discrimination is possible because the sounds can be amplified by modern hearing aids. It is also possible because detailed study of spectrograms reveal that even similar phonemes, such as /p/ and /t/, are different in intensity,

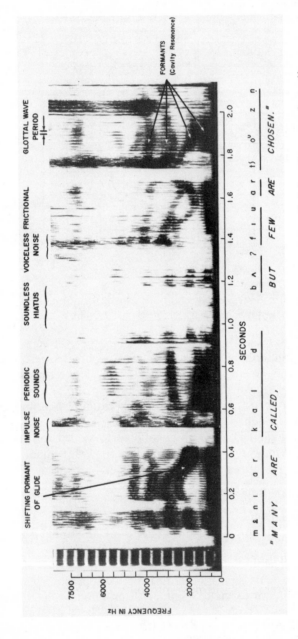

Fig. 12. Sound spectrogram of the sentence "Many are called but few are chosen" using wide band (300 Hz) analyzing filters. From Fletcher, 1970, p. 58.

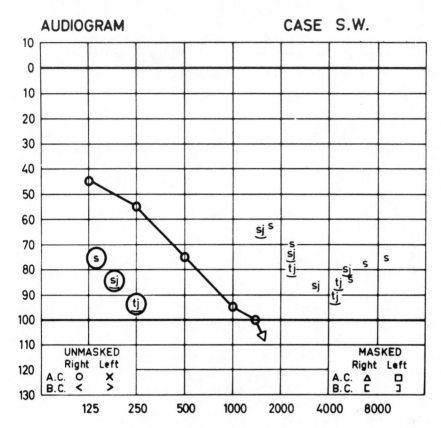

Fig. 13. Results of frequency transposition of the Swedish toneless consonants *s*, *sj*, and *tj*. The transposer hearing aid shifts the high frequency speech sounds into Staffan's auditory range as denoted by the symbols within circles. From Wedenberg, 1970, p. 329.

duration, and pattern of frequency distribution. At least some of these differences occur within those parts of the overall speech signal that still can be delivered into a restricted auditory area. Such differences may be perceived by the severely or even profoundly hearing-impaired person provided that appropriate amplification *and* training are implemented.

The suprasegmental phonemes—prosodic features of stress, intonation, and juncture—are also revealed as acoustic differences. Study of the detail of spectrograms for words and sentences reveals perceptible differences between such speech characteristics as well. Even an individual with a profound hearing loss may learn to perceive differences in stress and juncture. Depending upon his pitch perception for the sounds he can hear, this individual is likely to have more difficulty in identifying intonational changes. Learning merely to perceive stress patterns coupled with auditory discrimination of consonants, vowels, and diphthongs, however, provides a useful underpinning for acquisition of listening, speech, and language competencies.

VOCAL TRACT PHENOMENA

Figure 14 identifies the prosodic and phonetic (articulatory) features of speech. Stress and intonation are shown as variations of loudness–duration and pitch respectively. The phonetic features are subdivided into three voicing postures, two oral–nasal or velopharyngeal positions, three levels of restriction or manner of articulation, and three each of horizontal and vertical localities or places of articulation (Berg, 1972).

The first or most basic speech phenomenon, illustrated by the lower right circle in Figure 14, is stress or loudness–duration patterning. Stress is the relative vocal prominence of syllables, words, and larger units of speech. It contributes substantially to the intelligibility or meaningfulness of speech, particularly as it varies between the syllables of an utterance. There are four distinctive levels of syllable prominence, as exemplified by accent marks in the phonetic and prosodic transcription of the word *Mississippi*. Stress variations originate in the thorasic cavity as fine muscular contractions and convert into modulations of the air stream exhaled from the lungs into the vocal tract terminating at the front of the face.

The second basic speech phenomenon is the intonational contour of an utterance and its detailed pitch or melody variations between member syllables. The vocal folds depicted in the second circle from the bottom in Figure 14 vary in length and tension to modify intonation and pitch. General intonational variations and detailed pitch changes contribute considerably to the intelligibility or meaningfulness of speech. Four distinctive pitch variations occur within utterances and three at the ends of them.

The third basic phenomenon of utterance is whether or not the vocal folds are vibrating, separated, or approximated. These three vocal fold postures are shown in the next circle in Figure 14. By vibrating, the vocal folds add voicing to the exhaled air stream to produce vowels, diphthongs, and voiced consonants. During the production of the voiceless consonants, with the exception of the fricative /h/, the vocal folds are relatively separated. For the /h/ the vocal folds approximate and thus constrict the air stream passing through the larynx. The

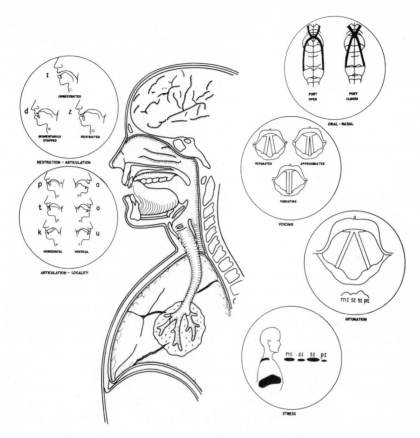

Fig. 14. The vocal tract and six associated prosodic and phonetic phenomena.

voiced versus unvoiced distinction particularly carries heavy responsibility in speech communication.

The fourth basic speech phenomenon is the oral–nasal distinction corresponding to the closing or opening of the velopharyngeal port. In the upper right circle of Figure 14, the left and right illustrations of muscular *pursestring* action show the open and closed port positions respectively. The velopharyngeal port should be closed, or nearly so, for the production of all vowels, diphthongs, and consonants with the exception of the nasals /m/, /n/, and /ŋ/. If the port is kept open during the time that it would ordinarily be closed, the voice quality will have an unnatural nasal sound. The oral–nasal distinction particularly affects the meaning of an utterance dependent upon differentiation between

/m/–/b/, /n/–/d/, and /ŋ/–/g/. For example, opening the velopharyngeal port during production of the first phoneme of *bat* will result in the pronunciation of this word as *mat*.

The fifth basic vocal tract phenomenon affecting speech intelligibility is the degree of restriction of the exhaled air stream through the oral cavity, the mouth. The schematic illustrations of the upper left circle in Figure 14 reveal the presence of three distinctive degrees of restriction: relatively open for the vowels and diphthongs, relatively closed for the glides and fricative consonants, and momentarily shut off for stops or stop-plosives and the nasals. The restrictive oral phenomenon is illustrated by the voiced phonemes /i/, /z/, and /d/, characterized by the linqua–alveolar articulation.

The sixth and last basic speech distinction is locality of articulation within the region immediately surrounding and including the mouth. Articulation depends upon the positions taken by the mandible, lips, and particularly parts of the tongue in relationship to the upper teeth, alveolar ridge, hard palate, and velum to complete the production of all phonemes. The articulatory locality distinction is unlike that of oral restriction in that the former refers to place and the latter to degree or manner. The lower left circle of Figure 14 locates precisely the places where articulatory acts can occur. These places include horizontal and vertical locations: anterior, central, and posterior; and inferior, medial, and superior. Three sounds illustrative of horizontal distinctions are the similar sounding /p/, /t/, and /k/; three examples of vertical distinctions are the back vowels /ɑ/, /o/, and /u/.

A question arises about relating the number of phonetic and prosodic clues perceived to the terms *hard of hearing* and *deaf*. For example, there are possibly 40 segmental phonemes and 12 suprasegmental phonemes in English. It has been the author's experience that if a child can be trained to perceive some of the speech features or phonemes, he should be able to learn to discriminate most of them. In the meantime the child is on the borderline or in the gray area between functioning as a deaf youngster or a hard-of-hearing individual. With additional perceptual learning, he will become hard of hearing.

The study of Staffan Wedenberg is a case in point (Wedenberg and Wedenberg, 1970). At age two and one-half, Staffan's hearing loss was confirmed. At that time he neither understood speech nor spoke. After 14 months of auditory training, however, he was able to decode auditorily and to speak 25 words. A year later he could understand and speak short sentences. Discriminating most phonetic and prosodic features of speech, he had become by definition a hard-of-hearing child.

Under conditions of extreme noise and reverberation, even a normal-hearing child may function as a deaf youngster. Therefore the definitions are based upon the probability of what is typical. However a child might be hard of hearing in a clinical teaching situation and deaf in a classroom that is not acoustically treated. Even in the latter situation, this same child may become hard of hearing again if a wireless amplification system is provided to permit the speech signal to bypass room noise.

Table 8 suggests the relative contributions of visual and auditory speech clues to the listening process. The hypothetical subject of this table has a profound bilateral hearing loss, with a corner audiogram extending only to 1000 Hz.

Table 8

Hypothetical Sensory Comparison of Perception of Prosodic and Phonetic Features of Speech by One Profoundly Hearing-Impaired Client

Vocal Tract Phenomenon	Vision	Audition
1. Stress	Not perceived	Probably two to three of four levels of stress perceived
2. Intonation	Not perceived	Broad changes probably perceived but usually not refined pitch variations
3. Voicing (voiced or voiceless phoneme)	Not perceived	Probably perceived in most if not all instances in stressed or audible syllables; clue often given primarily by durational differences
4. Oral–nasal (velopharyngeal port closed or open)	Not perceived	Probably perceived in many instances in stressed or audible syllables
5. Restriction of articulation (unrestricted, restricted or momentarily stopped)	Probably perceived in many but not in most instances of stressed or audible syllables	Probably perceived in most instances in stressed or audible syllables
6. Locality of articulation (primarily tongue but also lips, mandible, and other points of articulation)	Features of articulation perceived at front of mouth, but often confused due to homophenicity or similarity among speech sound productions	Probably perceived in many if not most or all instances in stressed or audible syllables

The table includes only hypothesized information. These data are based upon the auditory training experience of the author. It should be mentioned that the audiogram or extent of the auditory area itself would not account for all variables affecting the auditory discrimination of specific hearing-impaired children. More data on many more hearing-impaired children and adults would clarify the comparative contribution of the modalities, as shown in Table 8.

LISTENING CONSIDERATIONS

Communication training with hearing-impaired clients includes *listening instruction* and *speech remediation*. Listening instruction may be defined as training in decoding speech by use of auditory clues, visual or lipreading clues, and/or combined auditory–visual clues. It encompasses what is called auditory training, visual communication training or lipreading instruction, and combinations of the two.

Listening instruction may be differentiated from speech remediation in two ways that are related to speech perception. First, the clinician and client are at conversational distance in listening instruction rather than next to each other. Therefore the client cannot perceive as much visual speech detail on the face of the clinician as he can in speech remediation. A second difference between listening instruction and speech remediation relates to the purposes of each. An objective of listening instruction is improvement in understanding the messages of the clinician and other speakers. A corresponding purpose of speech remediation, on the other hand, is imitation of prosodic and phonetic features of speech.

Sanders (1971) defines *auditory training* and *visual communication training* within the context of information processing and perception. Auditory training constitutes a systematic procedure designed to increase the amount of information that a person's hearing contributes to his total perception. Visual communication training is a systematic procedure designed to increase the amount of information that a person's vision contributes to his total perception.

These definitions are based upon the need of the hearing-impaired listener to approach as normal behavior as possible in decoding speech messages. A normal listener can often perceive speech originating under eight conditions: nearby, face-to-face, in quiet; nearby, face-to-face, in noise; nearby, face turned away, in quiet; nearby, face turned away, in noise; distance, face-to-face, in quiet; distance, face-to-face, in noise; distance, face turned away, in quiet; and distance, face turned away, in noise. The hearing-impaired person fails to decode the message as often as a normal listener because auditory clues are absent or diminished, or incomplete. Furthermore, visual clues may not compensate for loss or lack of auditory clues. In addition, the speaker's face may be hidden, and the auditory noise of the environment may mask the auditory clues of the signal. A final problem in decoding messages is that the listener may have deficient language and/or misunderstand concepts of the message.

Even with normal hearing, the task of decoding a message can be foiled by combinations of still other factors: speech, language, and/or communication problems of the speaker; lack of redundancy in the message; high reverberation and/or poor lighting; and competing visual stimuli. Ordinarily, however, the normal listener has a comfortable redundancy of clues available for decoding speech messages.

> When we listen under favorable conditions, the clues available are far in excess of what is actually needed for satisfactory recognition. Indeed, general context is often so compelling that we know positively what is going to be said even before we hear the words. This is why under normal conditions we understand speech with ease and certainty, despite the ambiguities of acoustic cues. It is also the reason that intelligibility is maintained to such an astonishing extent, despite the variability of speakers, in the presence of noise and distortion. (Denes and Pinson, 1963, p 146)

Of particular importance in listening training is the utilization of the remaining auditory clues as well as the visual clues that may seldom be used by the normal listener. As necessary, the hearing-impaired client should also be trained in speech and language so that these communicative components do not counteract gains in perception of sensory clues. In addition, the client should be encouraged to develop a store of contentive information on life that contributes understanding to the speech messages conveyed.

CURRENT LISTENING STATUS

Many hearing-impaired children have used relatively few auditory clues in the perception of speech. Five reasons for such disuse are proposed.

1. Their parents and/or teachers may not recognize the extent to which their residual hearing exists and can be utilized for learning and communication (Vernon, 1972).
2. Auditory training procedures may not be within the expertise of most of the specialists who are educating them (Costello, 1958).

3. Hearing aids and auditory training units are often in a state of dis-repair or are not utilized optimally (Olsen and Matkin, 1971).

4. High noise and reverberation levels in many if not most regular and special classrooms or educational facilities tend to mask auditory clues, whether they are amplified or not (Ross and Giolas, 1971).

5. Hearing-impaired children who have not been conditioned to utilize auditory clues of speech learn to rely on and function with visual clues, although less successfully than if they had audition (Wedenberg, 1954).

Listening or decoding speech by use of visual instead of auditory clues is fraught with other difficulties. The speaker may not be facing the listener or may be too far away to be lip-read. Furthermore the vocal tract activities that produce the prosodic and phonetic features of speech are only partially visible on the lips. And most speech sounds look like or are similar to one or more other speech sounds. For example, the listener may not visually distinguish *me* from *be* and from *pea*.

These difficulties, associated with the perception of auditory and visual speech clues, have led to the use of manual communication with a great many hearing-impaired children, even hard-of-hearing youngsters.

REDUNDANCY, CONTRAINTS, AND NOISE

In order for listening training to be successful, auditory and visual speech clues learned in the remedial space must also be utilized in conversational and other learning settings. Such carry-over can be facilitated by designing clinical training sessions that simulate natural situations. Practice in decoding sentences can include fading out more and more visual clues and adding more and more competing auditory noise (Brown, 1974).

Sanders (1971) suggests that as listening instruction proceeds, speech stimuli should be presented to the hearing-impaired person under conditions of decreasing redundancy. In other words the pool of auditory and visual clues should be systematically decreased in size. Situational, contextual, and/or linguistic clues that help in predicting the message should be made less and less available to the client. Ordinarily, an excess of clues is available for decision making in speech perception. This informational redundancy is much less accessible to the hearing impaired person. He must be trained to get along with a minimum of clues.

Sanders (1971) relates the terms *redundancy* and *contraints* to auditory training and visual communication training. The term *contraint* refers to the restrictions placed upon the possible interpretations of a message by a situation, a context, and/or an utterance structure. We are aware that a situation often signals the message before the speaker utters it. Knowing the topic of discussion also greatly assists the listener, and being able to decode certain words or even phonemes of a sentence facilitates total perception of a message.

In listening training the concept of signal/noise ratio is important also. A child with normal hearing can select the signal or desired sound from a noise background when it is less intense than the noise. But for the wearer of a hearing aid, the signal must be more intense than the noise. By definition, signal/noise ratio is the difference in decibels (dB) between the intensity of the signal and that of the noise. For example, if the intensity of the speech signal reaching the ears of the listener is 70 dB, and the noise level is 70 dB, the signal/noise ratio is 0 dB—a ratio undesirable for a hearing aid user. Continual attention must be given to keeping the room noise level down unless a wireless transmission system is being used by speaker and listener (Gengel, 1971).

Another important consideration in listening training is whether or not a binaural hearing aid is being used by the hearing-impaired client. Having two ears enables the normal-hearing person to identify the source of the signal and to sort it out from surrounding or competing signals and noise. Evidence also exists that a child wearing two ear level hearing aids enjoys similar benefits (Ross et al., 1974). In group situations such localization and selection are particularly important because the *listener* cannot follow speech moving rapidly from person to person by use of lipreading or visual speech comprehension.

AUDITION AND VISION

In an educational audiology approach to case management, more attention is given to employment of residual hearing than to that of vision. This focus is understandable inasmuch as residual hearing provides the potential for utilization of greater numbers of relevant sensory speech clues than does vision (Berg, 1972). At its peak hearing combines a refined versatility for processing the speech signal with an uncanny competence for receiving it from any location within talking distance. In contrast, vision is a unidirectional sense that simply supplements audition in providing sensory speech clues. Its value, however, should not be underestimated: some hearing-impaired individuals with linguistic skills can decode a great many speech messages through visual clues when auditory clues are absent (Berg, 1970).

During the listening process the hearing-impaired person often has access to both auditory and visual clues of speech. Whether the individual is an adult who has lost some hearing or a child who has never had normal audition, the combined modalities make more clues available than either sense by itself. Hypothetical examples of the use of both modalities are related to persons with varying degree of auditory sensitivity below.

Faint loss, 11–25 dB. Distant or quiet speech is not completely audible. The client has to look at distant speakers to understand their messages.

Mild loss, 26–40 dB. Speech at 6–12 feet, particularly with competing room noise and reverberation, is often difficult to hear. The client depends upon looking at the speaker in even more instances than the person with a faint loss.

Moderate loss, 41–55 dB. The client has been fitted with a hearing aid which permits him to listen about as well as the individual with a faint loss.

Moderate-to-severe loss, 56–70 dB. Without an aid the client can only hear nearby speech well. With an aid he may function like the person with a faint loss. In either instance under normal noise conditions, he may need to look toward the speaker who is 12 feet away.

Severe loss, 71–90 dB. Without an aid the client may not hear conversational speech or a teacher giving instructions, even at 3–6 feet. With an aid the client might function like the individual with the mild loss.

Profound loss, 91–110 dB. Without an aid the client can only hear *ad concham* stimulation. With an aid he can detect the presence of nearby speech and can ordinarily perceive significant amounts of it after training. He relies on whatever lipreading clues and auditory clues he can get. A wireless auditory training system helps him particularly with communication from 12 feet away (Ross and Giolas, 1971).

VISUAL INNOVATIONS

Notwithstanding the advantages of being hard-of-hearing, the education of the hearing-impaired child since its beginnings has given precedence to utilization of visual modes of communication. Perhaps as a result, most children in special schools and special classes function as deaf children. The fruits of the failure to utilize residual hearing are linguistic retardation, unintelligible speech, and breakdown in communication with persons who do not use sign language.

The history and development of unique visual forms of communication is a fascinating study of ingenuity. A brief description and rationale for these communicative forms is described below.

American sign language (Ameslan). Hand, arm, and body positions, and movements are given arbitrary meaning as words and thoughts (Fant, 1973).

Signed English (Ameslish). The same system as that above, except that the signs are refined or modified and are sequenced to conform closely to the detail and syntax of our native language (Bragg, 1973).

Finger spelling. Finger positions and movements are established for each of the 26 alphabet letters needed to spell English (Scouten, 1972).

Visible speech movements. Positions and/or movements of the lips, mandible, and visible part of the tongue and teeth are watched during speech (Pratt, 1968).

Cornett cues. Hand configurations and hand positions on the neck and face are used during speech (Cornett, 1967).

These five visual forms or modes can be combined with auditory speech clues in *total communication* (Ameslan or Ameslish), in the *combined* or *Rochester* method using finger spelling, in the *oral* or lip-reading method, and in *cued speech* which employs Cornett cues and lipreading.

Historically these visual innovations were introduced or developed apart from auditory considerations, with the founding of the first school for the deaf in 1817 (Silverman, 1970). For at least 50 years signs and finger spelling or a manual approach predominated. Beginning in 1867 and continuing on for a century, the oral method and combined approaches came into prominence, particularly as day schools and day classes were established (O'Connor, 1967; Waite, 1967). During the last seven years, the Ameslish type of total communication and the cued speech method have gained many adherents (Bird, 1974; Cornett, 1975).

At this time the two predominant communicative approaches are the oral or aural method and total communication. Utilization of these two methods is illustrated in Figure 15. The exact percentages of children being educated in special classes with these two methods is unknown. However, lately the pendulum has swung from oralism toward total communication.

At least four generalizations can be derived from study of visual communicative forms in the education of the hearing-impaired child. One is that opinions differ as to the relative worth of particular methods, but objective evidence or hard data are barely emerging. Another is that the effectiveness of a particular method depends upon the extent to which it is used for communication throughout the days, months,

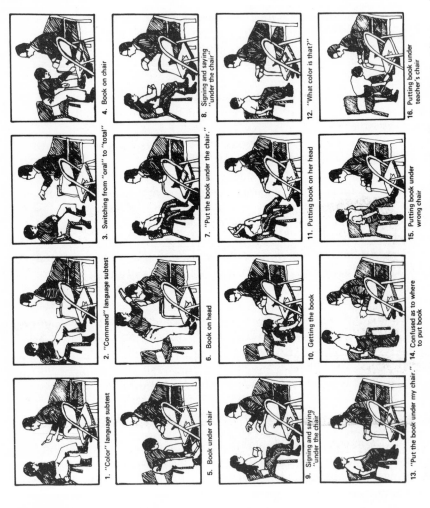

Fig. 15. Sequence of illustrations of training procedures with three hearing-impaired children using oral and total communication methodology. Compliments Utah State University, Logan.

1. "Color" language subtest
2. "Command" language subtest
3. Switching from "oral" to "total"
4. Book on chair
5. Book under chair
6. Book on head
7. "Put the book under the chair."
8. Signing and saying "under the chair"
9. Signing and saying "under the chair"
10. Getting the book
11. Putting book on her head
12. "What color is that?"
13. "Put the book under my chair."
14. Confused as to where to put book
15. Putting book under wrong chair
16. Putting book under teacher's chair

and years of the life of a given hearing-impaired child. A third generalization is that all of these methods have tended to relegate audition to a minor or supplementary avenue for the acquisition of language, speech, and listening skills. Finally, the use of a particular method should begin in the very early years of the child's life.

Notwithstanding the mode of visual communicative input, within each of the communicative methodologies—total, combined, oral, or cued speech—a primary training objective has been the systematic correlation of visual clues with the phonemes of the English language. In the instance of the total approach, for example, Cornett (1975) points out its use is based on the expectation that the child will either (1) think expressively in sign language and syllabic–verbal language simultaneously, or (2) think in one language and translate into the other during nearly simultaneous expression in the two languages. The simultaneous use of speech and manual communication may require knowledge of both rather than development of a hybrid language or mixture of the two. Cornett suggests that speech and manual languages are not mutually supportive. The English words must be taught by separate association with each of the corresponding signs, for example, by writing the equivalent.

Cornett (1975) lists five criteria for an adequate communicative method. One is that it should be oral so that there is complete use of and dependence on the information available from the lips. A second criterion is that any information added to that available from the lips must be compatible (in meaning, rhythm, etc.) with spoken language. A third is that the method must make evident all the essential details of spoken language, contributing to the gradual absorption of full understanding of language from the act of communication. A fourth criterion for an adequate communicative method is that it must be capable of being learned by a very young child through the simple process of exposure to communication in the home, without formal teaching. Finally, it must be capable of being learned by average parents who are willing to make a reasonable effort to help their child.

On the surface it appears that cued speech comes closest to meeting these criteria, with the Rochester or combined method second, and the Ameslish type of total communication third. Without audition, however, the prosodic or suprasegmental phoneme detail is not present. Also, parents have more difficulty in learning cues, signs, and/or finger spelling than they do in becoming competent with a strictly auditory approach. In addition, it is audition that facilitates spontaneous speech acquisition during infancy, whereas the visual signs or clues do not. Cornett and hearing-impaired students using cued speech are illustrated in Figure 16.

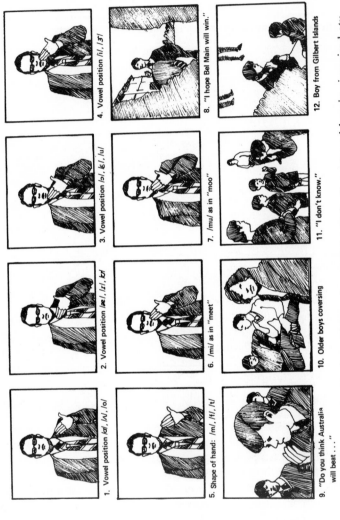

Fig. 16. Illustrations of use of cued speech by Orin Cornett and hearing-impaired students of a school for the deaf. Compliments Gallaudet College.

58

Giving precedence to any visual input system including lipreading has a limitation within the sensory system itself. If audition is not established initially as the primary input and acquisition system, the communicative skills of language, speech, and listening will be impeded. A rationale for such limitation is provided by Wedenberg and Wedenberg (1970) based on their experience in training their son Staffan and many other hearing-impaired children.

> In our opinion the natural synergism between hearing and the visual sense, which exists in normal persons, is highly disturbed in these cases of impaired hearing. Approximately 90 percent of the conceptions of a person with completely normal senses are based upon the visual sense. The complete or partial loss of the auditory sense results in an even greater concentration on the other senses and an intensification of their use. The unimpaired visual sense appropriates the greater part of attention to the detriment of the impaired auditory sense. The residual hearing that exists is not rationally utilized. On the contrary, the peripheral damage is augmented by an inability to use the hearing which, especially for a child building up his speech, is fatal. The task is to restore the synergy as far as possible by giving the child an auditory pattern through the normal channel. The hearing sense, although defective, should be used at every opportunity. Speech reading (lipreading) should not be extensively introduced until after the child has acquired this auditory pattern, which he demonstrated by approaching and wanting to have words spoken into his ear; in other words, not until he has the listening attitude. The child's vocabulary may then be rapidly increased. Lipreading had already begun to play an important role for this boy. It was, therefore, necessary to discourage it because, in our opinion, if he grew too dependent upon speech reading he would never learn to listen (Wedenberg and Wedenberg, 1970, pp 322–323).

The Wedenberg's references to over-dependence on speech reading could be generalized to include signs, finger spelling, and Cornett cues as well.

The author advances two basic communicative approaches for the education of hearing-impaired children. One is to utilize the auditory approach, as exemplified by Wedenberg and Wedenberg (1970). It should be used for most hearing-impaired children. The typical hearing-impaired child in a special school or class can be educated as a hard-of-hearing child. Once audition or the listening attitude is established through exposure and conditioning, visual means can be used to fill in spoken language elements that are inaudible or partially audible, such as word endings and unstressed syllables. Although visual speech clues or lipreading as well as print are usually sufficient, when they are not, Cornett cues or finger spelling can be employed (Cornett, 1975).

The other approach the writer suggests is to utilize primarily visual input for those hearing-impaired children who cannot acquire language, speech, and listening skills through an auditory modality. Lipreading supported by residual hearing or vibrotactile input might be tried initially. If the child does not progress sufficiently by this oral approach, then signs could be introduced also to establish and expand a communication system between infant and parents. Soon afterwards, cued speech or refined signs from the Ameslish system, or even the Rochester method, could be added. In all instances sensory input via the hearing aid should still be provided, at least until it has been established that audition does not exist. Even then, electrotactile clues available from low frequency amplification would facilitate speech and spoken language perception.

It is relevant that Cornett (1973) is developing an automatic cuer to present electrovisual or electrotactile clues to supplement what is seen on the lips during speech. He has demonstrated that a deaf person can understand speech through a combination of lipreading and vibratory cues transmitted through the fingers, if the cues follow the principles of cued speech. The visual cues of the cuer will be in the form of flashing lights reflected into the eye by a concave mirror in such a way as to appear to be on the face of the speaker. Again it should be emphasized that such a visual system will present certain phonetic or segmental features (consonants, vowels, and diphthongs) but not the prosodic detail of stress and intonation that most facilitates the development of spoken language.

Another device designed to facilitate listening is called an Eyeglass Speechreader. It has been designed and used by Upton (1968), who is hard-of-hearing himself. Five display lamps, mounted on an eyeglass lens which also frames the speaker's face, light in response to voiced sounds, unvoiced fricatives, unvoiced stops, voiced fricatives, and voiced stops. The Upton analyzing device, which employs integrated circuitry, is concealed beneath the clothing. Upton reported that he was a poor lipreader unless he used his speech analyzer.

An updated Upton Eyeglass Speechreader is shown in Figure 17. Pickett, Gengel, and Quinn (1975) note that the new system includes seven light bars. One is a voice level light bar which varies in brightness depending on the overall intensity of the speech signal. The other six bars are lighted one at a time. The output indications are only moderately correlated with the sound classes indicated in the figure.

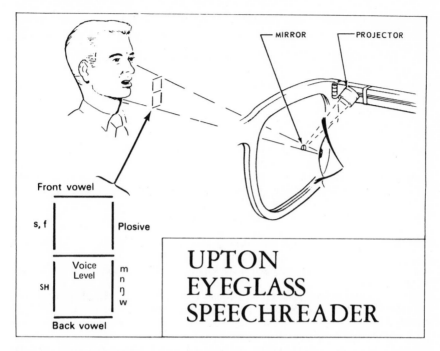

Fig. 17. Relative locations of seven light bars on the lens of the Upton Eyeglass Speechreader. Compliments Bell Helicopter Company.

SUMMARY

The education of the hearing impaired should give precedence to the utilization of residual hearing but not to the exclusion of visual forms of input. Presentation and discussion of the various visual modes of communication suggest that hearing-impaired children tend to be educated as if they are deaf. The features of total communication, the Rochester method, the oral method, and cued speech are explained briefly, and the author advances two basic communicative approaches to meet the individual needs of hearing-impaired children.

REFERENCES

Berg F: Educational audiology, in Berg F and Fletcher S (eds): The Hard of Hearing Child. New York and London, Grune & Stratton, 1970, pp 275–318

Berg F: Sensory Aids in Speech Remediation for the Hearing Impaired. Logan, Utah State University, 1972

Bird P: A Report on Total Communication. Gooding, Idaho School for the Deaf, 1974

Bragg B: Ameslish—our American heritage. A testimony. Am Ann Deaf 118:672–673, 1973

Brown K: A stimulus control, programmed conditioning format for auditory training. M.S. Thesis, Logan, Utah State University, 1974

Cornett O: Cued speech. Am Ann Deaf 112:3–13, 1967

Cornett O: An integrated approach to early education of the hearing impaired. Calif J Comm Dis 2:Fall, 1971

Cornett O: Contract signed and work proceeding on development of automatic cuer. Cued Speech News 7:1–2, 1973

Cornett O: The learning of English by the deaf. Teaching English to the Deaf 2:1, Washington, DC, Gallaudet College, 1975

Costello MR: Realistic goals in auditory training. Report of the Proceedings of the 39th Meeting of the Convention of American Instructors of the Deaf. Washington, DC, US Government Printing Office, 1958 pp 133–145

Denes P, Pinson E: The Speech Chain. Murray Hill, New Jersey, Bell Telephone Labs, 1963

Fant G: Analysis and synthesis of speech processes, in Malmberg B (eds): Manual of Phonetics. Amsterdam, North Holland, 1968, pp 173–277

Fant L: Why Ameslan? Unpublished manuscript. Northridge, California State University, May 1973

Fletcher S: Acoustic phonetics, in Berg F and Fletcher S (eds): The Hard of Hearing Child. New York and London, Grune & Stratton, 1970, pp 57–84

Fry D: Prosodic phenomena, in Malmberg B (ed): Manual of Phonetics. Amsterdam, North Holland, 1968, pp 365–410

Gengel R: Acceptable speech to noise ratios for aided speech discrimination by the hearing impaired. J Audiol Res 11:219–222, 1971

Johansson G: A new coding amplifier system for the severely hard of hearing. Proceedings of the Third International Congress on Acoustics. Amsterdam, Elsevier, 1961, pp 655–657

O'Connor C: Lexington school's first century of oral education. Vol Rev 69:128–136, 1967

Olsen W, Matkin N: Comments on modern auditory training systems and their uses. Bulletin of AOEHI. Washington, DC, AG Bell Assn Deaf 2:7–15, 1971

Pickett J, Gengel R, Quinn R: Research with the Upton eyeglass speechreader. Proceedings of the Speech Communication Seminar, Vol. 4. Stockholm, Almquist & Wiksell; New York, Wiley, 1975

Potter R, Kopp G, Green H: Visible Speech. New York, Dover, 1966

Pratt G: Oral education for deaf children. Reprint No. 769. Washington, DC, AG Bell Assn Deaf, 1968

Ross M, Giolas T: Three classroom listening conditions on speech intelligibility. Am Ann Deaf 116:580–584, 1971

Ross M, Hunt MF, Kessler M, et al: The use of a rating scale to compare binaural and monaural amplification with hearing impaired children. Vol Rev 76:93–99, 1974

Sanders D: Aural Rehabilitation. Englewood Cliffs, New Jersey, Prentice Hall, 1971

Scouten EL: Total communication in new perspective. Louisiana School for the Deaf. Baton Rouge, Louisiana. The Pelican 92:1–2,4

Silverman SR: From Aristotle to Bell and beyond, in Davis H and Silverman SR (eds): Hearing and Deafness. New York, Holt, Rinehart and Winston, 1970, pp 375–383

Upton H: Wearable eyeglass speechreading aid. Am Ann Deaf 113:222–229, 1968

Vernon M: Mind over mouth: A rationale for total communication. Vol Rev 74:529–538, 1972

Waite H: 100 years of conquest of silence. Vol Rev 69:118–126, 1967

Wedenberg E: Auditory training of severely hard of hearing preschool children. Acta Otolaryngol [Suppl] (Stockh) 94:1–129, 1954 (Suppl)

Wedenberg E, Wedenberg M: The advantage of auditory training: A case report, in Berg F and Fletcher S (eds): The Hard of Hearing Child. New York and London, Grune & Stratton, 1970, pp 319–330

3

Auditory Trainers and
Hearing Aids for Children

Among hearing-impaired children, success in listening without *ad concham* stimulation is critically related to the availability and utilization of electroacoustic amplification equipment. Since the advent of electronics, hearing aids and auditory trainers have been developed that can present a relatively undistorted signal, enabling many if not most profoundly hearing-impaired children to learn to perceive speech. Before the electronic age, children with just moderate hearing impairment were often functionally deaf. Basically, a hearing aid or auditory trainer amplifies the speech signal so that it can be heard unless masked out by surrounding or competing noise.

A large variety of electroacoustic devices is currently available for use by hearing-impaired children and adults. Ordinarily, children with a bilateral (two ear) loss 30–40 dB or more or adults with a loss of 40 dB or more are candidates for amplification. Individuals with unilateral hearing losses have not worn hearing aids in the past, but increasing numbers of such persons are doing so now. It may be true that at least 80 percent of the youngsters in special schools or special classes for the hearing impaired (often called deaf) can benefit from use of electroacoustic amplification (Wedenberg, 1967). Most youngsters educated in these special settings are unable to sense speech auditorily, except for sounds delivered right near the ear, unless they are using hearing aids or auditory trainers. Increasing percentages of deaf and hard-of-hearing children are also being educated in regular classes alongside normal-hearing children. Many hearing-impaired children in regular classrooms are also candidates for amplification.

Amplification Types

Brief descriptions of the main types of commercially available amplification devices are given below.

In-the-ear devices are cosmetically appealing but impractical for all but the mildest hearing losses. They are currently more of a gimmick than an aid, and are monaural or binaural.

Over-the-ear aids are relatively small and lightweight and suitable for mild, moderate, severe, and possibly severe–profound losses. They provide up to 50–60 dB of amplification, but their gain and frequency responses are not as suitable as those in body-model aids or auditory trainers. Over-the-ear aids are either monaural or binaural. See Figure 18.

Eyeglass hearing aids are the same as over-the-ear aids except that they are packaged inside or as an extension of a pair of glasses that the person also needs. They are also either monaural or binaural.

Body-type or pocket devices are larger than previously mentioned units. They are suitable for children with even losses of 90–110 dB, and provide up to 75 dB of amplification. Their frequency response is broader or more suitable than that of other aids, and they come in both monaural and binaural models. See Figure 18.

Fig. 18. Artists' drawings of over-the-ear hearing aid in foreground and body-type aid in background (Berg, 1971, p 21).

The CROS (contralateral routing of signals) type is for unilateral (one ear) losses. Sound is routed from the bad ear side of the head to good ear side for input. These units are similar in other characteristics to eyeglass or over-the-ear aids. A discussion of the CROS hearing aid and its many variations is presented by Michael Pollack (1975a).

The desk-type trainer is larger than any of the above wearable aids. It uses headphones or body-type aid receivers and is suitable for children with even losses of 90–110 dB. The desk-type provides up to 75 dB of gain or amplification, its frequency response is even broader than that of body-type aid, and it is either monaural or binaural. This aid is particularly applicable for initial auditory training when it is desirable to have a maximum number of undistorted auditory clues. One of the finest desk model auditory trainers, the EB-43 unit of Ekstein Brothers, is illustrated in Figure 19. Nearly a decade ago, Jeffers wrote an instruction manual to aid the clinician in using this type of EB unit.

Hard wire systems rely on wires to interconnect teacher, microphone(s), amplifier, headphones, or body-type receivers of children. The gain is adjusted on individual control boxes, and recorded input is optional. Its amplification and frequency response features are similar to those of the desk-type trainer. These systems are either monaural or binaural and are relatively inexpensive.

Loop, magnetic induction systems employ a microphone wired to

Fig. 19. Console of Ekstein Model 43 binaural desk-model auditory training unit. Compliments Ekstein Brothers.

an amplifier. The signal is broadcast electromagnetically from a loop driven by the amplifier and is received by a coil in the body-type aids of children. Its gain and frequency response features are similar to those of the previous two units mentioned, but it is monaural.

Loop, radio frequency systems depend on a microphone wired to an amplifier. The signal is broadcast by radio transmission from a loop serving as the antenna and is received by miniature antennas of radio receivers included within enlarged body-type aids of children. Gain and frequency response features are similar to those of last three units mentioned. This loop system is also monaural.

In the wireless, radio frequency system, the teacher wears a wireless microphone transmitter which broadcasts her speech signal by radio transmission. The signal is received by the same system as the one described immediately above. Gain and frequency response features are similar to those described for the last four units. The wireless system is monaural for radio-transmitted signals, and monaural or binaural for signals detected from the environment or sound field.

Amplification and Maintenance

In Figure 20 a series of 12 illustrations depict features of the process of amplification, the operation of a body-type hearing aid, and related problems and considerations. Similar description and guidelines might be advanced with respect to utilization and maintenance of other types of hearing aids and auditory trainers. The relevance of each illustration will be described in order.

1. Sound energy is transduced into electrical energy, amplified, and delivered through the cord to the receiver.
2. The receiver transduces the amplified electrical energy back into sound, which is now amplified and delivered via the ear insert into the outer ear.
3. A switch turns the aid on or off. It also functions as a continuously adjustable volume or gain control.
4. Another switch with three positions permits the hearing aid to incorporate the microphone, a coil for telephone reception, or a combination of microphone and telephone reception.
5. If the aid is "dead," the battery should be removed and checked.
6. If the battery is functioning, the cord between the console unit and the receiver should be twisted to check for a break.
7. The clinician should put the receiver to his ear, turn on the aid, and turn up the gain. He should then vocalize and listen to determine the fidelity of the sound being amplified by the aid. This is a listening check.

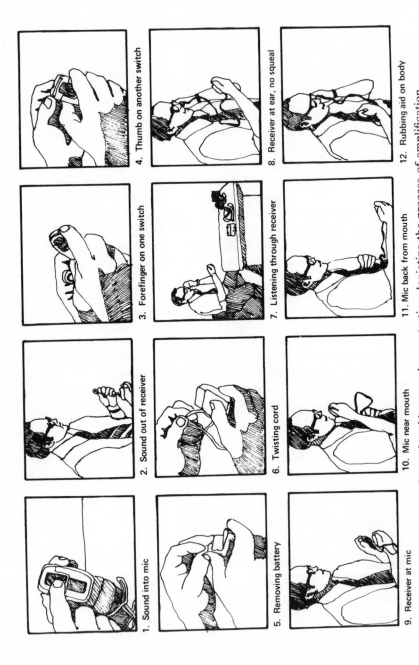

1. Sound into mic   2. Sound out of receiver   3. Forefinger on one switch   4. Thumb on another switch

5. Removing battery   6. Twisting cord   7. Listening through receiver   8. Receiver at ear, no squeal

9. Receiver at mic   10. Mic near mouth   11. Mic back from mouth   12. Rubbing aid on body

Fig. 20. Drawings of a videotape demonstration depicting the process of amplification, the operation of a hearing aid, and related problems and considerations.

8. In the same situation the clinician should also turn up the gain even more to determine whether a squeal will result. It may not if the ear insert is snug in the ear canal and coupled well with the receiver.
9. A squeal can be demonstrated with the receiver close to the microphone.
10. When the microphone or console is placed close to the mouth, the sound output from the receiver will be relatively loud.
11. When the microphone or console is moved back from the mouth, the same sound output will be relatively soft.
12. If the console or main part of the aid rubs against clothing or the body, an unwanted sound will be amplified along with the desired sound.

A body-type hearing aid, specifically the console or main part of it, may be worn in a shirt pocket. A body-type hearing aid designed specifically for children, the HC 527 Phonic Ear, is shown in Figure 21. Features of this aid include recessed controls, rechargeable nickel cadmium batteries, small size, broad frequency response, a 60 dB signal/noise ratio, linear compression, and a "child-proof" microphone.

Selection Guidelines

A number of guidelines might be applied to the selection of amplification units for particular hearing-impaired children and educational settings. Basically, the aid should permit the child to perceive as much of the prosodic and phonetic aspects of speech as possible. Therefore the device should at least faithfully amplify frequencies of sound between 200 Hz and 3300 Hz. However, if the auditory area of the given child does not include hearing across this entire critical range, the aid should amplify those frequencies that can be detected. It should be mentioned that audiometric measurement may not assess the entire auditory area of an individual with a very profound hearing loss. The audiometer simply does not generate sufficiently high intensities at all frequencies to reach the greatest hearing losses.

The aid should also allow the youngster to hear both his own voice) as well as the speech of others. This means that it should have sufficient gain or amplification. In addition to standard gain and acoustic output control, the device should permit detailed frequency response adjustments so that its characteristics can conform to the hearing response of the individual child. Thus the specialist should be able to make adjustments beyond simply varying a tone control or moving a tone switch from high to low positions. Factory personnel should not have the only option to make the acoustical adjustments that will have to be made for the child. Guidelines for these adjustments should be included with the aid.

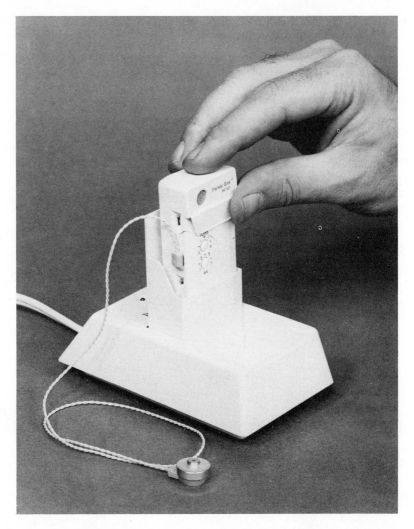

Fig. 21. The HC 527 Phonic Ear body-type hearing aid being placed in a battery charging unit. Compliments HC Electronics, Tiburon, California.

The device should also be relatively small and portable. This requirement suggests that the desk-type trainer, the hard wire system, and loop systems should be given relatively less consideration.

Finally, the amplification unit should be adaptable to use in a binaural system of amplification. The closer to ear level that aids can be positioned, the better. Current arguments for use of binaural amplification with most hearing-impaired children with bilateral hearing losses are compelling. Over-the-ear and eyeglass aids come closest to meeting this requirement. Body-type systems can be effectively positioned on young children for binaural listening. It should be mentioned that a wireless aid must be used as a body-type aid to be binaural.

Because of these considerations at least one exemplary facility for the hearing impaired, the Willie Ross School, provides two over-the-ear or eyeglass systems for children with lesser hearing losses. These aids are used both in school and out. In addition, wireless binaural systems are utilized for each of the children with relatively greater hearing losses. Outside of school these same youngsters ordinarily use body-type aids (Ross, 1974).

This school has been remodeled so that each classroom is acoustically treated. With acoustic treatment and adequate classroom management, the children with over-the-ear and eyeglass aids can perceive the teacher. The noise and reverberation problems are alleviated. Furthermore the children with more serious losses using the wireless systems are not bothered by any remaining noise and reverberation problems because a radio-transmitted signal bypasses these interferences.

Additional Considerations

The rationale for utilization of binaural hearing aids is explained below. First, a normal listener uses two ears to localize, perceive spaciousness, distinguish speech from background noise and competing signals, and decode messages conveyed rapidly by individuals in a group. On the other hand a person with a unilateral hearing loss or a hearing-impaired person using a conventional hearing aid on one ear does not perform these functions adequately. However parents and teachers have substantiated that children wearing binaural hearing aids adjust and learn better than youngsters fitted monaurally (Ross, Hunt, Kessler, et al., 1974).

Yonovitz (1974) placed two noise sources 60 degrees to the left and right of 20 hearing-impaired children who were tested individually. The speech signal source originated directly in front of them. It was a recorded version of the WIPI test, which requires a picture-pointing response from the child (Ross and Lerman, 1971). Two channels of signal in noise were recorded at five signal/noise (S/N) ratios using microphones placed in the ear canals of a given subject. The children were tested with earphones under all S/N ratios with both monaural and binaural input. The results demonstrated binaural superiority under all S/N ratios.

Ross (1975) advanced other considerations relevant to use of amplification. He stated that only a minority of hearing-impaired children do not hear at all. Because there is no way of knowing who these youngsters are, it makes sense to require hearing aids for all hearing-impaired children at the earliest age possible. Initially these are body-type aids because over-the-ear aids usually will fall off an infant.

Ross also notes that audiologists do not recommend "hearing aids" for young children but *electroacoustic systems*. The brand of an aid is not important, but acoustic requirements are. Whatever brand is purchased, the system should meet requirements specific to the hearing problems of the individual. A hearing aid with 10 percent or more harmonic distortion should be excluded from consideration.

Initial information on the residual hearing of the child may be limited. Therefore an aid is required whose electroacoustic characteristics can be modified to reflect audiometric data on the child that are obtained later. A Y cord arrangement is often recommended with a body-type aid when the auditory status of the two ears is insufficient to proceed directly to binaural fitting. In this arrangement the output of the aid is delivered to receivers and molds at both ears.

More recently, binaural fitting has been recommended instead because most children have bilaterally symmetrical losses and aids can be adjusted for gain and output with a moderate degree of imbalance of sound input. Also, parents are less likely to accept a recommendation for two aids after their child has adjusted to one aid. And occasionally a child himself resists a second aid after using and adjusting to one.

It is a problem to ensure that the receiver–mold combination stays in the ear of the child. Children's ears are small, soft, and smooth. The receiver mold easily drops out. Possible solutions are taping the receiver to the pinna; bending the cord up and around the back of the pinna and taping the cord to the mastoid process; or using a shell mold with tubing and an adapter for the receiver, which is then either taped behind the ear or hooked to the collar of the child's clothing. The clinician should teach parents how to insert and properly seal the earmold, how to operate the hearing aid, how to troubleshoot it, and how to remove it. Langford (1975) details and illustrates the technical procedures of coupling amplified sound from the hearing aid receiver to the ear canal.

Gain or amplification can be set in various ways. Ross (1975) prefers increasing the level until acoustic feedback or squeal occurs, and then reducing the gain just a bit until feedback is eliminated. Another method he combines with the first is estimating level on the basis of knowing hearing loss, signal input level, and gain. For example, if the loss averages 90 dB, the input 70 dB, and the gain 50 dB, the sensation level is 30 dB above threshold or 70 + 50 − 90. If the sensation level is too low, the child will not receive a sufficient degree of amplified sound. If it is too high, the setting may traumatize him.

The hearing-impaired listener, particularly the person with a sensorineural hearing loss, is more sensitive to the masking effect of noise while wearing a hearing aid than is the normal-hearing person. Tillman, Carhart, and Olsen (1970) indicate that many instances occur in which hearing aid users cannot understand their companions even though all signals are sufficiently amplified and competing background sounds are so faint that a person with normal hearing would disregard them easily. Gengel (1971) noted that persons using 10 dB S/N ratios found listening so difficult that they would rather not use their hearing aids. It cannot be overemphasized that acceptable noise level for normal-hearing listeners may not be acceptable for hearing-impaired persons.

Low frequency amplification should be de-emphasized with a hearing-impaired child who demonstrates residual hearing through the higher frequencies. Evidence exists that perception of the first formants of speech can interfere with perception of the more critical second formant consonant transitions. If a youngster, however, possesses only low frequency residual hearing, he will not hear the second formants anyway. Therefore it makes sense to exploit the low frequency area for such a child. Ross (1975) suggested that an engineering thrust be made to provide more amplification in hearing aids at the higher frequencies, those beyond 4000 Hz. He noted that recent engineering with electret and ceramic microphones has focused only on exploitation of the low frequencies of 100 Hz and below.

It is questionable whether or not pathological damage occurs as a result of prolonged sound input from hearing aids set at high gain and output levels. Ross (1975) noted that residual hearing can deteriorate in some instances. However he stated that amplification should not be permanently withheld from a child who is completely unable to function auditorily without an aid.

The care given to hearing aids is all too often deplorable. Beginning with a study by Gaeth and Lounsbury (1966), one investigation after another has revealed that only about 50 percent of hearing aids are functioning at all or adequately. Ross (1975) indicated that it seems to be easier to walk on the moon than to design "child-proof" hearing aids. Olsen and Matkin (1971) and others have made similar findings about the state of disrepair of auditory trainers in special classrooms for the hearing impaired.

Ross (1974) anticipated that improved types of amplification systems will be devised as a result of the rapid developments now occurring in the hearing aid industry. He described one such aid: The amplification system consists of a miniaturized microphone located at each ear. Thus sound from the environment is intercepted in the same locations as the normal auditory system receives auditory input. Wires extend from each microphone to a miniaturized console unit located in a pocket against the chest of the hearing-impaired person. This console transduces the sound into electricity, amplifies it, and delivers it to two receivers located in the ears. The console also includes a radio receiver for detecting and decoding wireless transmission. The miniaturized hearing aid receivers are snapped onto earmolds for insertion into the ears. With such an amplification system, speech from the sound field of environment would be heard. Speech could also bypass the sound field as desired because of the wireless transmission capability. The miniaturized components of the system would be comfortable to wear and cosmetically appealing.

Currently, particular interest in the hearing aid industry is being focused on improvements in ear level amplification units. Such rapid development is exemplified by the Unitron-B-500 instrument shown in Figure 22. The Unitron aid features miniature size, a continuously adjustable directional microphone, protection from sudden loud noise, and relatively broad frequency response. A more detailed description of this aid is included in a technical report which may be obtained by writing to the company, located in Port Huron, Michigan.

Trends in wearable hearing aid sales during the past decade reveal that the demand for over-the-ear and eyeglass amplification is growing. In 1974 these types of aids accounted for 90.3 percent of sales. In 1963 the percentage had been 77.9 (Pollack, 1975a). Perhaps no more than 10 percent of the half million units sold annually in the United States,

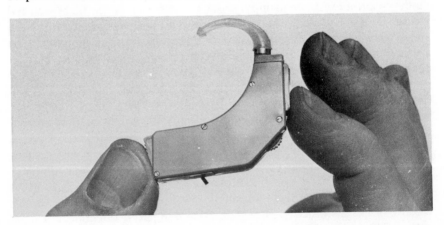

Fig. 22. The miniature Unitron B-500 over-the-ear hearing aid being held between the forefinger and thumb of a man. Compliments Unitron Industries LTD.

however, are fitted on hearing-impaired children. And most of these are not auditory training units. Thus less engineering and technological effort in the hearing aid industry has been expended on meeting the amplification needs of children.

WIRELESS SYSTEMS

During the past decade manufacturers of auditory training systems have become more and more convinced that hard wire and induction loop systems must give way to radio frequency systems, particularly those that are completely wireless, as illustrated in Figure 22. Although inexpensive, the hard wire systems are rarely seen these days. The magnetic induction loop systems are not found either, except when they are a part of what is essentially a radio frequency system. Advantages and disadvantages of these systems are detailed by Hetherington (1975).

Rationale

Ross and Giolas (1971) found that there is a rationale for the use of wireless radio frequency systems. They compared listening performance in ordinary classrooms of hearing aid users, non-hearing aid users with minimal hearing loss, and normally hearing children. The two experimental groups listened under three conditions: as they ordinarily did, with a wireless amplification system operating as a body-model hearing aid, and with a wireless system operating with both environmental sound input and radio frequency transmission. The speech stimuli were monosyllabic word lists administered as live voice. The speaker's lips were covered so that only auditory clues might be perceived. The stimuli were delivered at a distance of 12 feet from the desks of the children. One finding was that the mean speech discrimination score of the normal hearing group was 91.1 percent. The mean scores for the hearing aid users under conditions one, two, and three were 20, 10.9, and 41.1 percent respectively. The comparable mean scores for the non-hearing aid users were 46, 32.7, and 80 percent respectively.

Based upon these findings, Ross and Giolas (1973) concluded that the hearing aid users had depressingly low discrimination scores except when using the wireless system. They also noted that non-hearing aid users with minimal hearing losses had much more difficulty understanding speech in ordinary classrooms than is generally realized. However, when they used the wireless system, their discrimination scores approached those of their normal-hearing counterparts. It is of relevance that some hearing aid users scored zero or near zero percent in speech discrimination.

It should be mentioned that the ambient room noise was found to average 60 dB sound pressure level (SPL), and the speaker's voice was 65 dB SPL at the children's desks 12 feet away. Thus the signal/noise (S/N) level averaged 5 dB. The reverberation characteristics of the rooms were not described. The experiment points out the severe listening problems that hearing impaired children experience in ordinary classrooms, particularly if they cannot utilize lipreading clues as a supplement to auditory information.

When using a wireless system, however, the teacher or clinician may speak 6 inches from the microphone, where her signal is decoded and placed on a wave transmitted to the listener. The radio receiver of the listener receives the transmitted signal and converts it back into a speech signal. During this process of radio transmission and reception, the noise and reverberation of the classroom is bypassed. It is as if the speaker were speaking almost directly into the microphone of the hearing aid of the listener.

The concept of signal strength versus distance between speaker and listener should be explained further. At a distance of 3 feet, a 65 to 70 dB speech signal might be appropriate. A doubling or halving of this distance decreases or increases the sound intensity by about 6 dB, if the effect of reverberation is overlooked. Therefore at 6 feet the speaker has to increase his sound level by 6 dB, and at 12 feet by another 6 dB to be heard as if 3 feet away. As such distance increases, ambient noise and reverberation also interfere more and more with speech reception. The effect of distance upon speech intensity is best demonstrated by moving farther and farther away from the microphone of a loudspeaking system, or closer and closer to it. The effects are dramatic.

Many of us have tried to listen in a highly reverberant room. In such an environment we are receiving sound both directly and indirectly from the speaker. The room is literally echoing with sound energy which is not being absorbed as it should. The speech signal is bounding back and forth from wall to wall and between floor and ceiling as well. For example, the /b/ of *boat* is heard at one instant, and then reheard in the next moment as a reflected sound. However at this time the listener wants to have it quiet so that he can hear the /o/ phoneme. This overlapping or masking of one sound by another goes on and on. Its effect is lessened as the distance between the speaker and listener is decreased. A better solution is acoustic treatment of this room by use of tile, carpeting, and the like. The reverberation time of sound in a closed space should be a small fraction of a second. In many special and particularly ordinary classrooms it may be one or two seconds in length. It is no wonder that the hearing aid user can have a problem listening.

Description

A wireless system includes a microphone–transmitter, a receiver unit for each student, and a charging system for batteries. It is through the microphone–transmitter that the teacher or parent reaches each ear of each student, notwithstanding the distance between them. The receiver units provide the radio reception and hearing aid capability many students need. The batteries of the receiver units and often the microphone–transmitter units are recharged overnight or over a weekend in the charger unit. Costs during 1974 for microphone–transmitters ranged from $300 to $350, for each receiver unit from $350 to $550, and for a 10-unit charger from $290 to $300. Costs for an entire system for teacher and eight students ranged from $3400 to $5000.

Relevant components and controls of one wireless system, the HC 421 FM Phonic Ear, are depicted in Figure 23 as a series of tracings of photographs. A clarifying caption accompanies each tracing. The series is extracted from a videotape demonstration of Bob White, a Phonic Ear representative.

An extension of the Phonic Ear demonstration can be seen in Figure 23. It depicts procedures for fitting the receiver unit of the wireless system on a hard-of-hearing child. Selected highlights of the demonstration are also derived from videotape.

Clarification

It should be emphasized that a wireless auditory trainer is basically a monaural or pseudobinaural system. It is not a binaural system because sound input is delivered through only one microphone pickup and transmitted on only one radio frequency carrier wave. When picked up by the receivers, the speech signal is decoded from the carrier wave, amplified in the hearing aid, and fed to two earpieces.

The only way in which a commercially available wireless system is binaural is when the receiver units are used as body-model hearing aids. A three-position switch on a given receiver unit permits a listener using this device to decode wireless transmission of the signal, environmental transmission of sound (body-model aid), or a combination of the two. If the receiver unit includes two microphones for environmental pickup of sound, it will also include two separate amplifiers or

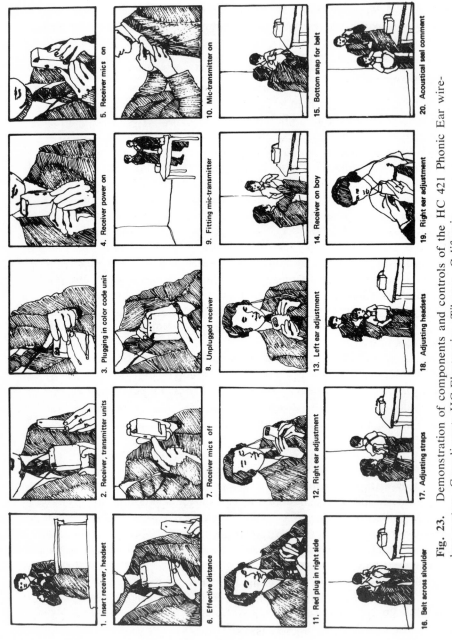

1. Insert receiver, headset
2. Receiver, transmitter units
3. Plugging in color code unit
4. Receiver power on
5. Receiver mics on
6. Effective distance
7. Receiver mics off
8. Unplugged receiver
9. Fitting mic-transmitter
10. Mic-transmitter on
11. Red plug in right side
12. Right ear adjustment
13. Left ear adjustment
14. Receiver on boy
15. Bottom snap for belt
16. Belt across shoulder
17. Adjusting straps
18. Adjusting headsets
19. Right ear adjustment
20. Acoustical seal comment

Fig. 23. Demonstration of components and controls of the HC 421 Phonic Ear wireless system. Compliments HC Electronics, Tiburon, California.

two hearing aids in one chassis or container. As a hearing aid, the receiver unit is binaural. With wireless transmission, however, it is not. Even as a hearing aid, the two microphones are not located near the two ears. Therefore they are not positioned for optimal realization of the binaural advantage. Instead the microphones are spaced only a few inches apart on the top of the receiver chassis.

Used as a hearing aid, a wireless system receiver is a quality device. Weighing 7 to 10 ounces, depending on the brand, it includes many desirable electroacoustic features. The gain and output capabilities meet the needs of children with very profound losses. The frequency response may be 175 to 5000 Hz with earphones and 250 to 4000 with insert receivers (H. C. Electronics, 1971). Harmonic distortion is 5 percent or less. The units also provide linear compression of the output if the input signal becomes so great that it ordinarily causes discomfort and distortion. In addition, the signal is typically 50 to 60 dB more intense than the noise of ambient electronics generated within the receiver unit.

Because the receiver unit weighs considerably more and is larger than even the body-model hearing aid, many hearing-impaired children do not favor using wireless devices for receiving environmental sound input outside of the classroom. It is the wireless feature of the system they appreciate, not using the receiver units in place of their personal hearing aids.

When the wireless transmission system is switched to combined radio frequency and environmental sound input for use in structured listening, speech, and language training, teacher input is optimal and other children can be heard relatively well. The use of environmental sound input also permits the child to hear his own voice optimally. However he cannot hear other children who are beyond five to six feet, particularly if the room is noisy and reverberant. It must be remembered that it is only the teacher who ordinarily has input through the microphone–transmitter unit.

Ideally, a wireless system should enable the clinician or teacher to adjust gain, maximum acoustic output, and frequency response. Current systems provide only a combined gain and output adjustment for each ear. Receiver units should also have the capability to switch between various frequency bands.

It is desirable that both the microphone transmitter and the receiver units permit recorded sound input in addition to transmitted and environmental speech. Often the teacher may want to have a group listen to a disk record or an audio cassette, or, better perhaps, to a sound filmstrip or the like. Or the clinician working with an individual may want to do likewise without disturbing other children in the same class-

Table 9

Comparative Analysis of Features and Costs of the EFI, Phonic Ear, and Biocoustics Wireless Auditory Training Equipment. Compliments Electronics Futures Incorporated.

Feature	EFI "TravelEar II" FM Transmitter	H. C. Electronics "Phonic Ear" FM Transmitter	Biocoustics FM Transmitter
72—76 mHz	Yes	Yes	Yes
Band width	Wide	Narrow	Narrow
Number of frequencies	8—signal/noise 55-60 dB down	32—signal/noise less than 40 dB down	32—signal/noise less than 40 dB down
Size and weight	3-3/4" L × 2-1/2" W × 1"D, less than 6 oz	7-1/4" L × 1-1/2"W × 1" D, 7 oz	6-1/2" L × 1-1/4" D, 6 oz
Hybrid circuitry	Yes	No	No
Throwaway battery	Yes	No	No
Automatic muting	Yes	No	No
Accepts other audio source	Yes	Yes	Yes
Dynamic compression	Yes—onset 2 Ms, release 150 Ms	Yes—onset 3 Ms, release 150 Ms	Yes—onset 4 Ms, release 40 Ms
Serviceable at customer location	Yes	No	No
Dual frequency capability	No	No	Yes
Hi/Lo power switch	Yes	No	No

Feature	Student Receiver	Student Receiver	Student Receiver	Student Receiver
Receiver Multichannel	Yes—3 frequencies on each receiver	No—must change module	No—must change module	No—must change module
Monaural/binaural in same package	Yes		No	No
Rechargeable batteries	Yes		Yes	Yes
Distortion	Less than 2%		Less than 5%	Less than 2%
Mic sensitivity control	Yes		No	No
MPO, binaural, and bass tone controls	Yes		No	No
Accepts any outside audiosource	Yes		No	Yes
Single switch for on/off and mic(s)	Yes		No	No
Hybrid circuitry	Yes		No	No
Serviceable on location	Yes		Yes, if boards are provided	No
Dynamic compression	Yes		Yes	Yes
Size and weight	3-3/4" × 2-1/2" x × 1", 7 oz		4-3/8" × 3-1/8" × 1-3/8", 10 oz.	4" × 2-1/4" × 1-1/4", 8 oz

Table 9 (continued)

Feature	EFI "TravelEar II"	H. C. Electronics "Phonic Ear"	Biocoustics
	Charging System	*Charging System*	*Charging System*
Time required	No	Yes	No
Built-in test meter	yes	No	No
Light indicators	Yes	No	No
Number of charge Receptacles	10 (monaural and binaural)	8 for binaural, 10 for monaural	10 (two separate five-unit chargers)
Feature	*Service Policy*	*Service Policy*	*Service Policy*
	90 days cords and batteries, 1 year parts and labor, backup boards provided; service contract $20 per unit after first year	90 days cords and batteries, 1 year parts and labor, backup units provided *only* under service contract at $40 per unit	90 days cords and batteries, 1 year parts and labor, backup units not provided

EFI–Monaural			*H. C. Electronics–Monaural*			*Biocoustics–Monaural*		
Model No.	Description	Unit Price	Model No.	Description	Unit Price	Model No.	Description	Unit Price
550	Microphone –transmitter	$350.00	421T	Microphone –transmitter	$300.00	60	Microphone –transmitter	$310.00

Typical 8-position classroom (continued)

Model No.	Description	Unit Price	Model No.	Description	Unit Price	Model No.	Description	Unit Price
150	Student receiver	$350.00	32IR	Student receiver with dual drivers	$350.00	70	Student receiver with dual drivers	$380.00
359	Dual drivers	$30.00						
90–95	10-unit charger	$300.00		10-unit charger	$300.00	51-2	10-unit charger	$290.00
Typical 8-position classroom		$3690.00	Typical 8-position classroom		$3400.00	Typical 8-position classroom		$3640.00

EFI–Binaural			*H. C. Electronics–Binaural*			
Model No.	Description	Unit Price	Model No.	Description	Unit Price	
550	Microphone–transmitter	$350.00	421T	Microphone–transmitter	$300.00	Biocoustics does not produce a binaural system.
152	Binaural student receiver	$480.00	421IRT	Student receiver with dual drivers	$550.00	
359	Dual drivers	$30.00	51-2	8-unit charger	$300.00	
90–95	10-unit charger	$300.00				
Typical 8-position classroom		$4730.00	Typical 8-position classroom		$5000.00	

room. Information on the ability of three wireless systems to accept other audio sources is provided in the competitive analysis sheet of Table 9.

The clinician must be familiar with and use the charging system after using the equipment. Specifically, the microphone–transmitter batteries and the receiver unit batteries may need to be charged overnight. Otherwise the units may not be ready for use the next day.

The clinician should also check the microphone–transmitter and receiver units daily. With the receivers this check includes testing the charge, setting the gain or volume controls on each side to a comfortable listening level, listening for distortion-free sound, and checking cords for continuity. With the microphone–transmitter, the specialist should listen for transmission by use of one or more receiver units. If a problem cannot be solved, units in question should be mailed to a manufacturer or service center without delay. Current air freight provisions commonly permit the return of a repaired unit within a week. In the meantime backup units should be available and used. It is interesting that H. C. Electronics (1973) provides an illustrated booklet on operating instructions for the HC 421 FM Phonic Ear. The addresses of eight manufacturers of wireless systems appear below.

Aurex "Sound Stage" and accompanying training aids, Aurex Corporation, 844 West Adams, Chicago, Illinois 60607

Biocoustics monaural wireless system, 12316 Wilkins Avenue, Rockville, Maryland 20852

Earmark Auditory Training System, 449 Putnam Avenue, Hamden, Connecticut 06517

EFI "Travel Ear II," Electronic Futures, 57 Dodge Avenue, North Haven, Connecticut 06473

HC 421 FM Phonic Ear of H.C. Electronics, 250 Camino Alto, Mill Valley, California 94941

Oticon Auditory Training System, P.O. Box 1551, Union, New Jersey 07083

Telex Direct Wireless FM System, Telex Communications, 9600 Aldrich Avenue South, Minneapolis, Minnesota 55420

Zenith Auditory Training System, 6501 West Grand Avenue, Chicago, Illinois 60635

Optional use of a wireless system depends upon the availability of an adequate service program from the manufacturer or dealer. The program of one company includes a service contract and an earmold contract (H. C. Electronics, 1973). If these contracts are purchased in addition to the equipment, the company guarantees continuing maintenance of units to ensure peak performance, backup units, ongoing user training, professional earmold impressions and periodic inspections and maintenance, and training to ensure the best acoustic seal. The cost is

$40 per unit. Another company provides a less expensive similar program as well as backup replaceable components at no cost (Electronic Futures Incorporated, 1974). The common warranty policy is 90 days for cords and batteries and one year for all parts and labor. Such service programs are necessary because auditory trainers of the past often fell into disrepair and consequent disuse.

REFERENCES

Berg F: Breakthrough for the Hard of Hearing Child. Smithfield, Utah, Ear Publication, 1971, p 21

Electronic Futures Incorporated: Competitive Analysis of Auditory Training Systems. North Haven, Connecticut, 1974

Gaeth J, Lounsbury E: Hearing aids and children in elementary schools. J Speech Hear Disord 31:283–289, 1966

Gengel R: Acceptable speech to noise ratios for aided speech discrimination by the hearing impaired. J Audiol Res 11:219–222, 1971

H. C. Electronics: Acoustics for Amplification. Mill Valley, California, 1971

H. C. Electronics: Operating instructions for the HC 421 FM Phonic Ear. Mill Valley, California, 1973

Hetherington J: Amplification in the educational system, in Pollack M (ed): Amplification for the Hearing Impaired. New York and London, Grune & Stratton, 1975, pp 373–385

Jeffers J: Instruction for Use of EB 43 True Binaural Master Auditory Trainer. Hawthorne, California, Eckstein Brothers

Langford B: Coupling methods, in Pollack M (ed): Amplification for the Hearing Impaired. New York and London, Grune & Stratton, 1975, pp 81–113

Olsen W, Matkin N: Comments on modern auditory training systems and their uses. Bulletin of AOEHI. Washington, DC, A G Bell Assn Deaf 2:7–15, 1971

Pollack M: Electroacoustic characteristics, in Pollack M (ed): Amplification for the Hearing Impaired. New York and London, Grune & Stratton, 1975a, pp 21–80

Pollack M: Special applications of amplification, in Pollack M (ed): Amplification for the Hearing Impaired. New York and London, Grune & Stratton, 1975b, pp 243–286

Ross M: Amplification considerations with hearing impaired children. Salt Lake City, Utah, Institute on Audition and the Hearing Impaired Child, 1974

Ross M: Hearing aid selection for the preverbal hearing impaired child, in Pollack M (ed): Amplification for the Hearing Impaired. New York and London, Grune & Stratton, 1975, pp 207–243

Ross M, Giolas T: Three classroom listening conditions on speech intelligibility. Am Ann Deaf 116:580–584, 1971

Ross M, Hunt MF, Kessler M, et al: The use of a rating scale to compare binaural and monaural amplification with hearing impaired children. Vol Rev 76:93–99, 1974

Ross M, Lerman J: Word Intelligibility by Picture Identification. Pittsburgh, Stanwix House, 1971

Tillman T, Carhart R, Olsen W: Hearing aid efficiency in a competing speech situation. J Speech Hear Res 13:789–811, 1970

Wedenberg E: The status of hard of hearing students in Sweden. Institute on the Characteristics and Needs of the Hard of Hearing Child. Logan, Utah State University, 1967

Yonovitz A: Binaural intelligibility: Pilot study in progress. Speech and Hearing Institute. Houston, Texas Medical Center, 1974

4

Programming Beginning During Infancy

Audiological programming for the hearing-impaired child should begin as soon as hearing loss is discovered. Recent findings from Fellendorf's survey (1975) indicate that a parent typically makes the diagnosis of hearing loss before the child is two years old. Before this time many behavioral signs exhibited by the youngster make parents suspicious of hearing loss. For example, during the first few months of life, sudden loud sounds startle a child who hears well, and by six months of age the normally hearing infant will attend to objects if they emit sounds. Cessation of babbling activity, common even to deaf infants early in life, is another indicator of hearing loss. During the second year of life, when words and even sentences are normally emerging, the parents become more and more convinced by lack of such development that their child has a hearing loss or some other handicapping problem.

The suspicions and diagnosis of the parents are confirmed when their child is tested in an audiological clinic. The audiologist presents various meaningful sounds to the child seated in the test booth. These auditory stimuli are produced by an audiometer at intensity levels up to 110 dB. When the sounds exceed the threshold of his auditory sensitivity, the child behaves as if he hears; he might stop what he is doing or turn his head. With repeated presentations it may become possible to estimate the degree of hearing loss. The audiologist might say to the parents, for example, that the child did not respond to speech until its intensity reached 90 dB. On this basis the audiologist might hypothesize that the child seems to have at least a severe and possibly a profound hearing loss. This specialist also recommends that the youngster be fitted with a hearing aid, and he administers tests to substantiate the loss and its permanence.

Behavior observation audiometry, without conditioning, may be replaced by careful application of operant principles for obtaining threshold and speech perception data on very young children (Eilers, Wilson, and Moore, 1975; Moore, Wilson, and Thompson, 1975; Wilson and Moore, 1975; Wilson, Moore, and Thompson, 1975). In a series of experiments being conducted at the Child Development and Mental Retardation Center of the University of Washington, significantly better thresholds are being obtained on children as young as six months of age by use of operant conditioning. Sound stimuli have included complex noise and warbled pure tones. Reinforcers that are proving effective are an animated toy animal and a food bit.

In a speech perception experiment, Eilers, Wilson and Moore (1975) tested as many as 10 speech contrasts among nine infants six to eight months of age in as few as three 20-minute sessions. The infants were presented with one member of the contrastive stimulus pair at the rate of one syllable per second at 50 dB sound pressure level. The infants were reinforced for head turns at changes of signals by activation of an animated toy. They had to respond appropriately five out of six times.

Electrophysiological procedures are also utilized in the early assessment of hearing sensitivity. The most successful of these has been averaged electroencephalic audiometry. However it is not as practical as behavioral audiometry because of the cost, time, and tracing interpretation experience needed. Furthermore in a number of cases the thresholds obtained with this procedure may vary by 20 dB or more from behavioral thresholds (Lowell, Lowell, and Goodhill, 1975).

Differential Diagnostic Behavioral Signs

Often overlooked in the early diagnosis of a hearing loss is an evaluative approach that goes beyond audiometric analysis to identify the cause of communicative retardation in the child. Under the topic of differential diagnosis, Fuller (1970) detailed the behavioral signs that identify whether the etiology (cause) of a speech and language delay is hearing loss, cerebral dysfunction (brain damage), emotional disturbance, or a combination of two or more of these handicapping conditions. Similarly, Myklebust (1954) described mental retardation as another handicapping condition leading to subnormal communication development. The Myklebust-Fuller approach is to isolate a particular one of these conditions by contrasting auditory, vocal, and visual behavior and social adaptation. Fuller interviews the parents, observes the child and parent, and uses audiometric and psychological testing procedures to elicit a large enough sample of behaviors to allow a differential diagnosis.

The relevance of looking beyond audiometric assessment to study of behavior can be understood by describing the children of a typical school for the hearing impaired. Many of these children have a handicapping condition in addition to a hearing loss. In most instances the problem is slow learning ability or perceptual learning disability. Superimposed upon hearing loss, the child is multiply handicapped and thus presents unique challenges to educational programmers. Having multiply handicapped children in special schools and classes, however, may not affect the relative capabilities that they have for learning via various sensory modalities or communicative methodologies. For example, if the child with an additional handicap has a 90 dB loss, he may still be a candidate for an auditory approach to language, speech, and listening development. His progress will be slower, as a rule, but it also may be slower under total communication.

Table 10 lists examples of comparative behavior presented by Fuller (1970).

In addition to differential descriptions of these handicapping conditions, the behaviors and adaptations of the slow-learning child are similar to those of the hearing-impaired child, except that responses may be slower and less sophisticated.

Otological Support

A child identified as having hearing impairment should also be referred to the otologist for medical diagnosis of ear pathology. If the otologist discovers that the outer ear and the middle ear of the child are nonpathological, he can then indicate to the parents that the loss stems from a problem within the inner ear or along the auditory pathway to the brain. If the problem is in the middle ear, however, medical and/or surgical treatment might alleviate at least a part of the hearing loss. The extent of hearing loss due to middle ear pathology will not exceed 70 dB. Often a hearing loss of 90 dB or greater is primarily or exclusively a sensory-neural (inner ear and/or auditory nerve) problem.

Move to Earlier Education

During the last 25 years hearing-impaired children have received earlier and earlier educational assistance (Education of the Deaf, 1965). In 1940 schooling typically began when the child was five to six years old or more. By 1964 half of the special programs for the hearing im-

Table 10

Contrast of Type of Behavior or Adaptation among Children with Hearing Impairment, Cerebral Dysfunction, and Emotional Disturbance

Type of Behavior or Adaptation	Hearing Impairment	Cerebral Dysfunction	Emotional Disturbance
Use of audition	Responds better to high than to low intensity sound	Frequently responds better to low than to high intensity sound	Responds best to sounds that have emotional significance
Use of voice	Imitates other voices when he can hear them; accuracy of imitation improves when given opportunity to speechread	May not be imitative; if so, imitates soft voice as well as loud; no conspicuous improvement with speechreading	Refuses to imitate; may act startled and anxious if his own vocalizations are imitated
Use of vision	Compensatory use of vision for environmental orientation; active visual scanning of the environment	Conspicuous visual distractibility	May act unaware of events in his visual environment
Social–emotional adjustment	Behavior generally well organized and purposeful; sensitive to social environment	Behavior often disorganized and haphazard; tasks started and left incomplete; abrasive to social environment	Ignores social environment; behavior satisfies autistic purposes, but is not related to surrounding activity

Extracted from Fuller, 1970, pp 209–214.

paired were providing preschool education beginning at ages two and one-half to four years. During the last five years increasing numbers of hearing impaired children six months to five years old have been receiving parent–home programming (Northcott, 1975).

Currently the U. S. Office of Education is giving priority to support of early education programs. Basic to such programming is increasing recognition that a child has a right to an education as soon as the diagnosis of a handicapping condition is established and at no cost to the family. Northcott (1975), a consultant with the Minnesota State Department of Education, described the components of educational practices in the management of infant and preschool hearing-impaired children. These include parent guidance counseling and education, aural (listening) and oral procedures, experiential inductive approaches to learning, early amplification and training in utilization of residual hearing, and group educational experiences with hearing children. As a result of early identification, parent training, and focus on what the child can hear and what he can do during the preprimary years, large numbers of hearing-impaired children are ready for placement in regular classes during the elementary school years.

Simmons (1971) suggested why special supportive assistance should be provided to hearing-impaired children from infancy. She noted that it is during the first years of life that language learning ordinarily advances rapidly. She also indicated that language learning is inextricably linked with auditory experiences. Simmons stated that delayed identification of hearing loss and delayed utilization of residual hearing prolong the time it takes a child to progress through the various invariant stages of language development.

It may be true, however, that lack of early utilization of residual hearing has an inherently devastating effect upon speech acquisition rather than upon language development. During the last decade evidence has been accumulating that utilization of either cued speech or Ameslish facilitates rather rapid language development, at least among many young hearing-impaired children (Clark, 1975; Cornett, 1973).

Utah Project

Many of the latest techniques in infant–preschool programming for the hearing impaired have been incorporated into the Utah Statewide Program for Identification and Language Facilitation for Hearing Handicapped Children Through Home Management, Ages Birth to Six (Clark, 1975). The present author has served as Evaluator of this U. S. Office of Education funded program called Project SKI-HI. Developed as a demonstration program in Utah between 1972 and 1975 and now expanding into other states, the project has the following chief features.

Audiological assessment. Baseline and periodic measures of hearing are obtained until thresholds are pinpointed.

Hearing aid evaluation and fitting. Two aids are often selected and fitted soon after an audiological estimate of the degree of hearing loss has been ascertained. The benefits of use of one ear or the other are monitored. Ear impressions are made and earmolds are custom fitted and refitted.

Parent orientation. Parents are familiarized with and provided group counseling and instruction in relevant aspects of adjustment to hearing loss and components of parent home intervention.

Parent home management. Home advisors prepare parents to become competent and independent in providing hearing aid management, listening, and language programming.

Individual evaluation. Data are obtained, recorded, and placed on an individual profile form for each child. The profile form includes categories of demographic information, significant dates, audiometric information, speech input, hearing aid specifics, and longitudinal data on several measures of child progress and parent progress.

Parent Evaluation

The unique feature of Project SKI-HI has been the development of a parent–home management model of delivery of services (Clark, 1975). Communicative disorders specialists are trained as parent–home advisors, and they in turn train parents in hearing aid management, listening development, and language development. They typically visit the homes of hearing-impaired infants or preschoolers on a weekly basis in order to render assistance within the environment in which the parents and children live rather than in a clinic or a demonstration home. Table 11 indicates the success of this program within 41 homes of Utah.

The areas of parent competence that have been subjects of training include hearing aid management, directed or supervised auditory development, independent auditory development, directed language development, and independent language development. As Table 11 shows, parents have generally attained very substantial competency in all of these communication management areas (Berg, 1975). Within the overall parent training scheme, the program focuses first on hearing aids, then on developing listening through audition, and finally on language acquisition.

Table 11

Percentage of 41 Homes or Parents Attaining Various Levels
of Competency in Each of Five Areas of Home Management

Area of Competency	Percentage of Homes at Each Competency Level*					
	0	1	2	3	4	5
Hearing aid management	0	2.5	14.7	9.8	24.4	48.8
Directed auditory development	0	2.5	17.1	17.1	26.8	36.6
Independent auditory development	0	14.7	12.2	26.8	34.1	12.2
Directed language development	0	4.9	19.5	17.1	41.5	17.1
Independent language development	0	7.3	26.8	22.0	36.6	7.3
Mean	0	6.3	18.5	18.5	32.7	24.4

*0: no competency; 1: minimal; 2: considerable; 3: substantial; 4: very substantial; 5: complete competency.

Once parents attain competency in assisting their hearing-impaired infants and preschoolers, the home advisors terminate their regular visits (Clark, 1975). However continuing contact is maintained between such homes and the project staff. Up to 14 specialists working part-time and living in various parts of the state of Utah provide sufficient parent–home support. After assisting certain parents in developing management competencies, these specialists move on to other homes in which children have been discovered to have substantial bilateral hearing loss. Hearing aid management and listening training are often mastered within six months. Training parents to provide children with language facilitation and support may take another six to 12 months. Other staff and university audiologists provide administrative, clerical, evaluative, and audiological assistance.

Methodology and Evaluation

Another important aspect of the SKI-HI project is evaluation of whether a particular child should be trained by means of an auditory method or through a total communication approach (Clark, 1975). Data on listening, speech, and language acquisition provide a basis for considering a shift between these two approaches. During 1972–1975 each child began the SKI-HI program with the auditory method. After an average of approximately nine months of parent–home management, about two-thirds of the 41 project children were still being auditorially trained. The remainder were being educated by means of total communication.

Video cassette recordings of total communication lessons have been prepared to train parents to use Ameslish signs. Video cassette recorders and recordings are then loaned to such parents. Hearing aids, however, are still worn by nearly all project children being trained by total communication. Project children who have entered the Utah School for the Deaf have demonstrated dramatically higher communication skills than youngsters who were enrolled before the SKI-HI project. State education monies are now being used to provide a continuation of the parent–home management program for hearing-impaired infants and preschoolers in Utah.

Child Evaluation

Month-by-month evaluation of the hearing-impaired child as well as of parents has been a part of the Utah SKI-HI project (Berg, 1975). Such evaluation with children has focused on measurement of progress or lack of progress in listening development and in vocal–verbal utterances of speech. Nine stages of each of listening development and of vocal–verbal development have been specified. The clinician judges within a given month the stage of the child on these two developmental scales. Plot points are graphed and interconnected to reveal changes of performance from month to month. Figure 24 illustrates the progress of one child in both areas over a four-month period. The accuracy of these data has not been subjected to validity and reliability controls.

The nine stages or levels of listening development evaluated in the SKI-HI training program for a hearing-impaired child are adapted and

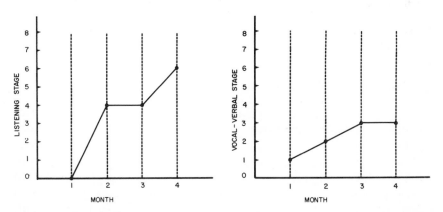

Fig. 24. Four-month progress of one SKI-HI child in the acquisition of listening and of vocal–verbal competencies. Compliments Utah State University, Logan.

extended from those identified by Pollack (1973). These adapted levels are listed below.

1. *Alerting.* Cessation of activity, widening of eyes, pointing to an ear immediately after a sound is produced.
2. *Searching.* Looking around for the sound source immediately after presentation of the auditory stimulus.
3. *Localization.* Finding the sound source without having looked at the object or event that produced it.
4. *Distance hearing.* Localizing to a sound produced from a source at least 20 feet away.
5. *Elevation hearing.* Localizing to a sound produced at an altitude requiring the child to look up and down; if up, including a sound made at least 20 feet away.
6. *Gross sound discrimination.* The child distinguishing, at close distance, one noisemaker from another without looking, e.g., a horn from a rattle.
7. *Voice discrimination.* The child distinguishing, at close distance, the father's voice from the mother's voice without looking.
8. *Prosodic discrimination.* The child distinguishing, at close distance, one tonal pattern from another, e.g., an angry voice from a soothing voice.
9. *Articulation discrimination.* The child distinguishing, at close distance, one word from another word when both are spoken with the same prosodic pattern, e.g., "Show me the *ball*. Show me the *fish.*"

A corresponding list of vocal-verbal stages has been generated by the author as a modification and downward extension of five levels of syntactic development described by Lee (1966). These nine stages, tentatively utilized for child evaluation in the SKI-HI project, are identified below.

1. *Vocal.* One syllable; limited articulation such as cry, coo, grunt.
2. *Vocal.* One syllable; prebabbling articulation emerging.
3. *Vocal.* Vocal play or babbling; repetitive syllables, e.g., *baba* (same) or *bado* (different).
4. *Verbal.* Single word, often functions as sentence; single or double syllable; does not have to be articulated correctly.
5. *Vocal.* Sentence-like jargon; nonlinguistic; tonal patterns across many syllables simulate adult speech and/or echolalia if it occurs.
6. *Verbal.* Two-word sentence; miniaturized language system; pivot open class might be typical but not inclusive, e.g., *a car, big car, car broken, not car.*

7. *Verbal.* Three to four words; noun phrase, e.g., *my big car, no more car, the other big car,* or designative, predicative, and verb phrase constructions, e.g., *it a car, the car broken, take car again;* also telegraphic, e.g., *finished went home.*
8. *Verbal.* Kernel sentences; designative construction, predicative construction, and actor–action sentence with or without article, e.g., *there's the car, the car is broken, car is broken, I see a car, I see car.*
9. *Transform.* Emerging transformation; revealed by substitutions of pronouns for noun phrases, use of interrogatives, employment of *and* to join series of words; affirmative, negative, and imperative constructions; complex sentences generated by rules of addition, deletion, permutation, and substitution within or among kernel sentences.

Two other relevant measures of child progress from month to month may also be kept in a program like Project SKI-HI (Berg, 1975). One is a cumulative record of articulation or of the segmental phonemes used. The other is a measure of prosodic patterning within vocalizations or verbalizations.

The clinician can keep a record of articulations that occur during the training program. Any new articulation used within a visit or sessions can be added to the record of phonemes that have been used before. Circles can be placed around symbols of phonemes that have been identified and verified as having occurred.

$$\text{h} \quad \text{p} \quad \text{t} \quad \text{k} \quad \text{f} \quad \theta \quad \text{s} \quad \int \quad \text{t}\int$$
$$\text{w} \quad \text{b} \quad \text{d} \quad \text{g} \quad \text{v} \quad \text{ɟ} \quad \text{z} \quad \text{ʒ} \quad \text{dʒ} \quad \text{m} \quad \text{n} \quad \text{ŋ} \quad \text{l} \quad \text{r} \quad \text{j}$$
$$\text{u} \quad \text{ʋ} \quad \text{o} \quad \text{ɑ} \quad \text{ʌ} \quad \text{i} \quad \text{ɪ} \quad \text{e} \quad \text{ɛ} \quad \text{æ} \quad \text{aɪ} \quad \text{aʊ} \quad \text{ɔɪ} \quad \text{ɪu}$$

Prosodic patterns that occur in vocalizations or verbalizations can also be recorded by the clinician. In Project SKI-HI three levels have been identified: (1) one loudness–duration and one pitch *or* abnormal stress variation and abnormal pitch variation within a syllable or from syllable to syllable; (2) appropriate stress pattern but inappropriate pitch variation within a syllable or from syllable to syllable; (3) appropriate stress and pitch change within a syllable or from syllable to syllable.

The specialist need only listen to the spontaneous or imitative utterances of the child to check the levels of prosodic patterns being used. If the stress and pitch of an utterance—be it a syllable or syllable sequence—stay on the same level or change peculiarly, the child may not be utilizing his residual hearing as a monitor of speech production. He has a level one prosodic pattern. When a child uses an utterance that is changing appropriately or naturally in stress but not in intonation, he is monitoring speech by use of residual hearing to some extent. His prosodic level is two. If the child utters a syllable or syllable series with appropriate pitch and stress change, his prosodic level is three. His residual hearing is sufficient to permit natural language, listening, and speech to emerge. In a month-by-month recording of prosodic levels, the clinician should check a sample of spontaneous utterances to note the types exhibited. Ordinarily, a child's prosodic level will be consistent. He will either be on level one, level two, or level three.

The utterances of a hearing-impaired child also provide additional evaluative information. For example, pitch level, loudness level, and voice quality can be assessed. Also an estimate of intelligibility can be derived by sampling the understandability of 50 or more utterances. Live observation or audio recording procedures can be followed by the specialist.

Early Swedish Contributions

Modern auditory programming for hearing-impaired infants and preschoolers is indebted to Erik Wedenberg of Sweden. Beginning with the discovery in 1939 that his two and one-half year old son Staffan was "deaf," Wedenberg conducted a pioneer investigation with 36 children that spanned more than a decade. His monograph (1954) and a book chapter (1970) describe many of his contributions.

Wedenberg predicted the consonants, vowels, and diphthongs that might be identified auditorially after a period of training. He correlated audiometric data on a child with spectrographic information to determine an order of presentation of segmental phonemes. He also initiated training immediately after confirmation of hearing loss. With his son Staffan, he began at age two and one-half years. A year or so later, a pure tone audiogram could be obtained. By age three and one-half, the boy had a 25-word vocabulary. The stimuli Wedenberg used were meaningful words and sentences, loaded with speech sounds relatively easy to hear. These sounds included first formants (250–850 Hz) and second formants (600–1600 Hz). Staffan's audiogram indicated that residual hearing existed in the lower frequencies up to 1600 Hz.

Initially Wedenberg utilized *ad concham* amplification, that is, speaking within an inch of the ear canal so as to generate 97 dB of SPL at conversational loudness input and 107–109 dB when input intensity is raised voice. Staffan's average hearing loss was 93 dB (75 at 500 Hz, 95 at 1000 Hz, and "no response" figured 110 at 2000 Hz).

Wedenberg assisted hearing-impaired children to develop a "listening attitude" rather than lipreading and/or manual communication skills. He conditioned children to respond when stimulated with words and with environmental sounds, whether the stimuli were in view or not. His clients became auditorially rather than visually oriented. In contrast, a deaf child relies upon vision to maintain homeostasis with the environment. Evidence of listening includes reiterating speech stimuli, talking during sleep, and ceasing restless roaming from one activity to another.

Play–talk associations were built up by utilization of both natural and contrived situations. Parents spoke *ad concham* as children participated in the many activities that were meaningful and natural to them. Many audible playthings as well as musical instruments were used. Children were trained to become aware of sound at increasing distances. They would respond to stimuli by turning around or by other overt actions. The piano and other musical instruments also provided sound stimuli, which were incorporated into games.

Wedenberg sought out hearing aid innovations that would enable Staffan to identify as many of the sounds of speech as possible. These developments included amplification of lower frequencies, transposition of the inaudible voiceless consonants into the lower frequency range, and binaural ear-level amplification. He also kept longitudinal record of vocabulary size, sentence types, speech intelligibility, and prosodic content of child utterances (Wedenberg, 1954). Finally, Wedenberg spearheaded the development of infant–preschool programs for the hearing impaired in Sweden, with the assistance of the Boy Scouts and eventually the government.

A chronology of events and programming derived from a case history of Staffan Wedenberg is presented in Table 12.

The achievements of Staffan during elementary and secondary schooling and beyond were underpinned by what took place during his early education in the home. His educational route did not take him to the school for the deaf because as a hard-of-hearing child he could function in regular classes and compete with hearing peers. The price paid for this innovative education was extensive guidance, stimulation, and tutoring from infancy well into the school years. "Looking back on his early days, he says he was always jealous of normal hearing children who were playing while he had to work with his vocabulary, even during summer holidays" (Wedenberg and Wedenberg, 1970).

Based on the success of the unisensory auditory approach with 36 hearing-impaired children with at least severe losses, preschools or early education centers for the hard of hearing were established throughout Sweden. Depending upon terminal achievement from preschool, hearing-impaired children enter either the regular schools, classes for the hard of hearing, or the schools for the deaf. Before the Wedenberg

Table 12

Age and Significant Events and Communicative Achievements of
Staffan Wedenberg

Age (years)	Significant Event or Achievement
2½	Parents recognize that Staffan is at least profoundly hearing impaired. They begin a unisensory auditory program of speech stimulation.
3⅔	Staffan now functions as a hard-of-hearing child. He has progressed through stages of sounds awareness, vowel perception, word perception, and sentence perception by use of audition only.
4	Staffan says his first sentence spontaneously, ''Toto, utta, aj-aj.'' The sentence is elicited by a fear that his dog Tutta will be trampled by a horse.
4½	Staffan learns to read or to associate sounds and letters.
5	He achieves a spoken or expressive vocabulary of 400 words, forms many sentences, and begins to use verbs in the perfect and future tenses. He speaks spontaneously but defectively, uses no signs, and is uninhibited, finding friends among normal-hearing children his own age.
6½	His spoken vocabulary includes at least 600 words.
7	Staffan enters ordinary school and later transfers to a class for hard-of-hearing children. He also learns to read piano music. In addition, he requests that his name be changed to Douglas because he cannot hear Staffan well. He also begins wearing a series of innovative hearing aids and receives speech instruction.
14	His vocabulary approaches normal. He has received better than passing grades in most of his subjects taken in junior high and high school.
17	Staffan's vocabulary compares favorably with requirements for intelligent adults.
30	Having completed a degree in forestry some years earlier, he speaks fluent Swedish and English. On a trip to the United States, his speech is as intelligible as that of his father.

era the main educational option open to a hearing-impaired child was the school for the deaf, where visual communicative methods were utilized extensively.

According to Wedenberg (1954) the goal of the unisensory auditory approach is for the hearing-impaired child to score within normal limits on the verbal scale of an intelligence test. In Staffan's instance it took 12 years of auditory training before he accomplished this goal.

Table 13 provides data on three other children who were clients of Wedenberg. It may be noted that two of these children, Cases 1 and 2 with severe rather than profound hearing impairment, attained at least a normal vocabulary before entering school. Their speech was defective, but their spoken language was spontaneous and reflexive. Whereas Staffan attended a class for the hard of hearing for perhaps four years, these two children attended ordinary classes throughout their schooling. The child with the profound loss whose training began at age five and one-half also developed vocabulary through hearing. However when he reached school age he was referred to the school for the deaf. It is apparent from this table that the variables of decibel loss, age at beginning of training, duration of training, and intelligence have impact upon language and speech attainment.

Vocabulary growth is an important dependent variable in the education of the hearing-impaired child. The number of words acquired by the growing youngster depends upon the number and meaningfulness of associations between environmental events and accompanying verbal description of these situations. A child with normal hearing can receive auditory and/or visual stimuli from any location within talking distance and associate events and descriptions of them almost effortlessly. In contrast, the individual with a profound hearing impairment will be decoding and associating fewer auditory and/or visual stimuli, unless an extraordinary effort is made in the home to facilitate this process.

The vocabulary growth of a normal-hearing child can serve as a measure against which the linguistic success of a hearing-impaired child can be measured. By 12 months of age a few words are emerging but

Table 13
Evaluative Data on Three Hearing-Impaired Children Who Were Given Auditory Training by Wedenberg

Case	dB Loss in Better Ear	IQ	Age at Beginning of Training	Duration of Training in Years	Vocabulary Following Training	Speech Intelligibility Following Training (%)
1	87	118	2½	3	Normal	76
2	85	132	1½	2½	Greater than Normal	27
3	95	93	5½	1½	150 Words	23

by 18 months perhaps only 20 are uttered. By two years of age, however, the normal expressive vocabulary typically includes 200 words. Thereafter about 50 new words are spoken per month, or 600 words per year. By the time the normally-hearing child enters school at six years of age, he has a spoken vocabulary of approximately 2500 words (Smith, 1926).

At least two generalizations may be drawn from these normative data. First, about two years of experience are needed before vocabulary really begins to emerge and sprout. Second, vocabulary growth is rapid once spoken language becomes a meaningful receptive and expressive communicative system for the child.

With Staffan, only one year of input resulted in a vocabulary that was the equivalent of that of a normal-hearing child who had received two years of auditory and visual experience. Thereafter it increased at about one-third the normal rate for two to three years, and then its acceleration became more rapid. With the two bright children with severe losses who were also clients of Wedenberg, the rate of vocabulary growth was at least normal.

The 10 dB difference between Staffan's degree of hearing loss and that of these other two children may not account for the dramatic differences in early vocabulary growth. It has already been noted that Staffan was able to hear only frequencies below 1600 Hz. This deficiency affected his auditory perception of voiceless consonants, which have considerable high frequency energies. Inasmuch as he had sufficient hearing to acquire articulate speech, particularly after receiving extensive speech instruction, Staffan might have been trained to identify voiceless consonants if they had been given special consideration. It should be remembered that the formant or frequency concentrations of the voiced and voiceless consonants are identical. However the noise characteristics of voiceless consonants tend to mask out auditory perception of formants. Auditory perception may be based more on the intensity and especially the durational characteristics of such phonemes (Berg, 1972).

Two additional factors may account for the delayed acceleration of Staffan's vocabulary. One is that his spoken language had to become articulate before he could perceive all of its components. Evidence is accumulating to support this motor theory of speech perception. The other factor is that Staffan had to acquire the morpho-syntactical aspects of his native language before he could read and thereby extend his vocabulary through this avenue.

Another possible factor accounting for Staffan's late acceleration of vocabulary relates to amplification (Wedenberg, 1970). Because of the electroacoustic limitations of wearable hearing aids of the late 1930s and early 1940s, *ad concham* amplification was used until Staffan was enrolled in school. This consisted of speaking at conversational (97 dB) or rather loud (107 dB) levels within an inch of the ear canal. Thereafter an ingenious engineer named Bertil Johansson cutom built a series of hearing aids for Staffan. The last of these featured unique decoding circuitry that transposed the 3000 to 6000 Hz frequencies into the lower frequency area where Staffan could hear (Johansson, 1966; Wedenberg, 1961). This permitted Staffan to hear the /s/, /ʃ/, and other voiceless consonants. In time he was wearing binaural ear level hearing aids featuring compression amplification. The reader should be cautioned, however, to question the relative superiority of frequency transposition for many hearing-impaired individuals with similar audiograms because of conflicting data noted in similar studies by other investigators including Ling (1968).

Listening and Talking Models

One of the current master clinicians in the development of educational audiology for infants and preschoolers is Doreen Pollack of Denver (1973). Figure 25 shows her mobilizing the residual hearing of a young hearing-impaired child. The captions under the scenes clarify the steps she incorporates in her listening program. In her clinic at Porter Memorial Hospital, she has stocked a variety of sound-making devices that support her procedures. The parent in Figure 25 assists Pollack and thereby learns to assist her own child. The first six scenes of Figure 25 are explained below.

1. Within the box on the table are many sound-making objects. Pollack initially stimulates the child with one of these objects before she lets him see it.
2. Immediately afterwards, Pollack quickly puts her hands to her ears and says, "I hear that." She may repeat steps one and two several times. The mother is also encouraged to put her hands to her ears whenever the sound stimulus occurs.
3. The child is then given the sound stimulator, which in this instance is a horn. He is encouraged to blow it. Each time he does Pollack and the mother place their hands to their ears and say, "I hear that."
4. Pollack next sounds a second object, which may be the snapper. She again puts her hands to her ears and says, "I hear that." The mother does likewise. This action may be repeated several times.
5. The child is then given the snapper and encouraged to make the sound. As mentioned before, Pollack and the mother again place

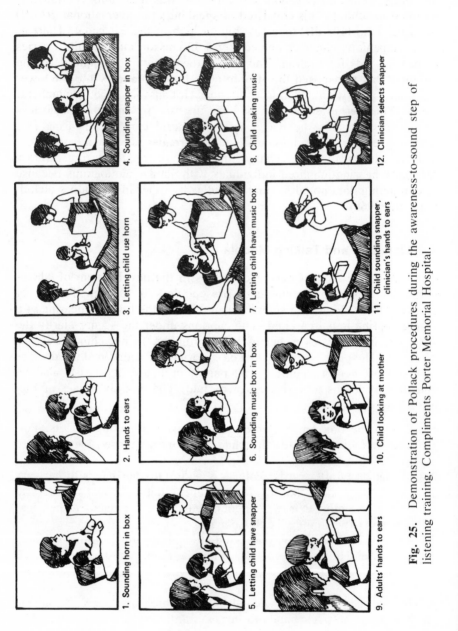

Fig. 25. Demonstration of Pollack procedures during the awareness-to-sound step of listening training. Compliments Porter Memorial Hospital.

their hands to their ears and say, "I hear that" when the child makes the sound. This procedure is repeated several times with this object.

6. The same procedures begin again when Pollack sounds a music box which is initially hidden from the child.

The sequence of scenes and procedures demonstrates the first stage of the Pollack listening program (Pollack, 1973). Whereas this stage concentrates on developing awareness of the presence of meaningful sounds, further steps include searching for sounds, auditory localization, distance listening, and then voice and speech discrimination. The procedures extend and systematize the listening program initiated by Wedenberg years earlier.

An infant–preschool program with refined procedures for perceptual or discrimination training is that of the Institute of Logopedics in Wichita, Kansas (Wait, 1975). The Pulsatone system of Perdoncini of Nice, France, is utilized as a major component of a comprehensive parent, home, and preschool training program. A Pulsatone device on the order of an audiometer produces pure tones of many discrete frequencies that can be varied in intensity and duration. The teacher or clinician utilizes this device to stimulate young hearing-impaired children with auditory signals. When a child hears the signal, he is conditioned to respond by raising or lowering his hand, using long or short hand movements, reproducing what he hears, selecting appropriate visual stimuli, and the like. Table 14 presents the auditory training sequence of this oral–aural program, including its six steps, the Pulsatone stimuli and responses, and associated classroom stimuli and responses.

In the first step of Pulsatone training the child discriminates between the presence and absence of sound by raising or lowering his hand. The frequencies 250 Hz and 500 Hz are used initially, then higher frequencies are used. A light is coupled with the auditory signal until the child responds to a sound alone. With auditory awareness established, the voice is also used as a stimulus.

The child is trained in the second step to judge the duration of the auditory stimulus. Pure tones of different durations are presented. Initially a short and a long sound are produced. Correspondingly, the child is conditioned to respond by making an abbreviated up-and-down hand motion or by swinging his hand out from his body. He is also taught to associate the duration with a short or long object and later with short or long sequences of written symbols. In addition, transition is made to use of speech signals as auditory stimuli.

The third step of Pulsatone training is called *rhythm* and is given particular precedence. The child is trained to discriminate between temporal patterns, which are made progressively longer and more com-

Table 14
Six Steps and Stimuli and Responses of Pulsatone and Classroom Training Characterizing the Perdoncini Oral–Aural Program

	Pulsatone		Classroom	
Auditory Training Sequence	Stimuli	Responses	Stimuli	Responses

Step 1—Sound and Silence	1. Pure Tones
	2. Voice
	  A. Nonsense syllables
	  B. Words
	  C. Phrases
	  D. Sentences
		1. Raises or lowers hand	1. Minipulsatone tone
			2. Music
			3. Noisemakers
			4. Environmental sounds
			5. Voice
			  A. Nonsense syllables
			  B. Words
			  C. Phrases
			  D. Sentences
				1. Raises or lowers hand
				2. Drops block in can
				3. Marches and stops to music
				4. Points to object or picture each time it is named

Step 2—Duration of Sounds	(Same stimuli at each step)	1. Long or short hand movements 2. Reproduces what is heard 3. Chooses concrete material of corresponding length 4. Relates to written symbol ——, U	(Same stimuli at each step)	1. Long or short hand movements 2. Reproduces what is heard 3. Chooses concrete material of corresponding length 4. Relates to written symbol

			...from objects or pictures
Step 3—Rhythm Patterns	(Same stimuli at each step)	1. Long and short hand movements 2. Reproduces what is heard 3. Relates to written symbol (Increasingly complex patterns used to increase auditory memory span)	(Same stimuli at each step)	1. Moves to music—walks, runs, skips, etc. 2. Reproduces number of sounds heard 3. Remembers and identifies objects named 4. Follows simple commands 5. Relates to written symbols 6. Imitates rhythm pattern
Step 4—Frequency	(Same stimuli at each step)	1. Raises left hand for low, right hand for high 2. Relates to color code; red for low, green for high 3. Tells *high* or *low* verbally	(Same stimuli at each step)	1. Raises left hand for high, right hand for low 2. Indicates *high* or *low* verbally 3. Matches pitch with teacher 4. Recognition of words with same duration on different sounds; therefore, different frequency components

Table 14 (continued)

Auditory Training Sequence	Pulsatone Stimuli	Pulsatone Responses	Classroom Stimuli	Classroom Responses
Step 5—Intensity	(Same stimuli at each step)	1. Raises hand to corresponding height 2. Tells *loud* or *soft* verbally	(Same stimuli at each step)	1. Raises hand to corresponding height 2. Selects or reproduces sound heard according to intensity 3. Indicates *loud* or *soft* verbally
Step 6—Combined Duration, Rhythm, Frequency, and/or Intensity	(Same stimuli at each step)	1. Combines all motor responses to indicate each aspect of the sound stimulus 2. Indicates verbally what is heard	(Same stimuli at each step)	1. Combines respones from each step 2. Discrimination of increasingly complex sentences

Prepared by the staff of the Institute of Logopedics, Wichita, Kansas (Wait, 1975).

plex. The patterns simulate the on-off syllable durations of connected speech. Initially, durational differences are exaggerated; then they are progressively shortened. The child also learns to identify the number of sounds in a series. He responds by reproducing a pattern with a switch at his control or by choosing among visual patterns. Later the child is required to reproduce patterns in writing similar to the dots and dashes of Morse code. He is also encouraged to respond with speech patterns and to relate them to phrases and sentences of spoken language.

In the fourth step the child learns to discriminate between any two frequencies from 150 Hz through 4000 Hz. What he achieves depends upon his potential for pitch discrimination and the extent of frequencies he can hear. He raises his left hand from table level for low-pitched sounds and his right hand for higher pitches. The child is similarly trained in the fifth step to discriminate intensity differences. He raises his hand from table level for no sound to high above the head for very loud sounds.

The sixth and final step in Pulsatone training utilizes combinations of duration, frequency, and intensity of sound. The instructor analyzes sentences into prosodic patterns that correspond to these basic sound parameters. He then assists the child in recognizing and reproducing these prosodic features. Pure tones and then speech signals are utilized in this training process.

Each step of Pulsatone training is correlated with speech and classroom activities. For example, the child beats time to music and marches and stops during step one. In step two he learns to recognize simple commands and to repeat nonsense syllables. In step three he marches in step to the sounds he hears and listens to simple commands emphasizing temporal patterns. During step four the child discriminates between syllables and words varying in frequency components. He also matches his pitch to that of the instructor. In step five he discriminates between voices, noisemakers, and instruments having different intensities. Step six requires the child to remember several named objects in order as well as to discriminate language structure that includes objective forms and modifiers.

Additional related activities assist the child in making discriminations during the Perdoncini program. These activities include work with form boards and simple principles of modern mathematics, manipulation of Montessouri materials, and stimulation with objects of different sizes, shapes, and textures.

During 1967 to 1969, an 18-month investigation was conducted in Wichita to evaluate the effects of the Perdoncini program. A control group of hearing-impaired children received traditional oral education or instruction. A matched experimental group received specific auditory training at the Institute of Logopedics. Auditory discrimination of frequency, intensity, and duration as well as speech intelligibility were measured before, during, and after training. By the end of the 18-month period, children in the experimental group scored higher than the control subjects on all tasks (McCroskey, 1975).

Since 1969, 55 children have completed the Perdoncini program at the Institute. Of these children, 49.1 percent have entered regular first grade classrooms at or near normal chronological age and have progressed with minimal speech and language assistance. Another 12.7 percent of the children have enrolled in special oral classrooms. Members of a third group of 9.1 percent have multiple handicaps that necessitate special education placement. Another 23.6 percent are enrolled in total communication programs that utilize Perdoncini instruction. A fifth group of 5.5 percent of the children are unaccounted for because of family relocation and the like (Wait, 1975).

Another center making a national impact upon programming for the hearing-impaired child is the Bill Wilkerson facility in Nashville, Tennessee. A spokesman for and innovator in this program, Horton (1973), states that most severely hearing-impaired children who were formerly called "deaf" have significant degrees of residual hearing. She indicates that such audition will facilitate the learning of aural and oral language, particularly when binaural hearing aids are utilized.

Wilkerson personnel have advanced 27 suggestions by which a clinician or parent can facilitate the development of communication skills in a young child. Known as "rules of talking," they are classified under five headings and are specified below.

The Rules of Talking

How to Get and Maintain the Child's Attention
1.   Get down on the child's level, as close to his ears as possible.
2.   Let your face and your voice tell your child that what you are doing is interesting and fun.
3.   Let the child actively participate. Language is best learned while doing.
4.   Tune into the child. Talk about what interests him.

What to Talk About
1.   Talk about the *here* and *now*.
2.   Talk about the obvious.
3.   At times, talk for the child.
4.   Put the child's feelings into words.

How to Talk to a Child Who Doesn't Yet Have Spoken Words
1.   Everything has a name. Use the name.
2.   Use short simple sentences.

3. When you use single words, put them back into a sentence.
4. Use *natural* gestures when you talk.
5. Tell, then show the child what you are doing.
6. Use repetition. Say it again and again.
7. Give the child a chance to show that he understands.

How to Help a Child Use His Voice to Make Sounds

1. Imitate the child's repeated movement and add voiced sounds to go along with the movement.
2. Vary the sounds you make to the child. Make it interesting for him to listen.
3. Give the child a chance to use his voice. Be a listener as well as a talker.
4. Imitate the sounds the child makes.
5. Reward the child when he uses his voice.

How to Talk when the Child Begins to Use Words

1. Reward the child when he attempts to say a word.
2. Repeat the child's word and put it into a sentence.
3. When the child uses telegraphic speech, repeat his thought in a complete sentence.
4. Expand the child's vocabulary by adding new words.
5. When the child uses incorrect language or speech, repeat it correctly.
6. Let the child hear new sentence forms.
7. When the child expresses an idea, expand his thoughts by adding new information.

——Lillie, Head Teacher

Still another program that has made an impact upon the early education of the hearing-impaired is the UNISTAPS project of the Minnesota State Department of Education, Division of Special Education (Northcott, 1975). Initiated in 1968, this project has provided family-oriented infant–preschool programming for 167 children. Eighty percent of these children have a severe or profound hearing loss. A guidebook on this project provides comprehensive and practical information on home and nursery school management of the very young hearing-impaired child (Northcott, 1972). This guide gives particular emphasis to the many components that contribute to the development of language and communication skills by hearing-impaired children. The contributive factors include an early start, a stimulating home environment, parent guidance and education, evaluative tools, individually prescriptive programming based upon developmental expectations, hearing aid fitting and management, auditory training and language training, and nursery school support (Northcott, 1972).

SUMMARY

Infant–preschool programming for the hearing impaired is becoming more and more prevalent. Within its context the auditory approach offers great promise for optimal development of language, speech, and listening competencies. At a very early age, special consideration must be given to the identification of hearing loss and of possible multiply handicapping conditions. The pioneering work of Wedenberg has provided a basic model and framework for the refinement of listening and language programming that has occurred in this country during the last decade. The data Wedenberg obtained on 36 preschool hearing-impaired children provided a rationale for an auditory approach. The innovative work of Pollack, Perdoncini, and of Horton and others is also noteworthy. In addition, the Utah SKI-HI project provides a statewide model of particular relevance for replication throughout the country. The UNISTAPS project of Minnesota is another useful guide.

Basic to success with these programs is the necessity of ensuring that the child can consistently perceive auditorily as much of the speech signal as possible. The audiologist's role is that of assuring that hearing tests, hearing retests, and hearing aid evaluation and fitting takes place. He must also monitor the fitting of the earmold and replacement until sound can be "fed" into the ear canal with comfort and continuity.

The clinician or home advisor must also assist with hearing aid management and must demonstrate features of the listening and talking programs to one or more parents and assist them in becoming competent in following these procedures. As month after month goes by, the clinician should also evaluate changes of listening behavior, vocal–verbal utterance, articulation, and prosodic patterning. In addition, she can "track" or assess other features of speech such as pitch, loudness, and quality. Her background in phonetic and prosodic evaluation can be invaluable to her in this endeavor.

Finally, the extent to which the listening, speech, and language competencies of the child can be developed within the natural environment of the home will determine the baseline from which communication remediation will be conducted in structured sessions of the clinics or in classrooms for the hearing impaired (Northcott, 1975).

REFERENCES

Berg F: Sensory Aids in Speech Remediation for the Hearing Impaired. Logan, Utah State University, 1972

Berg F: Evaluation Section, in Clark T (ed): Programming for Hearing Impaired Infants Through Amplification and Home Intervention. Logan, Utah State University, 1975

Clark T (ed): Programming for Hearing Impaired Infants Through Amplification and Home Intervention. Logan, Utah State University, 1975

Cornett O: Cued Speech News 6, No. 3. Washington, DC, Gallaudet College, 1973

Education of the Deaf. A Report to the Secretary of Health, Education, and Welfare by His Advisory Committee on the Education of the Deaf. Washington, DC, 1965

Eilers R, Wilson W, Moore J: Developmental Changes in Infant Speech Perception. Seattle, University of Washington, 1975

Fellendorf G: An Eduhealth Delivery Service Index: A Profile of Education and Health Services to Young Hearing Impaired Children and Their Parents. Washington, DC, AG Bell Assn Deaf, 1975

Fuller C: Differential diagnosis, in Berg F and Fletcher S (eds): The Hard of Hearing Child. New York and London, Grune & Stratton, 1970, pp 203–215

Horton K: Every child should be given a chance to benefit from acoustic input. Vol Rev 75:348–350, 1973

Johansson B: The use of the transposer for the management of the deaf child. Int Audiol 5:362–371, 1966

Lee L: Developmental sentence types: A method for comparing normal and deviant syntactic development. J Speech Hear Disord 31:330, 1966

Ling D: Three experiments on frequency transposition. Am Ann Deaf 113:283–294, 1968

Lowell M, Lowell E, Goodhill V: Evoked response audiometry with infants: A longitudinal study. Aud Hear Educ 1:32–37, 1975

Moore J, Wilson W, Thompson G: Visual Reinforcement of Head Turn Responses in Infants under Twelve Months of Age. Seattle, University of Washington, 1975

McCroskey R: Summary of the Perdoncini Method Research Project. Witchita, Kansas, Wichita State University, 1975

Myklebust H: Auditory Disorders in Children. New York and London, Grune & Stratton, 1954

Northcott W (ed): Curriculum Guide for Hearing Impaired Children, Birth to Three Years, and Their Parents. Washington, DC, AG Bell Assn Deaf, 1972

Northcott W: Normalization of the preschool child with hearing impairment. Otol Clinics North Am 8:159–186, 1975

Pollack D: Learning to listen in an integrated preschool. Vol Rev 75:359–367, 1973

Simmons A: Language and hearing, in Connor L (ed): Speech for the Deaf Child: Knowledge and Use. Washington, DC, AG Bell Assn Deaf, 1971

Smith M: Vocabulary development in young children. University of Iowa Studies in Child Welfare 3:(5), 1926

Wait D: Pulsatone. Perdoncini Oral/Aural Program. Wichita, Kansas, Wichita State University, 1975

Wedenberg E: Auditory training of severely hard of hearing preschool children. Acta Otolaryngol [Suppl] (Stockh) 94:1–129, 1954

Wedenberg E: Auditory training of the severely hard of hearing using a coding amplifier. Proceedings of the Third International Congress on Acoustics. Amsterdam, Elsevier, 1961, pp 658–660

Wedenberg E: The advantages of auditory training: A case report, in Berg F and Fletcher S (eds): The Hard of Hearing Child. New York and London, Grune & Stratton, 1970, pp 319–330

Wilson W, Moore J: Test-Retest Reliability of Visual Reinforcement Audiometry with Infants. Seattle, University of Washington, 1975

Wilson W, Moore J, Thompson G: Auditory Thresholds of Infants Utilizing Visual Reinforcement Audiometry. Seattle, University of Washington, 1975

5

Communication Training in Special Classes

Types of School Programs

Since the emergence of educational programs for the hearing impaired in the United States in 1817, several models of delivery of services have been developed (Education of the Deaf, 1965). Initially and until a decade ago, the programs were designed almost exclusively for deaf children. The needs of hard-of-hearing children were largely neglected. The original special program was the American School for the Deaf established at Hartford, Connecticut, in 1817. It served hearing-impaired children of that era's United States (Myklebust, 1964).

The American School was a public residential school or institution for the deaf. Soon after it was established it became apparent that the number of hearing-impaired children needing schooling had been underestimated. Within the next decade several other residential facilities were founded. As people settled farther and farther west and additional states were admitted into the Union, more and more such institutions were set up. Usually they were publically supported facilities but occasionally they were private schools.

A break from the residential model was made in 1868 with the establishment of the Boston Day School for the Deaf (Mulholland, 1968). Rather than residing at the school, children lived at home like most other school children. Similar day schools were established in other populated areas of the country. Typically these educational facilities were oral schools. On the other hand the residential institutions utilized some oral but predominately manual approaches for classroom instruction. In the latter facilities students characteristically communicated by use of signs and fingerspelling and approximated utterances outside of class.

Another innovation occurred during the last decade of the nineteenth century. Classrooms in regular public schools of Wisconsin began to be utilized for educating hearing-impaired children. This was the beginning of the day class programs that today enroll almost as many hearing-impaired children as the residential and day schools combined. Typically these programs are established in the relatively smaller cities and in the suburban counties of metropolitan centers. Many day class programs have lacked adequate supervision and curriculum. Until recently the communicative method of day class programs was exclusively oral (Mulholland, 1968). Now a great many of these day programs incorporate a total communication approach.

By 1975, 52,485 hearing-impaired children of the United States were enrolled in the following special classes (tabular summary, 1976).

Type of Facility	Number	Enrollment
Public residential schools	66	19,120
Private residential schools	13	1,212
Public day schools	76	7,024
Private day schools	17	445
Public day classes	467	22,132
Private day classes	32	678
Public classes for the multiply handicapped	43	822
Private classes for the multiply handicapped	31	1,052
	521	52,485

Rationale for Special Class

The rationale for a special class, whether it be in a residential or day facility, has been to design and implement an educational program unique to the characteristics and needs of the child with a moderate to profound or total hearing loss. If a deaf or hard-of-hearing child has been enrolled in a day program, he might leave there upon completion of the eighth grade and enter either a regular high school or the secondary phase of a state residential school for the deaf. Or the same child might be enrolled at the residential institution from the beginning of his education until the end. The typical special class enrollment has been seven to nine children.

Even before World War II increasing recognition of the importance of the preschool years for communicative development led to the establishment of special school programming for hearing-impaired children as young as 2-1/2 years of age. By 1964 as many as one-half of all deaf and moderately to profoundly hard-of-hearing youngsters had enrolled in residential and day preschool instruction (Education of the Deaf, 1965).

Before the past decade the design of preschool and elementary education in the special schools and classes typically focused on the development of language, speech, and visual listening or lipreading competencies. There were two reason for this emphasis on spoken communication skills: (1) spoken language skills ordinarily underpin the acquisition of reading, written composition, academic, and/or vocational skills, and (2) the child has to get along in a world of people who speak our language and listen to it. There was an accompanying lack of emphasis on the utilization of residual hearing.

During 1964 a committee chaired by Homer Babbidge, President of the University of Connecticut, made a thorough investigation of education of the deaf in the United States under the auspices of the Secretary of Health, Education, and Welfare (Education of the Deaf, 1965). A representative sample of residential, day school, and day class programs was visited and studied. In a summary of findings the Babbidge Committee noted that the American people had little reason to be satisfied with the education of their deaf children. They reported, for example, that the typical graduate of a residential school for the deaf had only an eighth grade education. The model of delivery of services notwithstanding, 60 percent of students in schools for the deaf who were 16 years or older read at a grade level of 5.3 or below. (Boatner, 1965; McClure, 1966). At about the same time, Furth (1966) reported the mean reading grade equivalent of a sample of 1075 deaf children aged 15-1/2 to 16-1/2 to be 3.5.

Soon afterward an office of demographic studies was established at Gallaudet College, a special postsecondary institution for the deaf located in Washington, D. C. As a result, detailed information on the academic achievement of each child enrolled in a special school or class has been recorded year by year. These data continue to reveal the devastating reading deficit of the deaf child. Furth (1966) clarifies the nature of the reading problem.

It should be noted that a 14-year-old deaf youngster with a reading level of Grade 3 is not comparable to a hearing peer who may have difficulty reading. The hearing individual enjoys a comfortable mastery of the language even though he may be retarded in reading. For the deaf, on the other hand, the reading level is his ceiling of linguistic competence. It is quite inappropriate to designate this latter condition as retardation in reading. It is properly termed incompetence or deficiency in verbal language, a condition rare among the hearing but almost universal among the deaf (Furth, 1966, p 15).

Aural and Total Communication Status

During the past decade total communication has replaced the oral method as the most frequently used communicative approach of the special classroom (Bird, 1974). Many factors seem to be responsible for this switch in focus. One factor is the rise of adult deaf influence in the educational decision-making process. It appears that many deaf adults have blamed the low educational achievement of their population on the use of the oral method during preschool and elementary schooling (Sanderson, 1969). Another factor influencing this changeover is a growing professional disenchantment with speechreading as the primary sensory avenue through which language and academic skills can be developed. A third factor is the rapid development of forms of signed English in place of the rudimentary signs used in the past (Anthony, 1972). A fourth factor is a professional belief that total communication is flexible enough to meet the individual communicative needs of children with varying degrees of hearing loss and varying learning needs. And another factor is the philosophical commitment to utilize also auditory clues within the total communication approach, particularly as they are needed by children with useful residual hearing.

The utilization of residual hearing and auditory clues, however, is currently being implemented most within the oral method and programs. Whereas speechreading clues were given precedence in the past, a new oral method is evolving in which audition is replacing vision as the basic sensory avenue for listening, speech, and language programming. Therefore the efficacy of total communication is beginning to be compared with an auditory or aural method rather than with an oral or speechreading method.

A "pure" comparison of methodologies by Holt (1976) seems to provide evidence that the pendulum of communicative approach may have swung to the incorporation of manual signs before objective evidence justified it. Holt carefully compared total communication and aural methodologies in a study of the learning of social studies by hearing-impaired students. During eight weeks of instruction using prepared scripts, transparencies, and overhead projectors, 14 classes of hearing-impaired children with second grade reading levels were taught the concepts of rules and locations. A criterion test was administered by teachers of 10 total communication classes and four aural classes. The classes taught with the aural communication system showed significantly higher achievement on the posttest than the classes taught with a total communication system that incorporated audition. Holt attributed these differences primarily to greater use of audition by the aurally trained children, although their mean hearing loss exceeded that of the total communication children. The intelligence of children and the level of teaching competence within the two groups were not measured but seemed to be equivalent.

Until additional data-based comparisons between communicative methodologies can be made, rationale for utilization of a particular classroom approach must be based on sound theoretical observations. This chapter provides a rationale for the continued use of an aural or auditory approach with those hearing-impaired children who can utilize auditory clues. Specific description of auditory training, speech instruction, and lipreading training is included. Emphasis is given to methodology that has already been developed.

The choice of a particular aural or oral approach to the education of a hearing-impaired child in a special classroom is described in a new book entitled *Speech and Deafness* (Calvert and Silverman, 1975). The authors refer to the Auditory Global, the Multisensory Syllable Unit, and the Association Phoneme Unit methods in a discussion of the three major current methodologies of speech teaching. This chapter also considers these approaches.

AUDITORY TRAINING

An outstanding American model for the practice of auditory training in special classes is the educational programming of the St. Joseph School for the Deaf in St. Louis. Systematic utilization of residual hearing among the hearing impaired has been practiced there with the aid of electroacoustic amplification equipment.

By the late 1940s, hard wire group auditory training systems were installed throughout the classrooms of this facility. Rather than letting these units fall into disrepair, as many educators were doing, the sisters of St. Joseph's saw to it that they were kept in operating condition. With the availability of amplification equipment, they designed and implemented procedures to ensure that the children were provided the auditory clues that were available within the context of a systematic curriculum which gave continuing emphasis to "good" speech, language, and listening skills. By the 1960s, St. Joseph's personnel had developed a systematic curriculum in auditory training (Hogan, 1961). In contrast to nearly all other special schools or special classes giving only token support to auditory training, the St. Joseph's staff supported it and discovered how to make it successful.

In 1961 a manual for classroom use with young "deaf" children was written by Sister James Lorene Hogan. Called *The ABC's of Auditory Training,* this guidebook describes a primary level program and details a series of exemplary lessons that have been field-tested at St. Joseph's. The lessons are prepared for three ages of children: five to seven, six to eight, and seven to nine. Success in auditory discrimination or successful utilization of auditory clues is correlated with three categories of severe to "total" hearing loss:

1. *75–90 dB.* Children are unable to hear above 4000 Hz. Auditory discrimination of lesson stimuli is extremely limited initially, but it is attained without speechreading by most children upon completion of the manual.
2. *85–100 dB.* Children are unable to hear above 3000 Hz. Auditory discrimination is difficult initially, then improves somewhat, but not as much with first group. Auditory clues supplement vision in attainment of speech, language, and academic skills.
3. *95–110 dB.* Children are unable to hear above 2000 Hz, and the pace of auditory training is slower still. Auditory discrimination improves very little with practice but aids vision in speech, language, and academic attainment.

The hearing loss categorizations above were not permanent or fixed. Lorene often shifted a child with a hearing loss from one category or group to another. Such shifts are necessitated because auditory sensitivity and auditory discrimination or learning are not highly correlated in the severely to profoundly hearing-impaired population.

The reader should not view these hearing loss categories as final indicators of what hearing-impaired children can achieve through auditory training. However they do describe what happened to many children attending one special school in which hard wire amplification was utilized. These children were initially trained to speech-read and to read the stimulus material before the training design called for auditory discrimination of the same content.

Of particular interest to the success that such children achieved is the fact that many of these youngsters may not have been fitted with hearing aids and provided with home programming in auditory training before they were enrolled at the St. Joseph Institute for the Deaf. This lack of infant–preschool training did not negate their candidacy for auditory training during their school years. However data from early

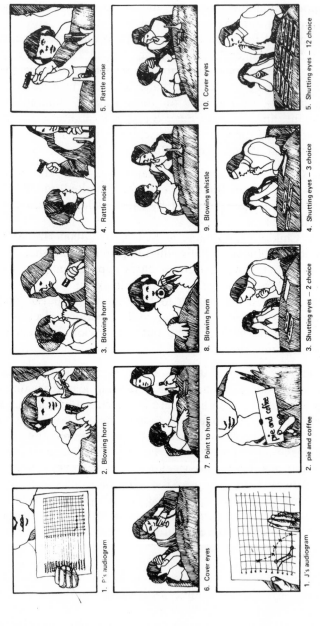

Fig. 26. Demonstrations of gross sound discrimination and speech sound discrimination procedures utilized at the St. Joseph Institute for the Deaf. Compliments Fontbonne College and the St. Joseph Institute for the Deaf.

education projects reveal that the speech, language, and listening competencies of hearing-impaired children are advanced if early and specialized home training is provided.

Earlier Wedenberg (1954) had studied the effect of early auditory training upon the development of vocal and verbal skills among infant and preschool children with severe and profound hearing impairments. He also categorized the children into audiometric classifications and correlated these with prediction of success. His five categories accounted for extent of intensity and frequency loss. Success with auditory training was also related to intelligence, age at which training began, and duration of training. Results were measured in terms of vocabulary and syntactic growth as well as speech proficiency. As a result of the training, some of the children were able to enter the regular Swedish schools by seven years of age, others required special class instruction for the hard of hearing, and still others entered special classrooms for the "deaf." Features of his methodology were described in the previous chapter. It is important to mention that Wedenberg's own son, Staffan, although having a hearing loss in Lorene's third category, was able to learn to perceive and produce speech and spoken language through a unisensory auditory channel, in contrast to the St. Joseph findings. Special emphasis in training, however, was given to initial perception of phonemes, words, and sentences "loaded" with voiced sounds, particularly those having formants or concentrations of energies between 0 and 1600 Hz, the upper limit of Staffan's hearing.

Figure 26 illustrates 16 scenes from two auditory training demonstrations of procedures used at the St. Joseph Institute for the Deaf. Captions are included to clarify the procedures. Scripts of all stimuli and responses follow. Frames 1–12 encompass gross sound discrimination procedures. Similar discrimination of speech stimuli is illustrated briefly in frames 13–16. The teacher's (T) stimuli are presented first, then the child's (C) response, and finally T's feedback or response.

These demonstrations were given years after the development of Lorene Hogan's (1961) auditory training manual. The second child had an audiogram similar to that of Staffan Wedenberg and was seven years old. The upper frequency limit of the audiogram for his better ear was perhaps no higher than 1500 Hz. The sound track from which the script was derived reveals that his voice and articulation were those of a severely hard-of-hearing child. The first child, however, was just beginning an auditory training program and functioned as a young deaf child.

Gross Sound Discrimination

Teacher's introduction. This is a lesson in gross auditory discrimination. This is a four-year-old student who has been in clinic class for one and one-half years, and in St. Joseph's in the regular preschool program for eight months. This is *P's* audiogram. *P* is a profoundly deaf child. He has learned to listen and to discriminate some noise-makers. In lessons in gross discrimination, it is very important that the child understands that he must listen. He looks so he knows what is happening, and then he learns to listen and to discriminate what he hears.

First noisemaker: horn

T:	Okay, we're going to blow the *horn*. Listen.	*C:*	listens and looks	*T:*	blows horn
T:	Okay, do you want to blow the horn and you listen?	*C:*	blows horn	*T:*	Good boy!
T:	Listen again.	*C:*	listens and looks	*T:*	blows horn twice
T:	Okay, don't look.	*C:*	listens, does not look	*T:*	blows horn
T:	Did you hear the horn? Blow the horn.	*C:*	blows horn	*T:*	Good boy!

Second noisemaker: rattle

T:	Now I have another one. Look. Listen.	*C:*	listens and looks	*T:*	swings a rattle
T:	Can you hear it? Can you do it?	*C:*	swings the rattle and it hits his head	*T:*	Oh, ow! We got hit on the head, didn't we? That's a hard one to do.
T:	Okay, now listen. Listen.	*C:*	listens and looks	*T:*	swings the rattle

Teacher's explanation. It is very important that the first two sounds that the child learns to discriminate are very different, like the horn and the rattle.

First and second noisemakers: horn and rattle on the table

T:	Okay, now look.	*C:* listens and looks	*T:* blows the horn
T:	What did I do? I blew the horn. Do you want to blow the horn? Blow.	*C:* blows the horn	*T:* Very good!

Teacher's explanation. First we have *P* watch so that he can see what I do, and then he will do the same thing.

First and second noisemakers: horn and rattle

T:	Okay. (swings the rattle, puts it down)	*C:* listens and looks	
T:	What did I do? Did you hear it? What did you hear?	*C:* points to the rattle and swings it	*T:* Good boy!
T:	Okay. Now you will listen. Okay? (blows the horn)	*C:* listens	*T:* puts hand over face
T:	What did I do? I blew the horn.	*C:* points to horn	*T:* Good boy!
T:	Okay. (blows the horn)	*C:* listens and points to horn	*T:* Good boy! (puts horn behind back)
		C: looks	*T:* Don't look.
T:	swings the rattle	*C:* listens	
T:	What did I do?	*C:* points to the rattle	*T:* Very good!
		C: swings the rattle	*T:* Ooo, very good!

Third noisemaker: whistle

T:	Okay, now for the third. Listen *P.* (blows the whistle)	*C:* listens and looks	
T:	Do you want to blow the whistle?	*C:* blows the whistle	*T:* Blow hard. Good boy!
T:	Listen *P.* (blows the whistle)	*C:* listens and looks	

T: Can you hear
the whistle?

T: Okay, now don't   C: listens   T: covers eyes
look. (blows the
whistle)

T: Did you hear the   C: blows the whistle   T: Good boy!
whistle? Blow the
whistle.

First, second, and third noisemakers: horn, rattle, and whistle

T: I want you to   C: listens
listen in threes.
(blows the whistle)

T: What did Sister *J*   C: points   T: No.
do?

                         C: points again   T: That's right.
                                                    I blew the
                                                    whistle.

T: Blow the whistle.   C: blows the whistle   T: Good boy!

T: Now listen again.   C: listens   T: swings the rattle
(swings the rattle)   behind her back

T: What did Sister *J*   C: points   T: No.
do?

                         C: points again   T: Yes.

                         C: swings the rattle   T: That's a boy.

T: Round and round.   C: swings it round
                            and round and
                            puts it down

Teacher's explanation. He's not discriminating between these
three, so we realize that he doesn't understand, or he can't discriminate. So we go back to the first noisemakers.

First and second noisemakers: horn and rattle

T: Okay. Don't look.   C: turns around   T: Good boy!
Turn around.

T: blows the horn   C: listens

T: Now, what did   C: points to the horn   T: That's right.
Sister *J* do?   She blew the
                                                    horn.

T: Blow the horn.	*C:* blows the horn	*T:* Good boy! Very good.
T: Turn around. I want you to listen.	*C:* turns around	
T: Listen. (swings the rattle)	*C:* listens	
T: Now, what did Sister *J* do?	*C:* points to the rattle	*T:* That's right.
	C: swings the rattle	*T:* Very good. Very good.
T: Turn around. Turn around.	*C:* turns around	
T: blows the horn	*C:* listens	
T: Now, what did Sister *J* do?	*C:* points	*T:* That's right. I blew the horn.
T: Blow the horn.	*C:* blows the horn	*T:* Good boy!

Teacher's summary. Now, that is all we will do with *P* today. When we work for gross discrimination, we begin with two very dissimilar noisemakers until the child is able to discriminate between them. Then we add another noisemaker. *P* is not ready for the third noisemaker, for example, the whistle that would sound like this [blows the whistle], which would be different from these two noisemakers on the table. Then we would eventually add a fourth noisemaker, such as the harmonica. *P* would be able to discriminate eventually between these four. Then we would add another noisemaker, for example, this high-pitched whistle. The last noisemaker we would add would be this horn [blows another horn]. We would be very careful in adding this noisemaker because this horn is very similar to the other horn that we blew and would be very difficult for the child to discriminate. So we must be very careful, and if the child has difficulty we would not put these two together [blows both horns] because this is a very fine discrimination for him.

Speech–Sound Discrimination

The child in the second demonstration, depicted in frames 13–16 of Figure 27, is already familiar with the vocabulary or meaning of the stimuli and can lip-read and read them. The purpose of the demonstration is to illustrate auditory discrimination of the speech stimuli that consist of compounds like *pie and coffee, ball and glove,* and *pen and pencil.* Initially, the child looks at the instructor as she says the word; the child also utilizes auditory clues delivered by his hearing aid. The instructor shows the child the printed form so that he has a perceptual set. Then she asks him to turn away. He listens auditorially but can refer visually to the printed options or choices of responses. Then he identifies the correct stimulus. Finally the instructor removes the structure or printed options to determine the competence of the child in discriminating auditorially between 12 stimuli including *pie and coffee.*

Teacher's introduction. I want you to look and listen and show me the picture on the chart.

T:	We're going to do *pie and coffee.* Will you say it? Pie and coffee.	*C:*	Pie and coffee.	*T:*	All right.
T:	Ball and glove.	*C:*	Ball and glove.	*T:*	All right.
T:	Do you hear?	*C:*	Yeah.		
T:	Shut your eyes. We're only going to do two. All right? Tell me which one. Shut your eyes.				
T:	Ball and glove.	*C:*	Ball and glove.	*T:*	Good.
T:	Pie and coffee.	*C:*	Pie and coffee.		
T:	Shut your eyes. Pie and coffee.	*C:*	Pie and coffee.	*T:*	Very good.
T:	I'm going to give you another one. Pen and pencil.	*C:*	Pen and pencil.		
T:	Shut your eyes. Pie and coffee.	*C:*	Pie and coffee.	*T:*	Very good.
T:	Ball and glove.	*C:*	Ball and glove.		
T:	Pen and pencil.	*C.*	Pen and pencil.		

Clarification. The instructor notes that the boy is identifying the stimuli through hearing only. If she were training the child to discriminate the items first, she would add them to the chart as she moved along and as the child progressed. This training would be conducted with the structure of the chart present.

T: Shut your eyes. Paint and brush.	*C:* Paint and glove.	
T: Oh, where do you see that? Where do you see *paint and glove.* Joe, shut your eyes.		
T: Paint and brush.	*C.* Paint and brush.	
T: Where is it. Come on, someplace here.	*C:* points to it	*T:* All right. Kind of slow.
T: Towel and wash-cloth.	*C:* Towel and wash-cloth.	*T:* All right.
T: Let's see how fast you can go. Table and chairs.	*C:* Table and chairs.	*T:* Good.
T: Bacon and eggs.	*C:* Bacon and eggs.	*T:* Ha!
T: Bacon and eggs. That's right. Where is it?	*C:* points correctly	*T:* Good.
T: Knife and fork. Show me. Knife and fork.	*C:* Knife and fork. (points correctly)	*T:* Good. All right.
T: Shoes and socks.	*C:* Shoes and socks.	
T: Needle and thread.		
T: Needle and thread.	*C:* What?	*T:* You looked.
T: Needle and thread.	*C:* Needle and—	
T: Needle. You know what that is. When you sew. Mother has a needle. Mother sews.	*C:* Sew.	*T:* Yeah.
T: Needle and thread.	*C:* Needle and thread.	*T:* I don't think you know that.

Clarification. The instructor indicates that the child does not appear to understand *needle and thread,* but she is not going to take time to teach its meaning now. She suspects he may not know *hammer and nails* either, but he does, so she moves into a phase of training requiring recall of the structure in addition to discrimination through audition only. She removes the structure by taking away the chart. The child is now required to repeat the compounds without pointing to pictures and/or printed forms of these stimuli.

T:	Shut your eyes. Ball and glove.	*C:*	Ball and glove.	*T:*	Good.
T:	Shoes and socks.	*C:*	Shoes and socks.		
T:	Pie and coffee.	*C:*	Pie and puppy.	*T:*	No.
T:	Shut your eyes. Pie and coffee. Something you eat.	*C:*	Pie and coffee.	*T:*	Good. Okay.
T:	Sh—Oh, you looked. Shoes and socks.	*C:*	Shoes and socks.	*T:*	Very good.
T:	Table and chairs.	*C:*	Table and chairs.		
T:	Pen and pencil.	*C:*	Pen and pencil.		
T:	Man and woman.	*C:*	Man and woman.		
T:	Knife and fork.	*C:*	Knife and fork.		
T:	Mother and daddy.	*C:*	Mother and daddy.		

Teacher's summary. The instructor points out that the last compound was a stimulus that was not in the structure from which the auditory training had proceeded. She notes that the child has been trained to use his residual hearing over a period of years and does very well for a child with a profound hearing loss.

These demonstrations from the St. Joseph Institute for the Deaf suggest that the basic activity to auditory training is presentation of a stimulus and elicitation of a response. Study of Lorene's manual indicates that a variety of verbal stimuli and response types may be utilized. The stimuli direct the child to point, repeat, answer questions, carry out commands, complete sentences, listen for particular phonetic or prosodic stimuli, give descriptions, and provide information. Types or levels of response include *imitative, associative,* short- and long-term *memory,* and *cognitive* (Hogan, 1961).

Curriculum

Auditory training in a special class program should be conducted within the overall curriculum activities. According to Taba (1962;

1967), a curriculum is a plan for learning and a plan for teaching. Its five major elements are objectives to be attained, selection and organization of content, choice and assembling of learning experiences, formulation and organization of teaching strategies, and evaluation. Auditory training at the Peninsula Oral School in California, for example, is incorporated within the Taba curriculum. Grammatico and Miller (1974) state that behavior objectives specify what children are expected to accomplish. They also note that the Taba curriculum is well suited to the development of the communication skills of listening, language, speech, and cognition. Grammatico and Miller point out that their behavioral objectives on the preschool level include the development of listening skills, spontaneous language, and correct speech sounds. These same objectives were among those specified earlier by Wedenberg (1954; 1970).

Verbotonal Considerations

Bellefleur (1967), a former audiologist at the Clarke School for the Deaf, has suggested that the student of auditory training should look closely at procedures used at a school for the hearing impaired in Zagreb, Yugoslavia. Directed by Guberina, this special facility enrolls many profoundly hearing-impaired individuals who generally have more natural-sounding speech than children with similar losses in American schools for the deaf. Guberina (1969) attributes his success largely to the utilization of a series of hearing aids named SUVAG. Each child begins his education at this school with daily auditory stimulation by SUVAG I, which amplifies sound energies from 0.5 to 15,000 Hz. After being mobilized to respond to auditory clues, the child advances to programming with SUVAG II.

SUVAG II is capable of selective amplification of various bands and peaks of sound energies. The large number of controls on the face of the device permits the clinician to isolate the specific intensities and frequencies at which each child discriminates speech best. It is at these settings that speech may be optimally identified or perceptually learned auditorially. While the child is not receiving individualized instruction, he is fitted with the body-model mini-SUVAG, which amplifies energies from 100 to 4,000 Hz. If a child has little or no residual hearing, he also receives speech and language instruction by use of an electrotactile device or vibrator that can be coupled to the mini-SUVAG. Both the Western Pennsylvania and the Tennessee schools for the "deaf" are currently experimenting with the Guberina method called verbotonal instruction (Asp, Berry, and Berry, 1973; Craig, Craig, and DiJohnson, 1972). Figure 27 shows a series of video photograph tracings and captions that picture and identify the various SUVAG aids.

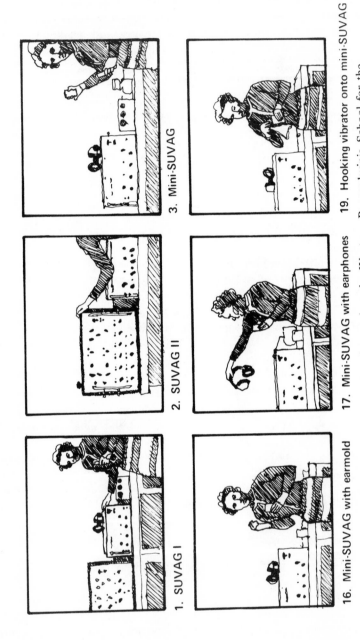

Fig. 27. Drawings of SUVAG units used at the Western Pennsylvania School for the Deaf.

Craig, Craig, and DiJohnson (1972) of the Western Pennsylvania school have studied the advantages of verbotonal instruction among hearing-impaired children in classes at that school. Comparing a verbotonal group with a control group of preschool children using established oral procedures, they noted that progress in speech favored use of the Guberina approach. The investigators described the overall experimental approach and speech results as follows.

The Verbotonal instructional approach, like the equipment, is geared toward maximizing auditory awareness in the development of language and speech, integrating the four procedural components of (1) body movement, (2) musical stimulation, (3) implementation (speech and language through body activities), and (4) individual work. Thus, in group work, the body movements broadly correspond to the tension of the articulators in producing various sounds and to the intensity or accent on units in a phrase sequence; the musical stimulation simultaneously uses movement (clapping) and speech to instill a feeling for the rhythm of phrases; and the implementation or language building sessions relate [sic] the sounds and words to meaningful language concepts. Individual sessions then provide tutoring in auditory perception, speech, and language production. . . . Observers who were familiar with the speech of preschool deaf children were in general agreement that, in addition to vocalizing more frequently, the Verbotonal group evidenced more normal intonation patterns and pitch contours than the traditionally trained children (Craig, Craig, and DiJohnson, 1972, pp 237–238, 244).

The aspect of the verbotonal approach that is particularly relevant to the present discussion is that of obtaining a prescription of the intensities and the frequencies that the individual child can best utilize for auditory perception. In contrast to findings of some investigators (Martin and Pickett, 1968), Guberina (1969) claims that, when amplified, the low frequencies of speech do not mask the high frequencies but actually facilitate their perception among profoundly hearing-impaired children. With the use of SUVAG II he has noted, for example, that the 300 to 3,000 Hz frequency band can be filtered out and speech will still be intelligible. The frequencies left in this instance are from 0.5 to 300 Hz and from 3,000 to 15,000 Hz. Guberina states that the frequencies above 3,000 Hz can be very important, as can those below 300 Hz. He indicates that the body itself is most sensitive to frequencies around 10 to 20 Hz.

Guberina's claims pertaining to the comparative advantage of low frequency amplification should be subjected to careful scrutiny. A series of follow-up experiments at the Western Pennsylvania School for the Deaf seem to reveal that the verbotonal approach may be no better than other auditory–oral methodologies currently in use. In careful comparisons in both the Middle School and the Upper School using experimental and control methodologies, improvements in speech, auditory discrimination, speechreading, and language generally were no greater for the verbotonal groups. Notwithstanding the auditory approach, however, communication tutoring resulted in significant speaking and listening gains. Furthermore the skills attained during tutoring or individual remediation were accompanied by a positive shift in students' attitudes about speech and listening (Craig, Craig, DiJohnson, 1973).

In a description of the rationale for continuation and expansion of verbotonal training at the Western Pennsylvania School for the Deaf, Craig, Craig, and DiJohnson (1973) suggest that the hearing-impaired children enrolled do not discriminate or sense frequencies higher than 500 to 1,000 Hz. They reason, therefore, that traditional amplification units discriminate against such youngsters. In addition, they indicate that temporal and intonation patterns of speech are incorporated in frequencies below 600 Hz.

These statements should be qualified or clarified. Actually most children in schools for the deaf are potentially hard of hearing. They can sense and be trained to perceive speech clues having frequency components up to 2,000 Hz and above. In addition, the second formants of the speech sounds in addition to the first formants carry the temporal and intonation patterns of speech. Depending upon consonant, vowel, or diphthong, the second formants are concentrated within the 600 to 2,300 Hz frequency range for males. They are located somewhat higher for females and especially for children. The first formants or intensity concentrations of speech sounds lie within the frequency range from 200 to 850 Hz (Wedenberg and Wedenberg, 1970).

However it is justified to emphasize exploitation of the very low frequencies among many children with profound hearing losses, averaging 90 to 110 dB. Most of these youngsters, comprising about 50 percent of students in typical schools for the deaf, characteristically have better auditory acuity in the first formant or the 200 to 850 Hz region than in any other frequency band of similar width (Wedenberg, 1970). Furthermore Ling (1964) compared the effectiveness of a hearing aid whose frequency response begins at 90 Hz with that of a typical amplification device whose response begins at 800 Hz. The profoundly hearing-impaired children he studied made significantly greater speech improvement using the experimental aid than those using the control aid. Currently, commercially available body-model hearing aids typically have frequency responses from 200 to 3,200 Hz. Thus they amplify both first and second formants. The fundamental frequencies of the human voice, varying from averages of approximately 135, 225, and 265 Hz for males, females, and children, carry relatively little energy that can be sensed or perceived in and of itself (Peterson and Barney, 1952).

Craig, Craig, and DiJohnson (1973) also rightly emphasize the reciprocal relationship between speech production and speech perception. The training focus on speech production and perception in the verbotonal method, however, was also a feature of Wedenberg's (1954) auditory methodology and of the Acoustic Method of Goldstein (1939) which was introduced from Vienna in 1893 (Wedenberg, 1951). Liberman (1957) presents data that indicate that sensory feedback from articulatory movements mediates between the acoustic stimulus and its perception.

The SUVAG II approach to determination of the best amplification response is based upon differential response to speech stimuli. The clinician keeps changing filter settings until the child achieves his most accurate speech perception scores. Enough stimuli are presented at each filter setting during successive auditory sessions to ensure rather objective results.

A similar procedure is pursued with the Auralometer developed at the Penninsula Oral School for the Deaf and manufactured by Audiotone of Phoenix, Arizona. With this master aid the clinician or teacher can vary gain, maximum power output, and slope and contour of frequency response. Such changes are made systematically and a record of responses to stimuli is kept. After repeated sessions conducted day by day, the specialist arrives at a combination of settings at which the child functions best. This information is then forwarded to the manufacturer. Custom-built aids that meet the individual need of the child are subsequently supplied on the basis of the forwarded specifications. The manufacturer also makes circuit changes and setting adjustments as often as requested to meet the changing needs of the child (Nielson, 1974).

SPEECH INSTRUCTION

During the preschool years or early school years, structured speech remediation is initiated with a hearing-impaired child. With or without previous programming in listening, such children have defective speech. The extent of the speech needs of each child varies. Careful speech evaluation determines where a structured program should begin. Concern is with degree of vocal, articulatory, and prosodic deviation. Typically, the deaf child errs in all three of these areas and the hard-of-hearing child errs at least in articulation (Berg, 1970).

Speech programming is structured when periods or sessions of time are used to focus on the remediation or development of specific vocal, articulatory, and/or prosodic competencies. A clinician or teacher interacts with a client or child, providing stimulation, feedback, and reinforcement. With baseline information the clinician writes specific objectives and prepares and/or selects a program. The clinician follows procedures but is flexible enough to redesign and reprogram as often as necessary.

The basic activities in speech remediation are presentation of stimuli by the clinician and imitation by the client. The stimuli vary from phonemes to syllables to phrases to entire sentences. During this procedure the clinician also prompts before the stimulus and reinforces after the imitated response. He continually encourages improvement in the accuracy of responses or consistency in responding at the "best" response level.

Sensory Clues

The imitated response of the client depends largely upon his speech perception. A hearing-impaired person does not perceive the phonetic and prosodic features through audition as well as the normal child does. Even with speech "packaged" into his auditory area, he cannot perceive the auditory clues that the normal child can. Because of reduced auditory perception, the hearing-impaired child should be provided clues from other sensory inputs.

Speechreading and Tactile Clues

In speech remediation the conventional nonauditory clues are provided by speechreading and tactile features. While the clinician is providing a speech model for imitation, the client is looking at his mouth and mandibular area. The client may also have his left hand and particularly his fingertips on the right side of the face of the clinician, or at times in front of the mouth of the clinician. The visual clues from speechreading and the tactile clues contribute to the perceptual pool which the client uses to facilitate accuracy of speech imitations and stabilization of correct response.

The clues available from speechreading include features of lip positioning, mouth opening, mandibular depression, and tongue positioning and contact. A different combination of these features characterizes the visual aspect of each phoneme. However the visual differences among consonant cognates are subtle. For example, the /f/ and the /v/ look alike, except that the point of articulation of the teeth on the lower lip may be located at a slightly different spot.

The articulatory information is only partially visible by use of speechreading. For example, the voiced–voiceless and the oral–nasal distinctions are hidden from view. In addition, closing the teeth hides the tongue positioning information that is related to the production of many phonemes. Furthermore it is impossible to note the glottal approximation for /h/ and difficult to see the lingua-velar articulation of /k/, /g/, and / ŋ/.

During speech modeling it is helpful to use a large mirror and to employ a directional light. Thus the client can compare his articulation of a given phoneme with that of the clinician. His visual perception also becomes more accurate.

As the client imitates speech, the stimulus is slowed down more than it is during speechreading instruction. Thus the client is able to study the formations and locations of the visible articulatory information and to couple these clues with the auditory speech clues that he may perceive. Furthermore tactile speech clues provide the child with still additional perceptual information for shaping speech sounds. It is during structured speech training that such a shaping and stabilization process can occur so that speech intelligibility, if not naturalness, results.

The tactile speech clues include vibration from the side of the throat or from one or more of the facial points to indicate voicing. Vibration from the side of the nose provides clues to nasal production. Air flow or expulsion from the mouth indicates a voiceless sound, and its amount and location even reveals production of a specific phoneme. Mandibular position, movement, and tension reveal information relevant to the production of specific phonemes, for example, /i/ versus /e/.

Although tactile clues assist the child in imitating the clinician, their use is largely restricted to the initial shaping of phonemes and core words. Thereafter, taction is phased out because it is cumbersome and tiring for the child to place his hand on the face of the clinician. Also tactile information is often less refined than other sensory input. For example, a child may tend to develop laryngeal tension with resultant voice disorder if the clinician is not cautious and conservative in utilizing tactile speech clues.

In short, tactile speech clues are valuable in the initial shaping of phonemes and core words, when the child needs as much information as possible about the vocal tract phenomena of voicing, velopharyngeal posture, and restriction and locality of articulation. However they need not be used when sufficient perceptual information is available from audition and speechreading, and when articulations are shaped so that habit patterns are established. By this time the clinician can utilize notations or can even point to specific anatomic locations to signal that a particular vocal tract phenomena is being omitted or should be included. Table 15 includes the speechreading and tactile speech clues for the specific phonemes.

Some clarifying points should be added to the above description of speechreading clues and tactile speech clues for specific phonemes. Hyoid bulging refers to a protrusion of fleshy tissue under the chin in the area of the hyoid bone. It can be felt with the fingertips and corresponds to the production of at least four tense vowels: /i/, /e/, /u/, and /o/. In many instances during the production of phonemes, tongue positioning is hidden from view. Ordinarily it can be viewed before actual articulation. For example, the tongue can be protruded from the mouth, cupped, retroflexed, and pulled back into the mouth before the lips are squared and the /r/ phoneme is produced. The clues detailed above ordinarily refer to articulation of the phonemes in isolation. In the context of words, phrases, or sentences, even if speech is slowed, the articulation is modified.

Table 15
Speechreading and Tactile Speech Clues for Each of 41 English Phonemes

Phoneme	Speechreading Clues	Tactile Speech Clues
h	Invisible articulation, mouth open depending upon formation of the following vowel	Flow of air emitted from the oral cavity
hw	Invisible articulation initially, lips pursed and then separated	Slight flow of air emitted from the oral cavity at the beginning, then vibration at side of throat
p	Lips shut and separated	Pulse of air explosively emitted from the oral cavity
t	Tongue tip to alveolar ridge, sides of front of tongue spread, then forepart of tongue drops	Pulse of air explosively emitted from the oral cavity
k	Back of tongue to the velum and separated	Pulse of air explosively emitted from the oral cavity
f	Upper teeth to lower lip	Flow of air emitted between articulation

Table 15 (continued)

Phoneme	Speechreading Clues	Tactile Speech Clues
θ	Tongue tip between teeth or against back of upper front teeth	Flow of air emitted between articulation
s	Teeth approximated, high front tongue position can be shown initially	Sharp flow of air emitted centrally between teeth
ʃ	Lips squared, teeth approximated, midelevation and flattening of front of tongue can be shown initially	Diffuse flow of air emitted between teeth
tʃ	Lips squared, teeth approximated, mandible dropping; lingua-alveolar position of tip of tongue can be shown initially	Diffuse pulse of air explosively emitted from the oral cavity
w	Lips pursed and then separated afterwards	Vibration at side of throat, mandible drops from high position to lower position depending upon following vowel
b	Lips shut and separated	Vibration at side of throat, mandible as above
d	Tongue tip to alveolar ridge, sides of front of tongue spread, the forepart of tongue drops	Vibration at side of throat, mandible as above
g	Back of tongue to the velum and separated	Vibration at side of throat, mandible depressed
v	Upper teeth to lower lip	Vibration of lower lip and at side of throat
ʝ	Tongue tip between teeth or against back of upper front teeth	Vibration of front of tongue and at side of throat
z	Teeth approximated, high front tongue position can be shown initially	Vibration of front of tongue and at side of throat
ʒ	Lips squared, teeth approximated, midelevation and flattening of front of tongue can be shown initially	Vibration of front of tongue and at side of throat

Table 15 (continued)

Phoneme	Speechreading Clues	Tactile Speech Clues
dʒ	Lips squared, teeth approximated, mandible dropping, lingua-alveolar position of tip of tongue can be shown initially	Vibration of front of tongue and at side of throat
m	Lips shut	Vibration at side of throat and at side of nose
n	Tongue tip to alveolar ridge, sides of front of tongue spread	As above
ŋ	Back of tongue to the velum	As above
l	Tongue tip to alveolar ridge, sides of front of tongue depressed	Vibration at side of throat
r	Can be shown initially that the forepart of tongue is raised high and the tongue tip is retroflexed or the midpart of tongue is humped centrally; lips squared, mandible depressed somewhat	As above
j	Teeth approximated and then separated; lingua-alveolar-palatal approximation of front of tongue can be shown initially	Vibration at side of throat
i	Lips extended, teeth approximated; lingua-alveolar approximation of front of tongue can be shown initially	As above, hyoid bulging
ɪ	Lips extended, teeth separated a little more than for /i/, mandible dropped somewhat; lingua-alveolar palatal approximation of front of tongue can be shown initially	As above, except that hyoid is not bulging
e	Lips extended, teeth separated noticeably more than for /ɪ/, mandible dropped noticeably more; midfront elevation of forepart of tongue can be shown initially	Vibration at side of throat, hyoid bulging

Table 15 (continued)

Phoneme	Speechreading Clues	Tactile Speech Clues
ɛ	Lips extended, teeth separated somewhat more than for /e/, mandible dropped somewhat more; midfront elevation of forepart of tongue can be shown initially	As above, except that hyoid is not bulging
æ	Lips extended, mandible dropped somewhat more than for /ɛ/, low-front elevation of forepart of tongue can be shown initially	As above
u	Lips rounded and protruded somewhat, small opening between lips	Vibration at side of throat, hyoid bulging
ʊ	Lips rounded and protruded only somewhat, somewhat larger opening between lips	As above, except that hyoid is not bulging
o	Lips rounded and noticeably larger opening than for /u/, can move next into /u/ or /ʊ/ position	Vibration at side of throat, hyoid bulging
ɑ	Lips extended and mandible depressed considerably more than for /o/; tongue appears to be lying flat on floor of oral cavity	Vibration at side of throat
ɔ	Lips rounded, noticeably larger opening than for /o/	Vibration at side of throat
ʌ	Mandible dropped approximately as much as for /o/ although lips are relaxed; tongue appears to be lying flat on the floor of the oral cavity	As above
ɝ	As for /r/	As above
aɪ	As for /a/ plus /i/ or /ɪ/; longer first part than second part	As above
ɔɪ	As for /ɔ/ plus /i/ or /ɪ/; longer first part than second part	As above

Table 15 (continued)

Phoneme	Speechreading Clues	Tactile Speech Clues
aʊ	As for /a/ plus /u/ or /ʊ/; longer first part than second part	As above
ɪu	As for /i/ or /ɪ/ plus /u/; longer second part than first part	As above

Auditory Clues

Audition may offer the greatest potential for contributing sensory information about articulation during speech remediation for the great majority of children in special classes and schools for the hearing impaired. When the speech signal is "packaged" optimally into the auditory area, varying numbers of significant features can be perceived, depending upon extent of hearing loss and amount of perceptual learning training. The auditory features include durational, intensity, and frequency information. These features correspond to the part of a given phoneme or suprasegmental sequence that can be perceived.

Auditory perception is particularly advantageous with the hearing-impaired population for at least two reasons. First, it reveals the deep as well as the surface vocal tract phenomena. As inaccurate or incomplete as auditory speech perception may be, the prosodic and the phonetic or articulatory features are present in the speech signal that is available. In contrast, the speechreading clues are limited almost entirely to articulatory activity in and around the mouth. Furthermore tactile speech clues are simply concomitant events to the speech act. Another advantage of auditory input is that it presents the speech signal over time more adequately than do speechreading and tactile sensory input. The ear keeps up with running speech, the eye loses track, and tactile speech clues are cumbersome to use. Audition, it should be remembered, is uniquely designed for speech communication. Once speech sounds are shaped and stabilized in the context of words and sentences, the hearing-impaired child can use kinesthetic or proprioceptive feedback clues to monitor utterances.

One of the finest speech programs in the country has evolved at the Clarke School for the Deaf since its founding in 1867. Five levels of speech instruction are utilized by the Clarke School teachers (Magner, 1971). During preschool years and up to the age of seven, emphasis is placed on encouraging children to use spontaneous speech and to develop a well-modulated voice. Thereafter the child receives intensive training to shape the consonants, vowels, and diphthongs, to associate them with phonetic symbols, and to incorporate them into connected speech. The last three levels of instruction begin when a child is approximately nine years old and ends about six years later when he graduates from the eighth grade. During the final six years the program is designed to refine vocal, prosodic, and articulatory skills and to teach the pronunciations and meanings of the child's expanding vocabulary.

Speech Programming

Extensive information on the production, development, and correction of each of the English phonemes is included in various books and curriculum guides (Calvert and Silverman, 1975; Haycock, 1941; Magner, 1971; Seamons, 1972). As needed by a given child, these phonemes are taught analytically, synthetically, or more often by a combination of synthetic and analytic approaches. The synthetic approach uses a meaningful combination of phonemes as a stimulus to be imitated. The analytic approach uses phonemes extracted from words or syllables as practice items.

Prosodic Notations

Prosodic and phonetic symbols constitute another form of visual information that a clinician uses to assist hearing-impaired children in speech training.

Spoken language or speech is characterized by suprasegmental phonemes or prosodic features as well as by segmental phonemes or phonetic phenomena. The supra phonemes or prosodic features include perhaps four levels of stress, four categories or levels of pitch within a phrase, and three terminal pitch phonemes or junctures between phrases. These features are linguistically determining and contribute to the intelligibility of speech.

As we speak we use phrases and pauses. The following sentence may be used to illustrate a pause, a phrase, another pause, another phrase, and a final pause. */Notations are introduced / as children progress in training./* The slash marks indicate the locations of the pauses. Each of the two phrases is a sequence of syllables varying in stress or loudness–duration and changing in pitch.

Conversion of this sentence to International Phonetic Alphabet (IPA) transcription and to prosodic notations can be seen in the first space of Figure 28. The numbers to the left and above each syllable indicate relative pitch level. A useful key to these pitch levels or phonemes follows (Pike, 1945).

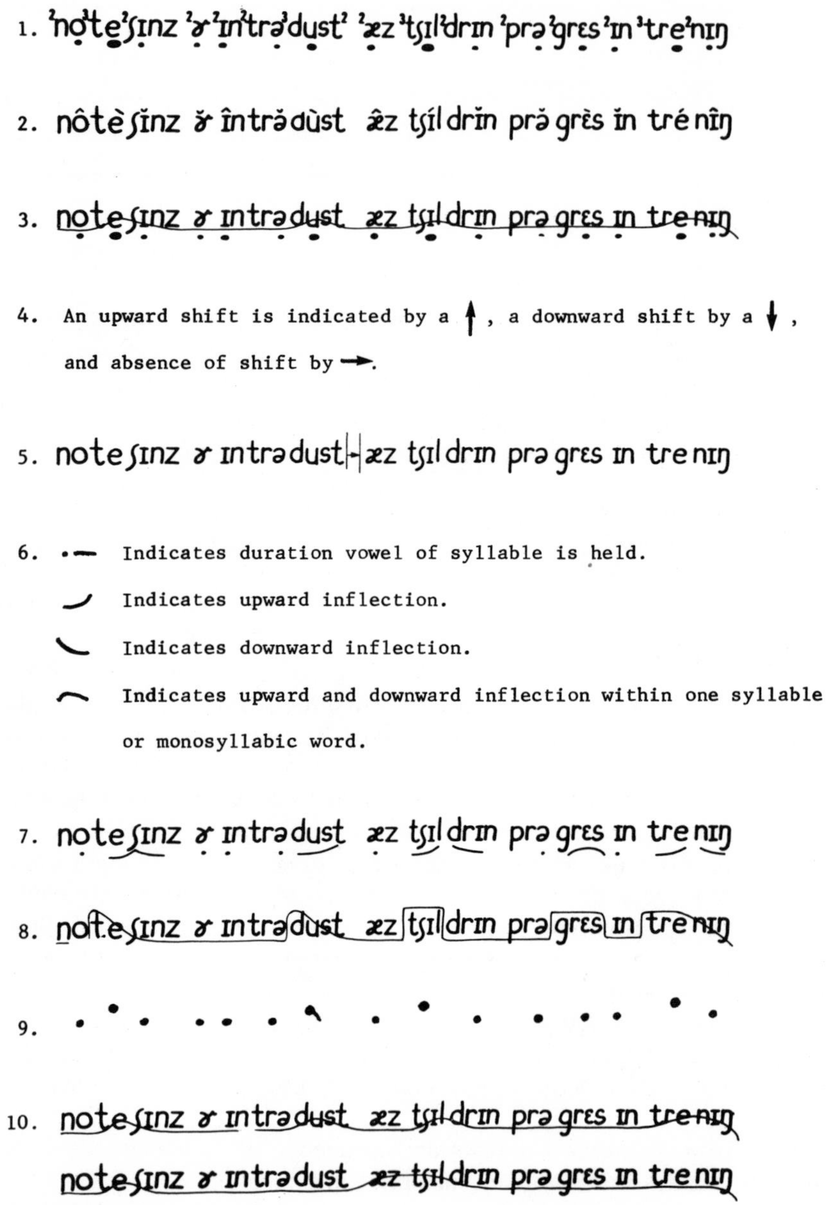

1. ˈn̥o̤teˈʃɪnz ˈɚˈɪnˈtrɜdṳstˈ ˈæz ˈtʃɪlˈdrɪn ˈprɜˈgrɛsˈɪn ˈtre̤ˈnɪŋ

2. nôtèʃɪnz ɚ̆ întrɜdùst æ̂z tʃɪldrɪn prɜ̆grɛs ɪn trénɪ̂ŋ

3. no̤teʃɪnz ɚ ɪntrɜdṳst æz tʃɪldrɪn prɜgrɛs ɪn tre̤nɪŋ

4. An upward shift is indicated by a ↑ , a downward shift by a ↓ ,
   and absence of shift by ➤.

5. noteʃɪnz ɚ ɪntrɜdust⊢⊣æz tʃɪldrɪn prɜgrɛs ɪn trenɪŋ

6. •— Indicates duration vowel of syllable is held.
   ⌣ Indicates upward inflection.
   ⌐ Indicates downward inflection.
   ⌢ Indicates upward and downward inflection within one syllable
   or monosyllabic word.

7. no̤teʃɪnz ɚ ɪntrɜdust æz tʃɪldrɪn prɜgrɛs ɪn trenɪŋ

8. no̤fte̤ʃɪnz ɚ ɪntrɜdust æz tʃɪldrɪn prɜgrɛs ɪn trenɪŋ

9. •   • •   • •   ◥   •   •   •   •   •   • •

10. noteʃɪnz ɚ ɪntrɜdust æz tʃɪ̷ldrɪn prɜgrɛs ɪn trenɪŋ
    noteʃɪnz ɚ ɪntrɜdust æz tʃɪ̷ldrɪn prɜgrɛs ɪn trenɪŋ

Fig. 28. Illustrations of various prosodic notational systems.

1 = *low*, as at the end of unstressed syllables, at the end of phrases, and for conveying certain special effects including the dropped voice

2 = *mid*, as used for the many unstressed syllables in a phrase

3 = *high*, as employed for most stressed syllables and for the raised voice

4 = *very high*, as used for surprise or for stress when the voice is raised.

The oblong patterns below each syllable convey four stress variations. The length and height of each pattern reveal duration and loudness respectively. These relative sizes suggest primary, secondary, tertiary, and quaternary levels of stress. The first two reveal stressed syllables and the last two unstressed syllables. The four levels of stress may also be indicated by the following symbols.

    ′ = primary stress, e.g., third syllable of the word *Mississippi*

    ˋ = secondary stress, e.g., first syllable of same word

    ˆ = tertiary stress, e.g., second syllable

    ˘ = quaternary of unstressed, e.g., last syllable

These marks, if used, are placed over the vowel of the syllables as noted in the second space of Figure 28.

It is easy to distinguish between stressed (first two levels) and unstressed (last two levels) syllables, relatively easy to distinguish between primary and secondary stress, but difficult to distinguish between tertiary and quaternary stress. The varying patterns of the speech we have developed are evidence that we perceive all four distinctions while learning our spoken language early in life.

Rather than using numbers, the author uses interconnecting lines that vary in elevation to depict the pitch changes of a phrase or utterance. This notational approach can be seen in the third space of Figure 28. Oblong patterns are placed below the syllables so that comparisons can be made between variations in pitch and loudness. It can be noted that pitch rises in many instances in which a syllable is stressed.

In notational applications, emphasis is also given to conveying information on pitch shift between phrases. Arrows indicate direction of shift from the last syllable of one phrase to the first syllable of the next phrase (Fairbanks, 1959). Arrows are illustrated in the fourth and fifth spaces of Figure 28. Such terminal pitch phonemes can also be indicated by two juncture marks: a double bar (//) indicates a sustained or rising shift from one phrase to the next; a double cross (#) indicates a falling shift that occurs at the end of a statement. These marks would replace the arrows of Figure 28.

Klinghardt has also developed a system of marking to convey prosodic or suprasegmental changes (Seamons, 1972). A description of
these marks is shown in the sixth space of Figure 28. Application of
the use of these marks is described in space seven of Figure 28.

A similar system of markings confined to pitch variations is that of
Pike (1945). These markings are illustrated in the eighth space of Figure 28. Pike observed that each phrase includes an intonation contour,
that is, a sequence of contrastive or relative pitch changes associated
with each fully stressed syllable. Some intonation contours carry meanings distinct from those communicated by the sequence of words included. Other contours do not.

An advocate of Pike's system, Woodward (1967), has developed
procedures and materials for training hearing-impaired children to learn
basic patterns of intonational contours. Her experience at the Central
Institute for the Deaf led her to believe that even profoundly hearing-
impaired children can learn to produce four pitch levels and to associate them with Pike markings. Woodward also suggested that once
such children develop flexible control of pitch, they seem to be able to
produce nuances like excitement and disgust.

A careful analysis of intonation variations of colloquial English has
been conducted by O'Connor and Arnold (1961). They use large dots
and small dots to indicate stressed and unstressed syllables. The dots
are located horizontally or on a time base corresponding to the sequence of syllables in a word, phrase, or sentence. The sequence of
dots also varies vertically, in relation to relative pitches in intonation
contours. When a pitch changes significantly within one or more syllables of a sequence, trace lines extend up or down from the circles. Application of this system of stress and intonation markings is shown in
the ninth space of Figure 28.

We also say the same words in many different ways. Each time we
give emphasis to a different word or sequence of words in a sentence
we change the prosodic patterning and to a lesser extent the phonetic
content. An example illustrated in the tenth space of Figure 28 reveals
the basic importance of auditory perception for the development of
highly functional speech. Whereas audition underpins prosodic variability, other sensory input supports articulatory or phonetic development
and refinement.

Phonetic Symbols

English is a relatively nonphonetic language. It is not characterized
by the use of one alphabet letter or spelling for one phoneme or speech
sound. There are 26 letters but about 40 consonants, vowels, and

diphthongs. Many different spellings exist for many of the sounds, and different sounds are associated with the same spelling. Examples of such phenomena are replete in the content of a phonetics course.

The nonphonetic characteristic of English as well as most other common languages has led to the development of phonetic symbol systems. The most common of these is the International Phonetic Alphabet (IPA). This system is used for transcription work and is studied in a phonetics course. The student becomes proficient in notating phonetically or phonemically the sounds of a word as it is pronounced or read orally. For example, *Mississippi* is transcribed /mɪsɪsɪpɪ/, and *chauffeur* /ʃofɚ/.

The IPA system is a valuable tool for the speech clinician. Its main function is to convey quickly the proficiency of the client in the articulation of isolated sounds, syllables, words, or sentences. The entire speech response of the client can be transcribed or a particular articulation can be symbolized. In the latter instance the symbol may be placed to the left of a slash mark. The correct symbol would be placed to the right of the slash mark. This comparative information would apply to a substituted response for the correct articulation, e.g., /t/ for /k/ or simply t/k.

Another phonetic symbol system frequently employed in speech development programming with hearing-impaired children is the use of common spellings. This system was pioneered by Caroline Yale (1946), a teacher at the Clarke School for the Deaf, and is called the Northampton system or the Yale spellings. It consists of a chart of symbols for consonants and one for vowels and diphthongs, as illustrated in Figure 29. The spellings are arranged in columns and rows. In the consonant chart the first column includes voiceless or breath sounds. The second column provides space for voiced cognates of the voiceless consonants. The nasals /m/, /n/, and /ng/ appear in the third column. Sounds that occur in the same rows are articulated in similar ways; for example, the /t/, /d/, /n/, /l/, and /r/ or five lingua-alveolar articulations appear on one row. In the vowel chart the first row includes back vowels, the second row front vowels, the third row central vowels plus a(r) as in *father*, and the fourth row diphthongs. The first two rows are arranged from left to right with high to increasingly lower tongue elevations.

In most if not all instances the spellings on top are the most common and the smaller letters placed underneath are somewhat less common but not exceptional. Rarely used spellings are not included in the charts, for example, *oe* as in *oboe* for /o/.

The charts are developed as the children learn symbols for specific articulations or speech sounds. The extent of development of a given

Consonants

h-				
wh	w-			
p	b	m		
t	d	n	l	r
k	g	ng		
c		n(k)		
ck				
f	v			
ph				
$\overset{1}{\text{th}}$	$\overset{2}{\text{th}}$			
$\overset{1}{\text{s}}$	z			
c(e)	$\overset{2}{\underset{\text{.}}{\text{s}}}$			
c(i)				
c(y)				
			y-	
sh	zh		x = ks	
	$\overset{3}{\text{s}}$			
	$\overset{2}{\text{z}}$			
			qu = kwh	
ch	j			
tch	$\overset{2}{\text{g}}$-			
	-ge			
	dge			

Vowels and Diphthongs

$\overset{1}{\text{oo}}$	$\overset{2}{\text{oo}}$	o-e	aw	-o-
(l)u-e		oa	au	
(r)u-e		—o	o(r)	
(l)ew		ow		
(r)ew				
ee	-i-	a-e	-e-	-a-
—e	—y	ai	$\overset{2}{\text{ea}}$	
$\overset{1}{\text{ea}}$		ay		
e-e				
	a(r)	-u-	ur	
		—a	er	
		—ar	ir	
		—er		
		—ir		
		—or		
		—ur		
		—re		

a-e	i-e	o-e	ou	oi	u-e
ai	igh	oa	ow	oy	ew
ay	—y	—o			
		$\overset{2}{\text{ow}}$			

chart is a measure of the progress of a class of hearing-impaired children in associating spellings and sounds.

The Northampton spellings are meaningful symbols for correlation of speaking and written tasks, particularly in the beginning years of formal instruction. Within one or two years of speech developmental work, the charts are essentially developed. The most common spellings have been written and many somewhat less common spellings have been added. As further vocabulary words are taught in speech and language tasks, the chart fills up rapidly.

Another chart in which the spellings may be placed has been developed by the author. Called the target chart, it includes series of circles including bull's-eyes for each of 36 critical articulations. This chart is illustrated in Figure 30. Moving from left to right, and from the upper row to the lower row, symbols for various groupings of speech sounds are presented. This chart is particularly applicable to the shaping of articulations and subsequent refinement.

Because of the nonphonetical nature of English, Sir James Pitman (1967) of England has developed a symbol system that is particularly applicable to the teaching of beginning reading skill. His symbols, called the Initial Teaching Alphabet (ITA), are similar to those of the International Phonetic Alphabet (IPA). These symbols are presented in Figure 31. All reading materials are converted from the 26 alphabet letters into the ITA symbols. Children learn to associate the sounds of words with these symbols more easily than with the 26 letters. Once the children can read by use of the ITA system, conversion to standard print is made. Hearing-impaired children who are familiar with the ITA symbols and who can produce corresponding articulations pronounce or sound out words. After conversion to standard printed materials, the ITA symbols can be placed over alphabet letters to facilitate pronunciation also. Currently the ITA system is not widely used in either regular education or schooling for the hearing impaired.

Once children can read somewhat, they are directed to use dictionaries. As youngsters look up meanings and pronunciations of words, they are aided by familiarity with diacritical marking systems. The accompanying comparative chart of Figure 31 also includes the diacritical marks of the Webster and the Thorndike dictionaries. It can be noted that these markings are added to the 26 letters of the alphabet to indicate the sounds to be pronounced or articulated. Often a speech program for the hearing-impaired child will require children to know

---

Fig. 29 *(facing page).* The Northampton charts with common spelling symbols. From Calvert and Silverman, 1975, pp. 12–13. Compliments Clarke School for the Deaf, Northampton, Massachusetts.

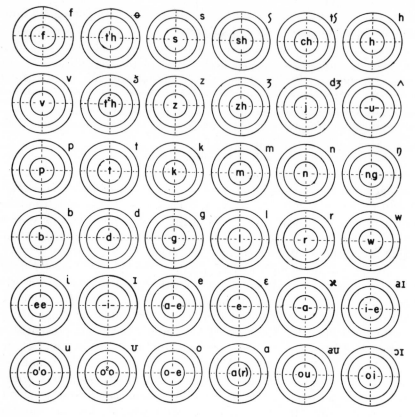

Fig. 30. Target chart for each of 36 phonemes critical to speech articulation.

the diacritical markings in addition to one or more basic phonetic symbol systems. It is especially important for the hearing-impaired child to learn the markings because his hearing loss puts him at a severe disadvantage in learning the pronunciation of words incidentally or in a natural way.

Two other phonetic symbol systems of at least academic interest are those developed by Alexander Melville Bell (1916) and A. Zaliouk (1954). Recognizing that alphabet letters do not naturally convey articulation information, Bell developed the visible speech symbols. Zaliouk went beyond Bell in devising static symbols to represent the hard palate, the tongue, the teeth, and the lips, *and* dynamic symbols to suggest movement during speech. He stated that speech is not a series of static positions but a blend of positions and transitions from one articulation to the next. Neither the Bell visible speech symbols nor the Zaliouk system of phonetic symbolization has found widespread use in the United States.

Prosodic and phonetic symbol systems both have a place in a speech development program for hearing impaired children. They are used to record or transcribe the speech utterances of individuals. They also indicate progress in the development of the prosody and articulations of speech. In addition, such symbols are essential in the learning of pronunciation of countless words of our language. Finally, the symbols themselves, if properly devised, might assist in prompting the child toward a correct or more correct speech response. Thirteen summary statements related to their use appear below.

1. The clinician or instructor familiar with notations will find them useful in speech evaluation, speech development, and pronunciation development.
2. Notations are symbols or markings that are written or inscribed to represent articulatory or phonetic as well as prosodic features of speech.
3. Articulatory or phonetic notational systems include the International Phonetic Alphabet (IPA), the diacritical markings from the dictionary, the Initial Teaching Alphabet (ITA), and the Northampton system of common spellings.
4. Each of these systems includes a written or printed symbol for each of the articulations or segmental phonemes. These symbols are shown in the comparative chart of Figure 31.
5. The IPA system is perhaps the most valuable tool for transcribing, evaluating, and training speech production.
6. The ITA system may be valuable in a beginning reading program.
7. The Northampton system may be valuable as an aid for the development of speech sounds, initial vocabulary, and sentence structure.
8. Diacritical markings relate to dictionary use.
9. Prosodic markings must account for suprasegmental phonemes of stress, pitch or intonation, and juncture.
10. Prosodic markings are perhaps most useful as they reflect what the client should perceive and eventually produce in speech.
11. Stress markings reflect up to four levels of loudness–duration.
12. Pitch markings represent four levels *within* utterance that can be perceived by a normal-hearing person and three levels *between* utterance.
13. Three juncture markings distinguish between fading, rising, and sustained levels between utterances.

	IPA	ITA	NH	TH	WB	Words
1.						
2.	h	h	h	h	h	hat
3.	hw	wh	wh	wh	wh	when
4.	w	w	w	w	w	was
5.	p	p	p	p	p	pop
6.	b	b	b	b	b	bib
7.	m	m	m	m	m	mom
8.	t	t	t	t	t	tot
9.	d	d	d	d	d	dad
10.	n	n	n	n	n	none
11.	l	l	l	l	l	lull
12.	r	r	r	r	r	roar
13.	f	f	f	f	f	fan, laugh, telephone
14.	v	v	v	v	v	vat, love
15.	θ	t͡h	t̔h	th	th	think
16.	ð	ϸh	t̓h	TH	TH	the
17.	s	s	s	s	s	sister, city, cent, cycle
18.	z	z	z	z	z	zoo, is
19.	ʃ	ϸh	sh	sh	sh	shoe, sugar
20.	ʒ	ʒ	zh	zh	zh	Zhivago, measure, azure
21.	tʃ	ch	ch	ch	ch	church, watch
22.	dʒ	j	j	j	j	judge, age
23.	j	y	y	y	y	yellow, onion
24.	i	ee	ee	ē	ē	feet, me, Eve
25.	ɪ	i	-i-	i	ĭ	hit, built
26.	e	æ	a-e	ā	ā	mate, bait, say
27.	ɛ	e	-e-	e	ĕ	met
28.	æ	a	-a-	a	ă	mat
29.	u	ω	do	ʊ	oo	boot
30.	ʊ	ɯ	oo	ʉ	oo	book
31.	o	œ	o-e	ō	ō	bone, bow, boat
32.	ɔ	ou	aw	o	ŏ	saw
33.	ɑ	ɑ	a(r)	ä	ä	father, on

34.	ʌ, ə	u	-u-	u	ŭ	up, above
35.	ɝ, ɚ	r	ur	ẽr	ẽr	further, sir, cur, her
36.	ɜ, ə	r	ur	er	er	further, sir, cur, her
37.	ɑɪ	ie	i-e	ī	ī	bite, high, my
38.	aʊ	ou	ou	ou	ou	house, cow
39.	ɔɪ	oi	oi	oi	oi	oil, boy
40.	ɪu	ue	u-e	ū	ū	cute, you

Fig. 31. Comparative chart of phonetic symbol systems.

Synthetic—Analytic Training

Once articulation training is begun, the clinician or teacher uses meaningful and familiar words as stimuli. As he presents a word or as the child spontaneously utters one, the clinician listens carefully to this response and judges its acceptability. If the articulation of the word does not meet the clinician's criterion for success, the child is required to repeat it a few times. During this procedure the clinician articulates the model, encourages the best or an improved response, and provides immediate feedback as to correctness or improvement. The child listens as well as he can, looks at the face of the clinician, places his hand on the clinician's face for tactile clues, and may even use a mirror to watch the visual aspects of his response.

The word does not necessarily have to be articulated precisely. It should, however, include the phonemes that identify it. If one of the phonemes cannot be identified, it then becomes the stimulus for analytic training. This misarticulation may be an omission, a substitution by another phoneme, the appending of another phoneme onto the desired articulation, a gross distortion, or a weakened production.

Analytic training is similar to synthetic training. The clinician provides the model and the child imitates it. He encourages the child to listen, to watch, and even to feel. In addition, he provides reinforcement or withholds it, depending upon accuracy of response or improvement in production. Repetition or practice is also included.

In analytic training particular focus is given to explaining and demonstrating how to articulate the phoneme in error, for example, the /t/ at the end of the word *boat*.

Ordinarily the task of producing a phoneme in isolation is easier than incorporating the phoneme into a word. The child is therefore more likely to be able to produce it through analytic procedures. Once the phoneme is articulated, practice is employed to stabilize its production. After the phoneme has been shaped and stabilized somewhat, it is placed in the initial or releasing position of a series of nonsense syllables. For example, the /t/ might be combined with vowels in *tee tee tee, too too too, to-e to-e to-e, ta(r) ta(r) ta(r).* After successful practice in these combinations, the /t/ would be inserted in the arresting position of a similar syllable series such as *eet eet eet, oot oot oot, o-et o-et o-et, a(r)t a(r)t a(r)t.* Perhaps practice would also be devoted to syllable combinations like *teet,* in which the error phoneme both releases and arrests syllables.

Practice in articulating the phoneme in isolation and in a series of nonsense syllable might be followed by word training again. The original word, for example *boat,* would become the stimulus to be imitated again. In many if not most instances, the child should be able to make the transfer of the /t/ into the word.

The /t/ would be practiced in other words and in phrases and sentences as well. However the specific vocabulary used as well as the complexity and length of syntactic structure employed would depend upon the child's development of language and expressive utterances. With some children only a few /t/ words would be utilized. With others many stimuli and sequences of words could be used as transfer items.

Order of Phoneme Development

There is no fixed order that should be followed in the development and correction of the phonemes of speech. The clinician should initially evaluate each child's speech competence and performance. Thereafter the clinician should design a developmental or remedial speech program utilizing this baseline information. Guidelines for determination of an optimal order to follow in shaping and refining speech sounds might include (1) determining the degree to which "packaging" of speech into the auditory area might facilitate speech acquisition; (2) studying the order in which phonemes emerge typically among normal-hearing children (Templin, 1957, p 51); (3) assessing the relative need of a child for a given articulation within his growing world; (4) selecting sounds or sound productions initially that are easier to articulate, for example, an initial or releasing /b/ is easy compared to an arresting or final /b/; (5) examining how any anatomic and neurological defects that may exist might affect articulatory acquisition; (6) staying within categories of distinctive features already developed. For example, if a child can articulate /f/ and /z/, he should be able to master /v/.

If a child can develop speech and language primarily through use of residual hearing, most of the consonants and vowels will be acquired without specific articulatory training. Other articulations may also develop as distortions or approximations of bull's-eye productions. The task of the clinician will be primarily to refine articulatory skills.

When the clinician is faced with a deaf child or a near-deaf youngster, the limited repertoire of articulations will signal the need for extensive articulatory training. Very few phonemes may exist. Features of voice–voiceless and oral–nasal distinctions, manner of articulation, and place of articulation may be largely nonexistent. Consideration of the guidelines above and examination of phoneme differences and similarities should be valuable.

If an order of development of phonemes for training is sought, the following sequence is suggested.

1. m	11. aɪ	21. ɔɪ	31. ʃ
2. ʌ,ə	12. w	22. ɪʊ	32. tʃ
3. b	13. j	23. n	33. v
4. o	14. h	24. f	34. ɟ
5. i	15. e	25. ө	35. z
6. ɑ	16. æ	26. s	36. ʒ
7. u	17. ɪ	27. k	37. ŋ
8. p	18. ɛ	28. g	38. Consonant clus-
9. t	19. ʊ	29. l	ters (blends) and
10. d	20. a,ʊ	30. r,ɝ,ɚ	abutting consonants

Consideration of this order and other factors suggests that the clinician should (1) alternate between consonants, vowels, and diphthongs during the first 22 items; (2) present the physiologically easy phonemes during the first 10 items and the increasingly complex phonemes later; (3) space the development of a particular distinctive articulatory feature, for example *alveolar,* across the gamut of items; (4) introduce voiced–voiceless and oral–nasal distinctions during the first 10 items; (5) shape the /u/ and /i/ vowels having the easier end-point articulations before vowels having the more difficult between-point articulations such as /ʊ/ and /ɪ/; (6) delay refinement of the voiced fricatives to items 33 to 36; (7) delay refinement of consonant clusters and abutting consonants until all simple consonants have been taught; and (8) combine all phonemes into meaningful words, phrases, and sentences.

During the first year of structured speech training, most of the phonemes that are not within the baseline repertoire of a child can be taught synthetically and analytically. For the next three years presentation and contextual application can be completed through the blends, particularly if the child advances rapidly in language development. A given remedial session might focus on the shaping of one phoneme or a few phonemes. An alternate approach is to focus on many phonemes.

The clinician or teacher should also be familiar with the detail of articulations or formations for each of the English phonemes. Within each phoneme he should be able to describe vocal fold posture, velopharyngeal posture, degree of articulatory restriction, and locality or place of articulation. He should also be able to draw an illustration of each phoneme articulation. This may be of value when assisting a child to produce a speech sound on target in isolation. Refinement of the production to bull's-eye accuracy would have to result from other competencies that will be described in chapter 6.

Association Phoneme Unit Method

An alternate approach to structured speech remediation for the hearing-impaired child is the Association Phoneme Unit method developed by McGinnis (1963) and revised and described by others (Kleffner, 1967; Monsees, 1972; Calvert and Silverman, 1975). This approach has been successful with children who have not made sufficient progress with the conventional method just described. Word and sentence programs have been developed (McGinnis, 1963).

In the McGinnis word program, a child learns to articulate each phoneme in isolation, to combine the phonemes into words and sentences, and to associate these words and sentences with meaning. In the word program, for example, the child initially learns to distinguish between /b/, /o/, and to a lesser extent /t/, and afterwards to combine them in the word *boat*. After the child articulates the word with little or no assistance, he is shown a picture of a boat and required to say it again, broken down into phonetic elements and smoothed. In later sentence programs, the child articulates combinations of the words he has acquired.

During the word program the child articulates most if not all of the consonants, vowels, and diphthongs in one or more contexts. A list of 77 typical words appears in Table 16. Releasing consonants of the words are located in the first column, and the vowels or diphthongs that are the nuclei of these monosyllabic units are positioned on the first horizontal row. The only phonemes not appearing in words on this list are the consonants /ə/, /ɟ/, /ʒ/ and /j/. The word program ordinarily is completed during the first year of structured speech and language instruction. The articulatory competence shaped during the learning of 50 to 100 words is also transferred into many other training contexts.

Two subprograms of the word program are of particular interest to the clinician. One is a beginning program in which 10 to 15 phonemes are shaped as well as 10 to 20 words. The other subprogram follows and incorporates the same phonemes and words and moves on to addi-

Table 16

Picturable Words Adaptable to the McGinnis Program

	i	ɪ	e	ɛ	æ	u	ʊ	o	ɑ,ɔ	ʌ	ɝ	aɪ	ɔɪ	aʊ	Total
h			hay	head	hat			hole						house	5
p	pea	pin		pen	pan			pole				pie pipe pile			8
t	teeth		tape		tack	tooth		toe	top			tie		towel	8
k	key		cake					coat				kite		cow	5
b	bee					boot	book	boat	ball	bus			boy		7
d									doll	duck					2
g			gate					goat							2
f	feet					food	foot				fur	file			5
v					vat										1
θ															0
j															0
s					sack			soap	sock	sun		sign			5
z						zoo									1
ʃ		ship				shoe									2
tʃ	cheese	chin													2
dʒ									jaw						1
l		lip		leg					lock			light			4
r	reel		rake					rope	rock						4
hw, w	wheel		whale						wall						3
m	meat				map	moon			moth					mouse	5
n	knee			neck nest				note		nut		nine			6
ŋ		ring													1
Total	10	5	6	5	6	6	2	9	9	4	1	9	1	4	77

153

tional ones. Items of these subprograms are detailed below. Each item corresponds to what a clinician draws in sequence on each page of a tablet perhaps 6″ × 8″. The numbers correspond to the pages in a tablet.

Beginning Program

1. Picture and name of child
2. /o-e/ appears several times together with a boy with his mouth rounded
3. /b/, as above, associated with another drawing
4. Syllable drill incorporating *bo-e bo-e bo-e*
5. Pictures and words for *bow, boat,* and *bone*
6. /ee/ as on pages 2 and 3
7. Syllable drill incorporating *bee bee bee*
8. Pictures and words for *bee, bean,* and *beet*
9. /oo/ as on pages 2, 3, and 6
10. /m/ as on pages 2, 3, 6, and 9
11. Syllable drill incorporating *moo moo moo*
12. Picture and words for *moon*
13. Syllable drill with *boo boo boo*
14. Picture and word for *boot*
15. Syllable drill incorporating *mee mee mee*
16. Picture and words for *meet*
    Etc.

Advanced Program

1. Picture and name of child
2. Six consonant spellings, e.g., /b/, /m/, /p/, /f/, /d/, /t/
3. Space for additional consonant spellings
4. Space for additional consonant spellings
5. Six vowel spellings, e.g., /o-e/, /ee/, /oo/, /a(r)/, /a-e/, /ou/
6. Space for additional vowel spellings
7. Space for additional vowel spellings
8. Syllable drills incorporating *bo-e boa bow, bee bea bee, boo boo boo, ba(r) ba ba(r)*
9. Pictures and words for *boat, bow, bone*
10. Pictures and words for *bee, beet,* and *bean*
11. Pictures and words for *boot,* and *ball*
12. Syllable drills incorporating *mee mea mee, moo moo moo, ma(r) mo ma(r), mou mou mow*
13. Pictures and words for *meat, moon, moth,* and *mouse*
    Etc.

In the McGinnis or Association Phoneme method, phonemes are shaped in isolation and then included in syllables, words, phrases and sentences. In addition, the child may be prompted to position his articulators before producing a given phoneme. This positioning provides anticipatory feedback to assist the child in the articulation of individual phonemes and combinations of them. For example, the child holds his lips together momentarily before producing /b/, increasing the likelihood of his making this articulation. Positioning as a procedure is phased out as soon as the child produces a given phoneme consistently in isolation and in context.

Common spellings are used as notational prompts in the articulatory shaping of each phoneme. The child learns to read, spell, and write as he learns to speak each phoneme, syllable, word, and sentence. In addition, the clinician draws pictures to relate words and core sentences.

The picture, the printed or written form, and the utterance itself become associated stimuli. Any one of these three becomes the stimulus for responding with one or both of the others. Initially, such stimulus response reaction is required when all are present. For example, when the child articulates *shoe,* he should be able to point to the word *shoe* written or printed in a notebook as well as to the picture of a shoe. Later the child is able to articulate or to write *shoe* from memory.

In the Associational Phoneme method, the unisensory stimuli of speechreading clues or of auditory clues are also associated with the articulation of a given word. For example, the clinician says *b-oa-t* and *boat* and the child repeats these broken and smoothed stimuli. If the input is speechreading, the clinician faces the child. If auditory stimulation is employed, the clinician speaks *ad concham* or the child uses a hearing aid.

This method can be used for individual, group, or class training. In individual training the clinician develops notebooks with the child and uses crayons to spell out phonemes, syllables, words, and sentences as well as to draw pictures. For group or class training the chalkboard and chalk are utilized. In such teaching the group or class learns by watching a clinician develop speech and associated competencies with one child at a time. Each child takes his turn in following specific procedures.

The entire McGinnis program may be divided into three parts: (1) a core of 50 to 100 vocabulary words that can be identified by use of picture stimuli, (2) a series of simple sentence forms, and (3) a sequence of more complex language forms. In a school program using the McGinnis approach, a child progresses from one of these subprograms to the next. Such a structure may be the core of the academic curriculum during up to eight years of schooling.

VISUAL COMMUNICATION TRAINING

A third type of communication training provided for school-age children with hearing impairments is speechreading instruction. Sanders (1971) defines such visual communication training as a systematic procedure designed to increase the amount of information that a person's vision contributes to his perception of a speaker's message. The clues of visual communication include facial, gestural, and situational phenomena associated with the speaking act. In a special classroom these visual phenomena contribute to message transmission within any of the communicative methods being advocated. As described in chapter 2, the visual speech clues are integral parts of the aural or auditory method, total communication, and particularly cued speech. If a child has been trained to develop listening, language, and speech skills through a unisensory auditory approach, he will utilize speechreading clues to further improve his listening and speech competencies. Even without specific speechreading instruction, the clues of visual communication will contribute to the perceptual pool from which he predicts the message of the speaker. Even a normal-hearing person must speech-read in order to listen in some situations. Without access to the full range of auditory clues, the hearing-impaired child must rely on speechreading clues in many more situations.

Sanders (1971) describes well the contributors and inhibitors to message transmission and reception during the speaker–listener act. These phenomena include redundancy, constraints, and noise. Redundancy refers to the aspects of a message that can be eliminated without loss of information. Constraints are the situational, contextual, and linguistic clues that limit the possible interpretations of a message. Noise includes the factors present in the speaker, the message, the environment, and the listener that interfere with message transmission and reception. When the contributions of redundancy and constraints exceed the interferences of noise, the listener can decode the message of the speaker.

Rationale

The need for visual communication training in the education of a hearing-impaired child can be understood by comparing the amount of redundancy normally contained in a message and the amount when hearing loss exists. If a listener has normal hearing, the auditory clues alone may far exceed the minimal amount of information needed to decode a message. When the listener has a hearing loss, speechreading clues must be added to the greatly reduced number of auditory speech clues present in order for a message be decoded. This is particularly true in the presence of (1) the normal amount of noise that exists in a classroom setting, and (2) the impracticality of continually incorporating structure or constraints into the teaching process.

The contribution of visual communication to the educational process should not be underestimated. In and of itself, it provides only partial clues for language acquisition and for speech development. However, once the hearing-impaired child has language, he can rely upon speechreading, as needed, to supplement auditory clues in decoding message after message. If this child has developed great skill in speechreading and utilizing residual hearing, he may be able to decode the message of a special classroom teacher better than if signs and fingerspelling are being used, particularly if the teacher is skilled in structuring her communication and teaching (Holt, 1976). It is particularly essential that speechreading skills be developed because the hearing-impaired child faces many situations in which he cannot rely upon manual forms of communication, simply because the world of speakers is not trained in the use of Cornett cues or signs and fingerspelling. When speechreading clues are added to auditory speech clues, most hearing-impaired children have a viable method for understanding most messages, in the special classroom as well as out of it.

Some of our finest speechreaders are persons who have never received any formal training to utilize visual speech clues. For example, one of these individuals, Staffan Wedenberg, was trained from early life to attend to auditory clues rather than to visual communication. Yet he became a phenomenal speechreader. His parents describe an illustrative anecdote.

> Staffan was called by a film company who had made a movie about a wild youth in Sweden. The sound tape had been destroyed, and there they were with a silent film. They asked Staffan if he could lipread the film. They intended to have a premiere in a month, so time was short. He lipread the whole film and new film stars were hired to speak in it. But he said to us: "The language the youngsters used was not the best" (Wedenberg and Wedenberg, 1970, pp 328–329).

The informal or natural learning of speechreading seems to have been an effective process for many person with acquired hearing losses. The author's own brother lost all of his hearing from spinal meningitis at age six. Afterward he learned to rely upon speechreading for communication with family members. It may be that his training at a school for the deaf did not facilitate his utilization of visual speech clues as much as did the need to communicate orally. Perhaps the main contributor to the utilization of speechreading clues for the person with little or no hearing is this motivation to communicate through speech.

Unfortunately the desire to communicate, in and of itself, does not make the speechreader. Authorities agree that speechreading requires a certain combination of cognitive abilities. It also requires visual perception and mobilization to utilize visual speech clues (Sanders, 1971). Among the competencies related to speechreading are synthesizing and associative abilities (Nitchie, 1951; Wong and Taaffe 1958). Currently, the extent to which such cognitive skills can be developed, if not sufficient at the time, is unknown (O'Neill and Oyer, 1961).

Speechreading Instruction

As speechreading evolved in this country, methods of instruction placed increasingly more emphasis on optimizing cognitive abilities as well as utilizing visual speech clues on the face, in gestures, and within situations (Nitchie, 1951; Morkovin, 1960). Such approaches were called synthetic methods rather than analytic methods. Edward Nitchie of New York was a pioneer in this early development. He had lost his hearing at age fourteen but was trained to speech-read. Having received speechreading instruction himself, he wanted to assist others with hearing losses to utilize visual clues and to be brought back into the mainstream of society. The Nitchie School of Speechreading in New York City is still operating after seventy years. An available Nitchie book on speechreading (1951) presents the classic lessons of the aural rehabilitative literature.

Until about 1940, speechreading instruction was often recommended publicly for persons who were deaf or hard of hearing. In the years thereafter the electroacoustic hearing aid, pioneered during the 1920s along with the audiometer, became commercially available and well advertised. Schools or classes for speechreading instruction, which were organized in large cities during the early decades of the century, became less popular. In a 1964 survey the author noted that fewer than two hundred of the four million people living in metropolitan Detroit were receiving speechreading instruction. The number of adults with hearing loss in that city was conservatively estimated at one hundred thousand (Berg, 1966).

In the education of the hearing-impaired child, speechreading clues for receptive communication has been a dominant feature of the oral method. Oralism was introduced into some of the early schools for the deaf during the 1840s. Previously, signs and finger spelling had been exclusively used in such educational settings. The first teachers to use an oral method and an oral philosophy were employed at the Clarke and Lexington Schools for the deaf, founded in 1867 (O'Connor, 1967; Waite, 1967). In these schools speechreading was taught as subject matter and was also utilized in and out of classes as the method of receptive communication. Varying degrees of skill in speechreading were attained by children enrolled in these and other oral schools and in classes that have been since established. The record of achievement of children in schools for the deaf where oralism prevailed was among the best attained in the field of education for the hearing impaired (Lane and Baker, 1974; Pratt, 1961).

Inhibitors and Contributors

An examination of factors that inhibit utilization of visual speech clues and of other factors that contribute to a rationale for speechreading is basic to the design of visual communication training. Inhibitors to speechreading will be described first.

It may be that the speechreader does not understand the language of a message. Even if he knows the language, he may not be able to perceive visually the information that bears prosodic features of speech. The vocal tract phenomena producing stress and intonation are located in the chest and larynx, hidden from the speechreader's view. The phonologically significant voicing and oral–nasal postures of articulation are also hidden from view. Only the place and manner of the features of articulation or utterance can be perceived, and the perception of these features is limited to activities of the mandible, lips, teeth, and the very front of the tongue. In addition, articulation of unstressed syllables is difficult to identify visually.

Most sounds of speech look like other phonemes to the speechreader. For example, the /p/, /b/, and /m/ are homophenous. The /t/, /d/, /n/, and even /l/, /s/, and /z/ look alike. It has been estimated that more than 50 percent of the commonly used monosyllabic words are visually equivalent to other words (Nitchie, 1951). For example, *Ted, ten, den, dent, debt,* and *dead* look alike to the speechreader. Even if each consonant, vowel, or diphthong were uniquely visible, the relative speed of their occurrence in conversational speech would preclude the visual identification of each during speechreading. Nitchie (1951) reported that the eye is capable of following eight to nine movements per second, whereas speech often moves at eleven to twelve phonemes per second.

The lip and mandibular movements of many speakers are limited and thus difficult to perceive visually. In addition, the speaker must be facing the speechreader to some extent in order to have his message decoded. Visual speech perception may not be as accurate if the distance between the speechreader and the speaker is less than three or more than 12 feet. Lighting also must be adequate for effective speechreading.

In spite of these limitations, speechreading is often possible, particularly if the child is linguistically competent. The speaking situation itself limits the possibilities of what information is incorporated in the message. In addition, if the speechreader knows the topic, further constraints are imposed upon possible interpretations. Because our spoken language is redundant, linguistic information is often repeated. For example, the italicized words in the sentence "Do *you* want *an* egg *for* breakfast?" are not necessary for transmission of the content of the message. Yet their presence eases the task of decoding each of the other words in the sentence. Each word that the child can decode in succession increases the probability of his perceiving further words in the sentence because of the word order and syntactic constraints of our language. For example, it is easier for the person to predict the *you* in the sentence above if he speechreads the first word, *Do*. Thereafter it becomes that much easier to predict additional words.

Particularly with practice, the speechreader is able to differentiate visually among the many words that have unique visual configurations. *Fish* and *which* are examples of such nonhomophenous words. The speechreader can also learn to perceive consistently increasing numbers of word combinations that are not homophenous and that present sufficient visibility. Examples are *How are you?* and *I'm fine.*

Speechreading Guidelines

Based upon contributing as well as inhibiting considerations, the author proposes nine guidelines for visual communication or speechreading instruction.

1. Speechreading instruction should be delayed until the child can articulate, on target if not within the bull's-eye, each of the consonants, vowels, and diphthongs in isolation and in the words of the language he is expected to perceive visually. With such a motor base of speech, the child has a perceptual set for training in speechreading.

2. Speechreading instruction should utilize stimuli that are within the linguistic repertoire of the child.
3. Ordinarily, the child should be trained to lip-read reflexively a large number of visually perceptible and nonhomophenous words and sentences.
4. Training should then proceed to groups of sentences that, step by step, include fewer and fewer nonhomophenous words.
5. Sentences might also be programmed to increase gradually in length and complexity. They should not, however, exceed the content of the linguistic code of the hearing-impaired child.
6. The child should be trained afterward to speech-read various speakers in life situations. During this stage of training, the child should learn to perceive situational and contextual clues.
7. The child should also be trained to speech-read a wide variety of messages and stories that are relevant to his life.
8. The child should participate in a program designed to improve continually his store of language and informational skills. Thus he will be better able to predict certain messages that are communicated through visual speech phenomena.
9. Each session of speechreading should also include auditory training and combined auditory–visual communication instruction.

Currently available speechreading materials are not optimally programmed to meet the training needs of hearing-impaired children. The need to develop updated materials, procedures, and strategies for speechreading instruction is critical. Until such improvements are made, the receptive communication skills of hearing-impaired children may never be maximally developed.

SUMMARY

The utilization of residual hearing offers great possibilities for eliminating or alleviating the underdeveloped listening, speech, language, and academic skills of hearing-impaired children in the special classes of the nation's schools. Models and innovations of auditory training, speech instruction, and visual communication training provide guidelines for breaking through long-standing educational barriers to adequate educational programming. Guidelines for the development of improved strategies in communication training have also been presented. Further models, innovations, and guidelines are described in chapters 6, 7, and 8.

REFERENCES

Anthony D: Seeing Essential English. A Sign System, Not a Sign Language. Denver, Community College of Denver, 1972

Asp C, Berry J, Berry C, et al: Auditory Training Procedures for Children and Adults. Knoxville, University of Tennessee, 1973

Bell A: The Mechanism of Speech. New York and London, Funk & Wagnals, 1916

Bellefleur P: Comments on European Programs for the Hearing Impaired. Institute on Characteristics and Needs of the Hard of Hearing Child. Logan, Utah State University, 1967

Berg F: Communication training for hearing impaired adults. Vol Rev 68:345–347, 384, 1966

Berg F: Educational audiology, in Berg F and Fletcher S (eds): The Hard of Hearing Child. New York and London, Grune & Stratton, pp 275–318, 1970

Bird P: A Report on Total Communication. Gooding, Idaho School for the Deaf, 1974

Boatner E: The Need of a Realistic Approach to the Education of the Deaf, Joint Convention of the California Association of Parents of Deaf and Hard of Hearing Children, California Association of Teachers of the Deaf and Hard of Hearing, and the California Association of the Deaf, Los Angeles, November 6, 1965

Calvert D, Silverman SR: Speech and Deafness. Washington, DC, AG Bell Assn Deaf, 1975

Craig W, Craig H, DiJohnson A: Preschool verbotonal instruction for deaf children. Vol Rev 74:236–246, 1972

Craig H, Craig W, DiJohnson A: Verbotonal Instruction for Deaf Children. Third Interim Report. Pittsburgh, Western Pennsylvania School for the Deaf, 1973

Education of the Deaf. A Report to the Secretary of Health, Education, and Welfare by his Advisory Committee on Education of the Deaf. Washington, DC, U.S. Government Printing Office, 1965

Fairbanks G: Voice and Articulation Drillbook. New York, Harper and Brothers, 1959

Furth H: A comparison of reading test norms of deaf and hearing children. Am Ann Deaf 111:461–462, 1966

Goldstein M: The Acoustic Method for the Training of the Deaf and Hard of Hearing Child. St. Louis, Laryngoscope Press, 1939

Grammatico L, Miller S: Curriculum for the preschool deaf child. Vol Rev 76: 280–289, 1974

Guberina P: The verbotonal method, questions and answers. Vol Rev 71:213–224, 1969

Haycock S: The Teaching of Speech. Washington, DC, AG Bell Assn Deaf, 1941

Hogan JL: The ABC's of Auditory Training. St. Louis, St. Joseph Institute for the Deaf, 1961

Holt B: The Relationship of Levels of Classroom Questions and Social Studies Achievement of Second Grade Achieving Hearing Impaired Children. Doctoral Dissertation. Logan, Utah State University, 1976

Kleffner F: Children's language disorders: Redefinition and reinterpretation. Proceedings of International Conference on Oral Education of the Deaf, vol 2. Washington, DC, AG Bell Assn Deaf, 1967, pp 1449–1459

Lane H, Baker D: Reading achievement of the deaf: Another look. Vol Rev 76: 489–499, 1974

Liberman A: Some results of research on speech perception. J Acoust Soc Amer 29: 117–123, 1957

Ling D: Implications of hearing aid amplification below 300 cps. Vol Rev 66:723–729, 1964

McClure W: Current problems and trends in the education of the deaf, Vol 18. Deaf Amer 8–14, 1966

McGinnis M: Aphasic Children. Identification and Education by the Association Method. Washington, DC, AG Bell Assn Deaf, 1963

Magner M: Speech Development. Northampton, Massachusetts, Clarke School for the Deaf, 1971

Martin E, Pickett J: Sensorineural Hearing Loss and Upward Spread of Masking. Washington, DC, Gallaudet College, 1968

Monsees E: Structured Language for Children with Special Language Learning Problems. Washington, DC, Children's Hospital, 1972

Morkovin B: Through the Barriers of Deafness and Isolation. New York, Macmillan, 1960

Myklebust H: The Psychology of Deafness. New York, Grune & Stratton, 1964

Nielsen B: Selection and use of custom fit amplification. The Utah Eagle 3:14–16, 1974

Nitchie EH: New Lessons in Lipreading. Philadelphia, Lippincott, 1951

O'Connor C: Lexington school's first century of oral education. Vol Rev 69: 128–136, 1967

O'Connor J, Arnold G: Intonation of Colloquial English. London, Longmans, Green, 1961

O'Neill J, Oyer H: Visual Communication for the Hard of Hearing. Englewood Cliffs, New Jersey, Prentice Hall, 1961

Peterson G, Barney H: Control methods in a study of vowels. J Acoust Soc Amer 24:175–184, 1952

Pike K: The Intonation of American English. Ann Arbor, University of Michigan Press, 1945

Pitman J: Can I.T.A. help the deaf child, his parents and his teacher? Proceedings of International Conference on Oral Education of the Deaf. Washington, DC, AG Bell Assn Deaf, 1967, pp 514–542

Pratt G: Oral education for deaf children. Vol Rev 63:480–483, 1961

Sanders D: Aural Rehabilitation. Englewood Cliffs, New Jersey, Prentice Hall, 1971

Sanderson R: Personal communication. Logan, Utah State University, 1969

Seamons B: Speech Curriculum. Ogden, Utah School for the Deaf, 1972

Taba H: Curriculum Development: Theory and Practice, New York, Harcourt, Brace, and World, 1962

Taba H: Teachers' Handbook for Elementary Social Studies: Reading, Massachusetts, Addison Wesley, 1967

Tabular Summary of Schools and Classes in the United States, October 1, 1975. Am Ann Deaf 121(2):144, 1976

Templin M: Certain Language Skills in Children. Institute of Child Welfare Monograph No. 26. Minneapolis, University of Minnesota, 1957

Waite H: 100 years of conquest of silence. Vol Rev 69:118–126, 1967

Wedenberg E: Auditory training of deaf and hard of hearing children. Acta Otolaryngol [Suppl] (Stockh) 94:1–129, 1951

Wedenberg E: Auditory training of severely hard of hearing preschool children. Acta Otolaryngol [Suppl] (Stockh) 94:1–129, 1954

Wedenberg E, Wedenberg M: The advantage of auditory training: A case report, in Berg F and Fletcher S (eds): The Hard of Hearing Child. New York and London, Grune & Stratton, 1970, pp 319–330

Wong W, Taaffe G: Relationships Between Selected Aptitude and Personality Tests of Lipreading Ability. Los Angeles, John Tracy Clinic, 1958

Woodward H: Intonation and the teaching of speech. Proceedings of International Conference on Oral Education of the Deaf, volume 1. Washington, DC, AG Bell Assn Deaf, 1967, pp 886–907

Yale C: Formation and Development of Elementary English Sounds. Northampton, Massachusetts, Metcalf, 1946

Zaliouk A: A visual tactile system of phonetical symbolization. J Speech Hear Disord 19:190–207, 1954

6

A New Speech Technology

During the past decade professionals have made advances in the design and implementation of speech remediation. This chapter describes many of these innovations, particularly as they apply to hearing-impaired clients. First the gathering of preliminary evaluative information on speech is discussed, then perceptual learning, next shaping and refinement, and finally transfer and generalization. Promising electro-sensory speech aids are also described. If clinicians utilize the innovations discussed in this chapter, they can facilitate precision in the speech of hard-of-hearing and deaf children. If specialists fail to keep up with technological change, the deaf will continue to be largely unintelligible and the hard-of-hearing generally imprecise in utterance.

PRELIMINARY EVALUATION

The evaluation of the speech of a hearing-impaired client provides a baseline for initiation of optimal training procedures. The objectives of speech evaluation include the identification and description of speech errors. Specifically, these errors may be omissions, substitutions, distortions, or additions of prosodic, phonetic, and vocal features of speech. If the hearing-impaired client is deaf, the clinician may anticipate errors in five general categories: timing and rhythm, pitch and intonation, nasality or denasality, articulation, and voice quality and loudness (Nickerson, 1975). When the client is hard of hearing, his speech errors characteristically are limited to hypernasality and misarticulation (Berg, 1970).

165

Prior to speech remediation the clinician should assess a sample of the life situational utterances of the client. This sample of natural vocalizations may be brief or extensive. The assessment can be ongoing or a tape-recorded sample. If the assessment takes place as the client is speaking naturally, the clinician must have reflexive skill in phonetic transcription and prosodic notation. If the assessment makes use of a tape recording, the clinician can replay utterances as many times as he wants.

Some clinicians use radio telemetry systems to record speech responses, no matter where the client is located within 200 feet of the recorder. A microphone transmitter is positioned on the client, and his utterances are transmitted via radio carrier wave, intercepted by a radio receiver, and then recorded on audio tape (Gardner, 1973; Hoshiko and Holloway, 1968).

McDonald (1964) indicates that many children will spontaneously produce enough speech to enable the clinician to note errors. Other children may have to be asked to name persons, days of the week, and similar information.

At least 50 utterances should provide examples of the vocalizations and verbalizations that exhibit the vocal and prosodic characteristic of the client and the "surface" of his sounds in error. The clinician can use this sample to judge timing and rhythm, pitch and intonation, nasality or denasality, articulation, and voice quality and loudness (Irwin, 1947; Longhurst and Grubb, 1974). The clinician can also identify omissions, substitutions, distortions, and additions of articulations of the client.

Structured Evaluation

The clinician also structures evaluative sessions to obtain detail on the speech of the hearing-impaired client. Isolated phonemes, words, and sentences are commonly used as contrived speech stimuli. The clinician presents each stimulus under one or more conditions: picture, graphemic, echoic, or combinations of these. The picture stimulus is an illustration used to prompt a spontaneous speech response. Graphemics are written stimuli. The echoic mode refers to imitation of a speech stimulus. When the echoic condition is used, the client looks at the face of the clinician and listens to him. Under this condition the client may also perceive tactile speech clues and electrovisual speech clues, if these sensory aid conditions are being utilized to prompt a "best" baseline response. A clinician may find it helpful to use a Floxite mirror lamp to illuminate and magnify the tongue, palate, and posterior pharyngeal wall. This speech aid is available from the Floxite

Company, P.O. Box 1094, Niagra Falls, N.Y. 14303. He may also utilize Pho-Vi cards as accessory stimuli. These cards show the lip and tongue positions of speech sounds with shadows eliminated. They may be obtained from the Communication Clinic, Department A, 2335 Burton, S.E., Grand Rapids, Michigan 49506.

Structured Tests

Many structured tests have been developed to provide detailed information on speech errors. Three tests of particular relevance to hearing-impaired clients are the author's shortened version of the full-scale Templin-Darley Test of Articulation (Templin and Darley, 1969), a Deep Test of Articulation by McDonald (1964), and the Goldman-Fristoe Test of Articulation (1972). The modified Templin-Darley test is recommended for initial evaluation of articulation, the Deep Test for clarification of error sound productions, and the Goldman-Fristoe Test for determination of susceptibility of an error sound to remediation. The Goldman-Fristoe Test also includes a story subtest that is valuable in assessing articulation in contexts that approximate conversational speech (Goldman and Fristoe, 1972). In addition, it has a word subtest that may replace the Templin-Darley Test.

The regular version of the Templin-Darley Test includes 141 articulations or stimulus items (Templin and Darley, 1969). Each articulation is tested with a picture or by having the client read a sentence. The clinician judges the accuracy of the client's production of test articulations at the beginning, in the middle, and at the end of the stimulus words, as they appear by themselves or in sentences.

The present author has extracted 67 items from the 141 pictures or words to form the shortened version of the Templin-Darley word subtest. The items of this shortened version sample all vowels and diphthongs; all single consonants in the initial position of words; the voiced stops /b/, /d/, and /g/; the sibilants /s/, /z/, /ʃ/, /ʒ/, /tʃ/ and /dʒ/, and glides /r/ and /l/ at the ends of words; and many blends incorporating /s/, /r/, and /l/ with other phonemes. Figure 32 illustrates the recording form and Figure 33 depicts the picture stimuli of this modified test.

The recording form of Figure 32 includes the word and the phoneme for each stimulus item of the modified test. A blank provides space for recording the accuracy of response for each of the 67 items. An omission is marked with a dash (—); a substitution with the IPA symbol for the error sound; a distortion with an asterisk (*); and an addition with IPA symbols, for example, də/d. The form also identifies the position in which the test item appears in a word. *I* refers to the initial position, *M* to the medial position, and *F* to final position.

1.	p (i)	pipe _____	34.	s (f)	mouse _____
2.	t (i)	two _____	35.	sm-	smoke _____
3.	k (i)	cat _____	36.	skr-	scratch _____
4.	b (i)	bicycle _____	37.	ks	socks _____
5.	d (i)	door _____	38.	z (m)	scissors _____
6.	g (i)	girl _____	39.	z (i)	zipper _____
7.	m (k)	mittens _____	40.	z (f)	ties _____
8.	n (i)	nose _____	41.	lz	nails _____
9.	ŋ (f)	ring _____	42.	ʃ (i)	shoe _____
10.	f (i)	fence _____	43.	ʃ (m)	dishes _____
11.	θ (i)	thumb _____	44.	ʃ (f)	fish _____
12.	v (i)	valentines _____	45.	ʃr	shred _____
13.	ð (i)	there _____	46.	ʒ (i)	Zhivago _____
14.	w (i)	window _____	47.	ʒ (m)	television _____
15.	tw	twins _____	48.	ʒ (f)	mirage _____
16.	b (f)	tub _____	49.	tʃ (i)	chair _____
17.	d (f)	slide _____	50.	tʃ (m)	matches _____
18.	g (f)	dog _____	51.	tʃ (f)	watch _____
19.	i (m)	feet _____	52.	dʒ (i)	jump _____
20.	I (m)	pin _____	53.	dʒ (r)	engine _____
21.	ɛ (m)	bed _____	54.	dʒ (f)	cage _____
22.	æ (m)	bat _____	55.	rdʒ	large _____
23.	ʌ (m)	gun _____	56.	ɝ	bird _____
24	ɝ	car _____	57.	r (i)	red _____
25.	ɑ (m)	clock _____	58.	r (m)	arrow _____
26.	ʊ (m)	book _____	59.	pr-	presents _____
27.	u (f)	blue _____	60.	dr-	drum _____
28.	o (m)	cone _____	61.	str-	string _____
29.	aʊ (m)	house _____	62.	mɝ	hammer _____
30.	e (m)	cake _____	63.	l (i)	leaf _____
31.	aɪ (f)	pie _____	64.	l (f)	bell _____
32.	ɔɪ (f)	boy _____	65.	gl-	glasses _____
33.	s (i)	sun _____	66.	-tl	bottle _____
			67.	-lt	belt _____

Key: omissions = - ; substitutions = / ; distortions = * ; slightings = ⟍ .

Fig. 32. Recording form for the 67-item, modified Templin-Darley test of articulation.

The Templin-Darley test materials include the stimulus items, recording forms, normative data, conversion tables, and rationale and background for the test. Certain items of the test form the Iowa Pressure Articulation Test. These items are designed to evoke articulations that are particularly susceptible to disintegration due to excessive nasality. Originally, the entire scale included 176 items with 43 segmental phonemes distributed as follows: 12 vowels; 6 diphthongs; 25 single consonants in 68 initial, medial, and final positions; 81 double consonant blends; and 9 triple consonant blends. The newer 141-item test includes the same number of vowels and diphthongs, 25 single consonant contexts, 64 double consonant blends, and five triple consonant blends.

The number of sounds and sound combinations correctly articulated during the 141- or 176-item tests may be equated with a particular articulation age norm. Table 17 includes normative data Templin derived from 480 three- to eight-year-old children. The positions of the dash marks indicate initial, medial or final places of words in which the articulations occurred.

As a clinician administers the modified or complete Templin-Darley test to a hearing-impaired person, he should mark distortions of articulation as well as omissions, substitutions, and any additions that occur. Clinicians often tend to check an articulation as correct when it is produced *near* the bull's-eye of a target rather than *on* the bull's-eye. Instead this close approximation of correct production should be marked as a distortion. The clinician must listen very carefully to identify slight distortions. If he does not mark these subtle differences on the recording form, he cannot plan to fully refine articulatory skills.

Articulatory distortions are prevalent in the speech of hearing-impaired individuals, particularly as they articulate the difficult-to-produce phonemes. The sibilants /s/, /z/, /ʃ/, /ʒ/, /tʃ/, and /dʒ/ are particularly susceptible to distorted production. Utilization of electrovisual speech clues in addition to other sensory input may noticeably reduce such articulatory distortion.

The clinician can administer the 67-item or modified Templin-Darley test in less than 10 minutes. He asks for repetitions of a response if he is uncertain about the client's production. He may use diacritical IPA marks in addition to substitution, distortion, and addition marks to clarify an error (Faircloth and Faircloth, 1973). The marking system, however, should be keyed so that other professionals who have case management responsibility can identify and describe the errors. It is necessary to check the reliability of each clinician who administers articulation tests. Clinicians must be trained to listen critically and to record responses precisely.

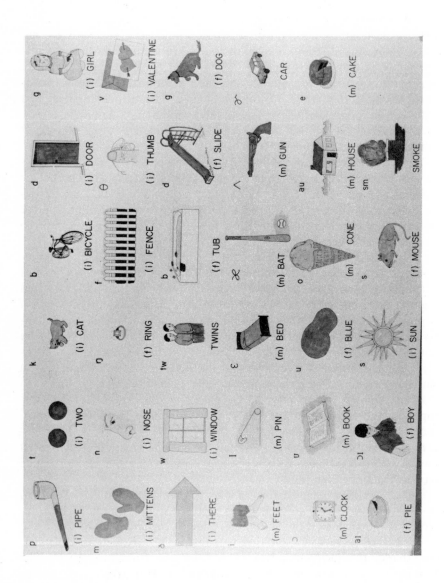

p (i) PIPE

m (i) MITTENS

θ (i) THERE

↑ (i) WINDOW

(m) FEET

a₁ (m) CLOCK

(f) PIE

t (i) TWO

n (i) NOSE

w (i) WINDOW

l (m) PIN

ʊ (m) BOOK

(f) BOY

k (i) CAT

ŋ (f) RING

tw TWINS

ʒ (m) BED

s (f) BLUE

(i) SUN

b (i) BICYCLE

f (i) FENCE

b (f) TUB

o (m) BAT

(m) CONE

(f) MOUSE

d (i) DOOR

θ (i) THUMB

d (i) SLIDE

ʌ (m) GUN

aʊ (m) HOUSE

sm SMOKE

g (i) GIRL

v (i) VALENTINE

g (f) DOG

e CAR

(m) CAKE

170

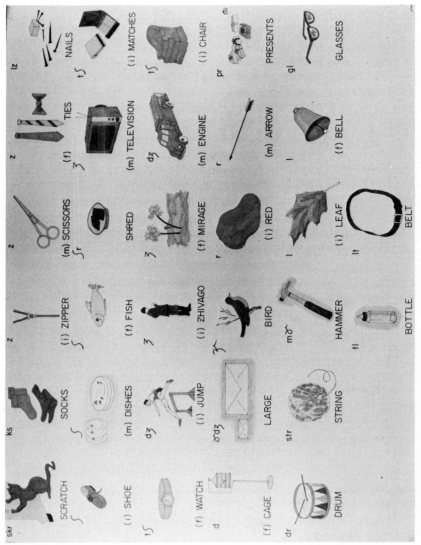

Fig. 33. Picture stimuli for the 67-item, modified Templin-Darley test of articulation.

Table 17
Earliest Age at Which 75 Percent of All Subjects Produced Each of 176 Tested Sound Elements Correctly

CA	Sound Elements
3	Vowels: ē, ĭ, ĕ, ă, ŏ, ŭ, o͝o, o͞o, ō, ô, ȧ, ûr Diphthongs: u, ā, ī, ou, oi Consonants: m-, -m-, -m, n-, -n-, -n, -ng-, -ng, p-, -p-, -p, t-, -t, k-, -k-, b-, -b-, d-, -d-, g-, -g-, f-, -f-, -f, h-, -h-, w-, -w- Double-consonant blends: -ngk
3.5	Consonants: -s-, -z-, -r, y-, -y- Double-consonant blends: -rk, -ks, -mp, -pt, -rm, -mr, -nr, -pr, -kr, -br, -dr, -gr, -sm
4	Consonants: -k, -b, -d, -g, s-, sh-, -sh, -v-, j-, r-, -r-, l-, -l- Double-consonant blends: pl-, pr-, tr-, tw-, kl-, kr-, kw-, bl-, br-, dr-, gl-, sk-, sm-, sn-, sp-, st-, -lp, -rt, -ft, -lt, -fr Triple-consonant blends: -mpt, -mps
4.5	Consonants: -s, -sh-, ch-, -ch-, -ch Double-consonant blends: gr-, fr-, -lf
5	Consonants: -j- Double-consonant blends: fl-, -rp, -lb, -rd, -rf, -rn, -shr Triple-consonant blends: str-, -mbr
6	Consonants: -t-, th-, -th-, -th, v-, -v, th-, -l Double-consonant blends: -lk, -rb, -rg, -rth, -nt, -nd, -pl, -kl, -bl, -gl, -fl, -sl Triple-consonant blends: skw-, -str, -rst, -ngkl, -nggl, -rj, -ntth, -rch
7	Consonants: -th-, z-, -z, -th, -zh-, -zh, -j Double-consonant blends: thr-, shr-, sl-, sw-, -lz, -zm, -lth, -sk, -st Triple-consonant blends: skr-, spl-, spr-, -skr, -kst, -jd
8	Double-consonant blends: -kt, -tr, -sp

*hw-, -hw-, -lfth, and -tl are not produced correctly by 75 percent of the subjects by eight years of age.

Templin, 1957, p 51.

Deep Testing

The error data on articulation provide the clinician with considerable information for setting objectives. The clinician should also test the error phonemes in phonemic contexts beyond those of the Templin-Darley or surface test items. A Deep Test of Articulation by McDonald is designed to test the articulation of 13 difficult-to-produce phonemes in an extensive number of phonemic contexts. For example, the /s/ appears before /v/ in hou*s*e *v*ase and before /ə/ in hou*s*e *th*umb. In the same depth test, the /s/ also appears after /v/ and /ə/ in sto*v*e *s*un and tee*th* *s*un. Access to McDonald Deep Test stimuli enables the clinician to test articulation of each of these difficult-to-produce consonants in as many as 49 different phonemic contexts.

The phonemes tested in depth by use of the McDonald materials are /s/, /z/, /r/, /l/, /ʃ/, /tʃ/, /dʒ/, /ə/, /ɟ/, /k/, /g/, /f/, and /v/. A picture booklet and a sentence booklet provide two options for presentation of stimuli. The examples of abutting contexts in the picture book have been given already. Examples of sentences testing /s/ in the same phonemic contexts are shown below.

> Is your fa*c*e *v*ery cold?   I ha*v*e *s*een a zebra.
> Thi*s* *th*ing is mine.   Bo*th* *s*aw the doll.

Each sentence is read from beginning to end so that the overlapping of articulatory movements is not interrupted. If necessary, however, a clinician can read the sentence aloud and the client can echo this stimulus. The clinician can also say the name of a picture stimulus and ask for an echoic response. If use of the echoic condition is necessary, the clinician can return later to the same item and seek a spontaneous response.

The rationale for testing an error sound in many phonemic contexts is twofold. One reason is to clarify the extent or consistency with which a client articulates the error sound. Evidence exists that a close correlation does not always exist between articulation in a surface test and in a depth test. For example, a client may misarticulate /k/ in all Templin-Darley Test contexts and articulate the same phoneme correctly in one or more depth contexts (McDonald, 1964).

Another reason for testing in depth is to identify all contexts in which an error sound may be articulated correctly. These contexts provide veritable nuggets for transfer of correct articulation to contents in which a phoneme is being misarticulated (McDonald, 1964).

Abutting consonants that are said quickly may present an articulatory task as difficult as producing consonant blends (McDonald, 1964). Both abutting consonants and blends are more difficult to articulate than single consonants. Producing any phoneme in a structured setting, however, may be less difficult than articulating it in a noncontrived utterance.

Stimulability Procedure

After a clinician evokes responses from a client during a Templin-Darley test, he can present the same items under an echoic condition to determine if the client will improve production from the baseline obtained. This stimulability procedure is used for items that have been articulated in error. The clinician uses sensory clues from audition, speechreading, taction, and if available electrovisual speech clues, to prompt an improved production. The susceptibility of a particular test item to improvement from baseline suggests its amenability to change during more extensive shaping and refinement procedures. If the clinician is administering the modified Templin-Darley Test and has marked 20 of the 67 items as incorrect, he can obtain stimulability data on the error sounds in an additional five minutes. He can then couple this evaluative information with baseline data from both the Templin-Darley and deep tests. Such a data pool is invaluable for planning speech remediation.

Goldman and Fristoe (1972) have also designed a 72-item stimulability subtest into their overall test of consonant articulation. The speech units of this subtest are syllables, words, and sentences. For example, one item includes pɪ, *pig,* and *The pig is fat.* The clinician orally reads the syllable, word, or sentence, and the client imitates this production. The 72 items incorporate 23 consonants in 61 initial, medial, and final phonemic contexts and 11 consonant blends. Goldman and Fristoe state that isolated phonemes should not be used as stimulability items. However they do not support this position with data. Training a client to articulate isolated phonemes has been described as a critical part of speech training procedures in chapter 5. Further rationale for training with isolated phonemes will be described later in this chapter and in chapter 7.

Words and Sentences

The Goldman-Fristoe Test of Articulation also includes a sounds-in-words subtest and a sounds-in-sentences subtest. In the first of these, 35 pictures or plates are used to elicit 24 of the 25 consonants in 74 phonemic contexts. The response form does not include space for recording accuracy in the articulation of the 18 vowels and diphthongs. However the words of the consonant items include vowel phonemes except for /ʊ/ and /ɔɪ/. A slight alternation of the test form would enable the recording of vowel and diphthong errors. The clinician needs to evaluate vowel and diphthong production when testing hearing-impaired children.

A third subtest of the Goldman-Fristoe Test is designed to assess the articulation of 18 consonants in 43 key words of sentences. Twenty-two key words and 17 sentences appear in the first of two stories told by the clinician. Twenty-one key words and 12 sentences are in the second story. Five plates or situational pictures accompany the first story. Four plates accompany the second. The clinician reads a story to the client and points to pictures or uses gestures to emphasize key words. Afterwards he asks the client to retell the story and reuses the same pictures to prompt articulation of key words. The clinician records articulatory accuracy in the key word section of the response form. Articulation errors that occur in the sentence subtest may be similar to those that a client produces in conversational speech. This information can be combined with data from life situational utterances of the client. It can also be compared with data from the sounds-in-words subtest of the Goldman-Fristoe Test.

In the National Speech and Hearing Survey directed from Colorado State University, data were gathered on the number of articulatory errors elicited from a stratified sample of 38,884 children. The word subtest and the stimulability subtest of the Goldman-Fristoe Test were used to obtain this information. Percentile rank norms for males and females, ages 6 to 16+, are included in Tables 7 to 10 of the Examiner's Manual (Goldman and Fristoe, 1972). By use of these tables, the number of errors that a particular child makes on either the word subtest or the stimulability subtest can be converted into a percentile rank. However the value of making this conversion for a hearing-impaired child is open to question because the norms emerged from the testing of children who generally were normally hearing. The same objection would be raised about using the Templin-Darley normative tables to interpret the articulatory data of a deaf or hard-of-hearing youngster.

Classification of Data

Once a pool of baseline and stimulability data on articulation is established, the clinician will find it valuable to classify this information. Table 18 suggests a format for transferring and recording overall test information. Space is provided for evaluative detail derived from natural situations, pictured words, stimulability procedure, and depth contexts. Subcategories include initial (I), medial (M), and final (F) positions of articulation in words as well as consonant blends. Depth or deep test contexts are subdivided into vowel, vocalic consonant, and voiceless consonant groupings. The marking system is evident from the hypothetical examples of error sounds presented. It may be noted that the /z/ phoneme is produced correctly in only some vocalic depth contexts. Misarticulations of /z/ vary from omissions, to distorted /s/ substitutions, to distortions of /z/. The /s/ errors include omissions and distortions. The spontaneous /ɪ/ articulations are neutralizations and the echoic production is a distortion.

Table 18

Hypothetical Baseline and Stimulability Data for Three Error Sounds Articulated by a Hearing-Impaired Client During Natural and Contrived Evaluation

Error Phoneme	Natural				Pictured Words				Stimulability				Depth Contexts		
	I	M	F	Blend	I	M	F	Blend	I	M	F	Blend	Vowel	Vocalic	Voiceless
/z/	—	—	—	—	s*	s*			z*	z*	s*		z*	mz, nz, lz	s*
/s/	—	—	—	—	*	*		s*p etc.	*	*	*	s*p etc.	*	* *	
/ɪ/		ə				ə			*						

I = initial position of word, M = medial position, and F = final position. A dash (—) indicates an omission and an asterisk (*) indicates a distortion.

Another worthwhile classification system for speech evaluation is distinctive feature analysis (Jakobson, Fant, and Halle, 1969). A list of 11 distinctive features and corresponding definitions is presented below. The terms and definitions are the author's modification of those used by Jakobson and associates.

Voiced. (+) = vocal folds in vibration; includes all vowels, diphthongs, and voiced consonants; (−) = voiceless.

Oral. (+) = velum raised to allow the air stream to be directed through the mouth; includes all phonemes except /m/, /n/, and /ŋ/; (−) = nasal.

Tense. (+) = Supraglottal musculature exerting considerable effort so that the articulators maintain their posture for a relatively long time; includes /u/, /o/, /i/, /e/, /æ/, /ɔ/, /ɪu/, and /t/; (−) = lax.

Rounded. (+) = lip orifice rounded; includes /u/, /ʊ/, /o/, /ɔ/, /w/, and /hw/; (−) = extended or relaxed.

Squared. (+) = lip orifice squared; includes /r/, /ɝ/, /ʃ/, /ʒ/, /tʃ/, and /dʒ/; (−) = extended or relaxed.

Restricted. (+) = more obstruction to air flow than for /i/ or /u/, but less than for the noise and buzz sounds; includes /l/, /r/, /j/, and /w/; (−) = unrestricted.

Noise. (+) = articulators positioned so that voiceless air stream is very obstructed but not stopped; includes /θ/, /ɟ/, /f/, /v/, /s/, /z/, /ʃ/, /ʒ/, /tʃ/, /dʒ/, and /h/; (−) = unrestricted.

Buzz. (+) = articulators positioned so that the voiced air stream is very obstructed but not stopped, and the tongue or lower lip is in vibration; includes /ɟ/, /v/, /z/, /ʒ/, and /dʒ/; (−) = unrestricted.

Stop. (+) = articulators momentarily dam off the air stream in the oral cavity (and explosively release it if the phoneme initiates a word); includes the voiceless sounds /p/, /t/, /k/, and /tʃ/, and the voiced sounds /b/, /d/, /g/, and /dʒ/; (−) = unrestricted.

High. (+) = body of the tongue elevated from the neutral or at rest position; includes the consonants /t/, /d/, /n/, /l/, /r/, /k/, /g/, /ŋ/, /s/, /z/, /ʃ/, /ʒ/, /tʃ/, /dʒ/, /j/, /w/, and /hw/, the vowels /i/, /ɪ/, /e/, /ɛ/, /u/, /ʊ/, /o/, and one or both parts of /ɔɪ/, /aɪ/, /au/, and /ɪu/; (−) = tongue not elevated from neutral position; includes /æ/, /ɔ/, /a/, and /ɑ/.

Front. (+) = tongue elevated anterior to the neutral position; includes the consonants /t/, /d/, /n/, /l/, /s/, /z/, /ʃ/, /ʒ/, /tʃ/, /dʒ/, and /j/, and the vowels /i/, /ɪ/, /e/, /ɛ/, and /æ/, and one or both parts of the diphthongs /aɪ/, /au/, /ɔɪ/, and /ɪu/; (−) = tongue elevated posterior to the neutral position; includes the consonants /k/, /g/, and /ŋ/, the vowels /u/, /ʊ/, /o/, /ɔ/, and /ɑ/, and one part of the diphthongs /au/, /ɔɪ/, and /ɪu/.

Table 19

Distinctive Features Normally Produced During the Articulation of English Phonemes

Phoneme	Vcd	Orl	Tns	Rnd	Squ	Rst	Ns	Bz	Stp	Hgh	Fnt	Total
/i/	+	+	+	−		−				+	+	7
/ɪ/	+	+	−	−		−				+	+	7
/e/	+	+	+	−		−				+	+	7
/ɛ/	+	+	−	−		−				+	+	7
/æ/	+	+	+	−		−				−	+	7
/u/	+	+	+	+		−				+	−	7
/ʊ/	+	+	−	+		−				+	−	7
/o/	+	+	+	+		−				+	−	7
/ɔ/	+	+	+	+		−				−	−	7
/ɑ/	+	+	−	−		−				−	−	7
/ʌ/	+	+	−	−		−					−	6
/ə/	+	+	−	−		−					−	6
/ɝ/	+	+	−		+	−						5
/ɚ/	+	+	−		−	−						5
/aɪ/	+	+	−	−		−				− +	+ +	7
/aʊ/	+	+	−	− +		−				− +	+ −	7
/ɔɪ/	+	+	−	+ −		−				− +	− +	7
/ɪu/	+	+	− +	− +		−				+ +	+ −	7
/h/	−	+				−	+					4
/hw/	− +	+		+		+	+			+	−	7
/w/	+	+	−	+		+				+	−	7
/p/	−	+	−	−					+			5
/b/	+	+	−	−					+			5
/m/	+	−	−	−								4

	/t/	/d/	/n/	/l/	/r/	/k/	/g/	/ŋ/	/θ/	/ð/	/f/	/v/	/s/	/z/	/ʃ/	/ʒ/	/tʃ/	/dʒ/	/j/
	7	7	6	6	7	7	7	6	7	7	7	7	8	8	8	8	9	9	6
	+	+	+	+	−	−	−	+	+	+	+	+	+	+	+	+	+	+	+
	+	+	+	+	+	+	+						+	+	+	+	+	+	+
	+	+			+	+										+	+		
									−	+	−	+	−	+	−	+	−	+	
									+	+	+	+	+	+	+	+	+	+	
						+	+												+
						+									+	+	+	+	
	−	−	−			−	−	−	−	−	−	−	−						
	+	−	−	−	−	−	−	−	−	−	−	−	−	−	−	−	−	−	−
	+	+	−	+	+	+	+	−	+	+	+	+	+	+	+	+	+	+	+
	−	+	+	+	+	−	+	+	−	+	−	+	−	+	−	+	−	+	+

Distinctive Feature Analysis

Table 19 identifies the distinctive features of the English phonemes. If a plus (+) or a minus (−) does not appear below a category, the feature is not present in that phoneme. A double plus, a double minus, or a combination of a plus and a minus signals a diphthong. The number of distinctive features varies among phonemes, from four for the /h/ articulation to nine for the affricates. The differing numbers of features for each phoneme suggest that the phoneme articulations vary in complexity.

When a phoneme is misarticulated, a circle can be placed around each feature in error. If the /i/, for example, is nasalized, a circle is placed around the plus below the oral category. When the error data of a speech evaluation appear in this distinctive feature table, the pluses and minuses circled reveal the detail of the articulation problem. A distinctive feature analysis combined with baseline and stimulability data provides the clinician with enough information to plan a sophisticated program of speech remediation.

McReynolds and Engmann (1975) detail the procedures for applying distinctive feature analysis to a client's misarticulations. They also demonstrate how information derived from this analysis can be utilized in remedial articulation programming. Particular focus is given to the 13 distinctive features proposed by Chomsky and Halle (1968). A detailed description of such features and comparison with other similar systems is provided by Singh (1975).

PERCEPTUAL LEARNING

It is assumed too often in speech remediation that a client begins the habilitative process with full perception of sensory clues. This is not at all the case. Perceptual learning must occur before sensory identification becomes optimal. Ordinarily, we can expect that baseline performance in the perception of speechreading, tactile, auditory, or electrovisual clues is below the client's potential sensory identification.

A speech remedial program with a hearing-impaired client should commence with perceptual learning of sensory clues. If the clinician expects full utilization of speechreading clues by the client, for example, this sensory modality must be mobilized by means of unisensory learning tasks. More importantly, if the clinician wants the client to use auditory clues or electrovisual clues, similar training must take place. Usually the hearing-impaired client is naturally mobilized to perceive speechreading clues rather than clues from the two latter sensory input systems. A hearing aid or an electrovisual speech indicator may be used by the clinician but bypassed or ignored by the client.

Rouzer (1972) performed an experiment in which two hearing-impaired children were intermittently provided with electrovisual clues during speech modeling. These sensory clues were additional to the speechreading and auditory input. Throughout a series of 16 therapy sessions, Rouzer noted that one child used the electrovisual clues to some extent, while the other did not. Preliminary practice in perceptual learning of these clues was not designed into the experiment. The children were like so many of us. We utilize the stimuli currently meaningful to us and ignore other potentially valuable clues.

Sensory Training

The author has developed a sensory training procedure that consists basically of repeated presentation of speech stimuli in various sequences. The stimuli can be isolated phonemes, words, or sentences. First, a list of items is selected. For example, 36 critical articulations may comprise the list. As stimuli, these items are presented repeatedly, but each time in a different one of four or more orders. During such presentation the clinician vocalizes the item, for example /p/, and the client is asked to repeat it. Feedback on the correctness of each response is provided. When an incorrect response is made, the clinician may also present discrimination practice using the correct stimulus and the error stimulus. The client might respond correctly to 6 of 36 items on the first block or presentation of the list, 13 of 36 on the second, and eventually 36 of 36.

Most of us have learned to identify auditory clues as a prerequisite to learning speech and spoken language early in life. These clues were environmental sounds and speech stimuli, presented repeatedly in conjunction with life situations. We did not identify these speech and situational clues initially. We learned them after considerable practice. If we had a hearing loss, we might have been deprived of auditory clues during the normal period of speech and language acquisition. Naturally we would turn to vision as a compensatory sensory input system, as imperfect as nonauditory clues are for learning speech. If identification and incorporation of speechreading clues were facilitated by our early environment, we were exposed to this visual input repeatedly. Perceptual learning would occur within the limitations of the visual modality. If speechreading was not encouraged or successful, we would learn instead to rely upon communicative signs revealed through gestures. If exposed to it, we would also learn the language of signs and fingerspelling. The natural inclination might be to lock into the communicative system or sensory modality that would be least ambiguous and most meaningful to us (Gaeth, 1971).

Case Study

In 1972 the author designed and conducted a perceptual learning experiment with an oral "deaf" college student with a profound hearing loss. The subject's audiogram was very similar to that of Staffan Wedenberg in that he could not detect the presence of sound frequencies at 2000 Hz or above. As the experimenter, the author set out to determine which sensory aid conditions might be most suitable for the subject during speech modeling or training. Before the experiment, the subject had been tested for both speech reception and speech discrimination in an audiometric test booth. He was unable to repeat any of the spondaic or phonetically balanced (PB) words used as test stimuli. However he could auditorily discriminate the number of syllables and simple stress patterns presented through a master hearing aid. The subject did not own a hearing aid, but he had used amplification sporadically in the past. His method of interpersonal communication was somewhat intelligible speech coupled with speechreading. He had a limited vocabulary and an underdeveloped linguistic code.

During the experiment three unisensory conditions and four multisensory conditions were compared; (A) auditory, (B) facial meaning speechreading plus tactile speech clues, (C) electrovisual or video patterns, AB, AC, BC, and ABC. The conditions were incorporated into perceptual learning tasks. Forty-nine tasks were presented in all, seven under each of the seven conditions. The conditions were counterbalanced in that one never appeared in the same order during a given training session. A training session included seven tasks and lasted approximately 45 minutes. Training sessions were held over a period of six weeks.

The stimuli of each task were 36 consonants, vowels, and diphthongs critical to articulation. They were presented in multiple sequences to prevent transfer of serial learning from one task to another. Each stimulus or phoneme was spoken carefully by the experimenter and imitated by the subject. During the auditory condition, the subject faced away from the experimenter and utilized his recently acquired body-model hearing aid. During the facial condition, he placed his left hand on the face of the experimenter to perceive voicing, oral-nasal, mandibular, air flow, and other possible tactile clues. He also looked at the experimenter for speechreading clues. During the electrovisual condition, the subject watched the screen of a Video Articulator as the experimenter uttered stimuli into the microphone of this unit.

The combined conditions were staged as follows. In the AB condition, the subject listened to, speech-read, and touched the face of the experimenter. In the AC condition, he looked at the Video Articulator screen and listened. Under the BC condition, he held his left hand on the face of the experimenter, speech-read, and watched the Video Articulator screen. And in condition ABC, the staging was the same as above, except that the subject also used his hearing aid.

The unisensory and multisensory stagings are shown in Figure 34. The experimenter spoke into a microphone of a desk-model hearing aid to provide the auditory clues noted in frames 2, 7, 8, and 10. He spoke into a separate microphone, which was inserted into a Video Articulator, to provide the video clues of frames 6, 8, 9, and 10. The facial condition of the experiment is shown in frame 3 as a combination of lipreading and tactile speech clues. Frames 4 and 5 depict use of the facial condition as lipreading and tactile subconditions respectively. The subject is seated approximately four feet from and to the left of the experimenter, as seen by an observer facing the remedial situation. The left hand of the subject for tactile conditions is well shown. Not well shown is the holding of two microphones by the experimenter for frames 8 and 10, in which auditory and video clues were provided simultaneously.

Before the perceptual learning experiment began, the subject had to perform two skills without error. One was to point to the appropriate International Phonetic Alphabet (IPA) symbol for each phoneme uttered by the experimenter. The second skill was to articulate all training stimuli until the experimenter could point to the corresponding symbols without making errors. Both the subject and the experimenter were able to look at and listen to each other.

At first the subject was unfamiliar with many of the IPA symbols, and he did not perceive or articulate all of the phonemes correctly. Within two hours, however, he recognized the symbols and perceived the phonemes by looking at the experimenter and by listening with his hearing aid. He also articulated the consonants, vowels, and diphthongs well enough for the experimenter to differentiate the phonemes he was saying. Considerable training in shaping certain articulations was required before the subject attained the second skill. At the same time the experimenter was being trained to correlate the subject's articulatory productions with the IPA symbols.

During the study itself, the experimenter recorded all responses by using check marks for correct imitations and IPA symbols for incorrect imitations. The data for each task were number of correct responses out of a possible 36. A total of 1764 responses were made during the seven presentations of each of the seven conditions. Whenever the sub-

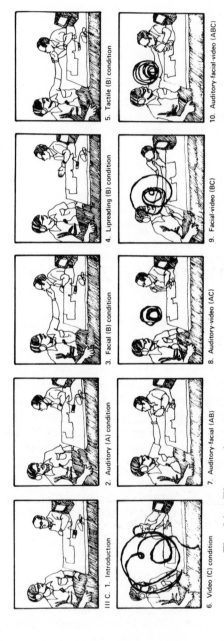

Fig. 34. Three unisensory and four multisensory stagings used in a perceptual learning experiment with a "deaf" college student. Compliments Utah State University, Logan.

184

ject made an error, the experimenter trained him to discriminate between the correct sound and the error sound.

Findings and Extensions

The experimental results revealed that the "deaf" subject learned
to perceive each of the 36 critical articulations under each unisensory
and multisensory condition. By the fourth session, after three weeks,
the subject achieved essentially errorless responding. Throughout the
sessions, performance was somewhat better under the multisensory
conditions. Responses under the auditory condition were relatively less
reflexive for certain stimuli, particularly during earlier training sessions.

As the experiment proceeded and fewer and fewer errors were
made, the experimenter asked the subject numerous times how he was
able to identify certain difficult phonemes. Each time the subject responded by indicating that there were differences between sounds, or
visual speech clues, or electrovisual patterns, or occasionally tactile
speech clues. He could perceive slight visual differences between the
homophenous /f/ and /v/ articulations, for example. He also learned to
distinguish auditorily between an /f/ and a /θ/, and electrovisually between the "splash" of a /p/ and the configuration of a /t/. These perceptual learning procedures should be replicated with many other
hearing-impaired children and adults.

Another unexpected finding of the experiment was that the subject
seemed to be refining speech articulation as well as improving speech
perception while the training proceeded. The experimenter noticed that
the subject was refining certain vowels, diphthongs, and affricatives.
On an occasion in which direct speech therapy was initiated, however,
the articulation of the subject retrogressed momentarily. The experimenter began to think that he might aid the subject's articulatory
refinement more by perceptual training than by speech shaping procedures.

A distinction might be made between the process involved in the
initial shaping of an articulation and the process involved in refining
phoneme production. It may be necessary to shape an articulation initially through direct speech training. Afterwards it may be necessary to
conduct perceptual training to assist in refining articulation optimally.
Such a distinction may hold true particularly for phonemes that are
inherently difficult to articulate, such as the /tʃ/ and /dʒ/.

One of the main findings of the perceptual learning experiment was
that the "deaf" subject could identify auditorily isolated phonemes.
Having discovered this, the experimenter then trained the subject with
30 consonant-vowel-consonant (CVC) words (Boothroyd, 1967). With

less practice than before, the subject learned to reiterate the words also. The CVC words were similar in length and phonemic content to the auditory discrimination stimuli of the PB test originally administered during the hearing aid evaluation. In contrast to zero performance on PB word identification, however, the subject was able on clinical retest to repeat most of the items correctly. Six weeks later the subject was retested using the CVC stimuli and again reiterated most items correctly. Months later, he once more successfully repeated most PB items.

The author has administered perceptual learning tasks to other hearing impaired clients since. For example, he noted that a "deafened" adult improved substantially in the identification of isolated phonemes, CVC words, and unrelated sentences. A student of the author, Stokes (1974) obtained similar results with three hearing-impaired children. One was nearly deaf, the second had a 95 dB loss in the better ear, and the third child had a 70 dB impairment.

Other Applications

Perceptual learning may be utilized not only in articulation training but also in prosodic and voice remediation. Durations, loudnesses, and frequencies have served as sound stimuli in the effective Pulsatone training of Perdoncini that has been incorporated into some aural–oral programs. James (1975) of the Institute of Logopedics believes that this sensory training contributes fundamentally to the aural–oral educational success generally achieved among children in the Institute's infant-preschool program for the hearing impaired. Similar sensory training with stimuli simulating degrees of hypernasality, harshness, and other vocal parameters could be incorporated into a program of voice training.

Goldstein (1939), an otologist who founded the Central Institute for the Deaf (CID) in 1914, introduced sensory training into the education of hearing-impaired children in America. His methodology was that of the Vienna Doblin School for the Deaf where he had studied with Urbantschitsch in 1893. Sensory or acoustic training introduced by Goldstein utilized musical tones, phonemes, syllables, words, and sentences. The methodology focused upon perceptual learning of these stimuli as well as on production of speech units. McGinnis (1963), who headed the CID program for so-called aphasic children, also utilized the auditory modality as well as other sensory input systems to facilitate the improvement of perception and production of speech stimuli among the hearing impaired.

Prosody and Rhythm

In 1962 DiCarlo reported that hearing-impaired children who discriminated audio frequencies in the 500 Hz region employed amplification quite well. He noted that 250 and 500 Hz did not incorporate much of the information-bearing features of speech. However these low audio frequencies do enable perception of prosodic features of stress and thereby enable establishment of natural speech rhythm.

The importance of perception of pitch as well as stress in speech and language development has received considerable emphasis in the professional literature during the past 25 years. As early as 1951, Lewis stated that the infant normally identifies gross pitch patterning initially, then finer intonational features as well as some articulatory components, and finally the remaining perceptual correlates of speech articulation. Lieberman (1967) stated that the intonation contour was the primary feature of the constituent phrase or sentence, which is the basic speech unit.

According to Pike (1945), intonation contours incorporate four relative pitch levels: *extra high* for surprise, unexpectedness, or raised voice; *high* for normally stressed syllables and for raised voice; *mid* for unstressed syllables before the end of an utterance; and *low* for unstressed syllables at ends of sentences and for the dropped voice. Pike also defines the intonation contour as a sequence of contrastive pitch changes correlated with each fully stressed syllable of an utterance. He accords primacy to stress as the organizing principle of both rhythm and intonation. Stressed syllables generally occur at regular intervals. The number of stressed syllables rather than the total number of syllables in an utterance is directly related to the length of a phrase or a sentence. Woodward (1967) indicates that because many deaf children have been taught to use syllable-timed speech, teachers can be effective in assisting them to maintain a basic rate of utterance.

Pike (1945) defines rhythm as a phrase unit or rush of syllables between pauses. He indicates that each phrase or rhythm unit is organized around one or more stressed syllables. The syllables closest to the stressed syllable tend to be uttered more rapidly than those farthest from it. An intonation pattern of an utterance generally includes a precontour and a primary contour. For example, in the utterance *I think it's John's book,* the precontour encompasses *I think it's* and the primary contour is *John's book*. The primary contour begins with the stressed syllable and includes all subsequent significant pitch variations before the next contour begins.

The present author prefers to use the term *prosody* or *prosodic unit* rather than *rhythm unit* to describe a pattern of pitch and stress variation within a phrase or sentence. Fairbanks (1960) defines rhythm as the recurrence in time of a pattern of vocal change. A prosodic unit must repeat itself to have rhythm. For example, the two lines *My country 'tis of thee, Sweet land of liberty* is rhythmic because the pitch and stress pattern repeats itself.

Serial Learning

If each syllable of speech were equally stressed, nearly all hearing-impaired clients would hear if not perceive each part of an utterance. In a doctoral study Berg (1960), the present author used a number of pure tones, each with the same intensity and duration, as stimuli in serial learning tasks. Each item of a task included one to five tones. A subject responded by saying *one, two, three, four,* or *five*. Each task included 12 items. An example of the number of tones in a task was 3, 5, 2, 4, 1, 5, 2, 1, 3, 4, 5, and 1.

Nine normal-hearing and nine hearing-impaired young adults individually learned the tasks by the serial anticipation method. The hearing losses of the experimental subjects ranged from 85 dB to 105 dB. Each could detect the presence of amplified pure tones, 1000 Hz, 2000 Hz, and 3000 Hz in frequency. In serial anticipation, only one item is presented at a time. As it is presented, the subject anticipates the next item by some type of overt response. Therefore each item is the cue to the one that follows. A given item also confirms or corrects the previous anticipation. The experimenter records all of a subject's responses as a series of items is presented until it is learned to a criterion of two consecutive correct renditions.

In the author's study, each of the nine tasks included a different frequency–duration combination. For example, the stimuli of one task were 1000 Hz tones presented at a rate of three per second. The stimuli of the other eight tasks were drawn from a pool of 1000, 2000, and 3000 Hz, occurring at rates of three, four, and five times per second. According to French and Steinberg (1947), the 1000 to 3000 Hz band is critical for the intelligibility of speech. Use of 1000 Hz as the lowest frequency also tended to ensure that the auditory sense would not be confused with the vibrotactile sense. The rates converted to one-sixth, one-eighth, and one-tenth second durations, with a tone–silence ratio of 50 percent. According to Stetson (1951), three, four, and five stimuli per second simulate slow to rapid rates of syllable utterance. At these rates the trains of one to five tones were usually identified as digits by even profoundly hearing-impaired individuals.

Figure 35 includes learning curves for seven of nine pairs of subjects. The hearing-impaired subjects learned the serial tasks almost as

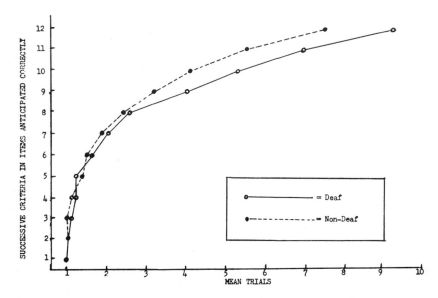

Fig. 35. Mean number of trials for seven normally hearing young adults and a matched group of hearing-impaired individuals to reach successive criteria in the serial acquisition of nine auditory tasks. Compliments Southern Illinois University and Gallaudet College.

rapidly as the normal-hearing subjects. The slight differences in favor of the control group can be attributed to certain misidentifications made by experimental subjects. The two hearing-impaired young adults with the most perceptual difficulty are not included in the comparative data. However they only misidentified 17 of 1548 items and seven of 972 items respectively. The mean number of blocks needed for the remaining seven hearing-impaired subjects to learn the tasks was 9.91. The corresponding mean for the control subjects was 8.29. The difference was not statistically significant at the five percent level of confidence.

Another relevant finding was that the number of trials needed to master the preliminary visual tasks and the auditory tasks decreased considerably with practice. For example, the number of blocks used by one hearing-impaired subject to master the visual series ranged from 24 to 10 from the first task to the third. Another hearing-impaired subject used 41 blocks to master the first visual task and only five blocks to learn the last auditory task. The visual task stimuli were one to five dots in domino patterns.

Before presentation of auditory tasks, each subject received training in discriminating one to five tones under the various frequency and duration conditions. In addition, the six visual tasks and three preliminary auditory tasks provided subjects with substantial practice in identifying stimuli and in learning serially. By the time the subjects were learning the last nine auditory tasks, they were relatively efficient in discriminating the number of tones and in learning by the serial anticipation method. Age, sex, intelligence scores, and visual task performance was used to match an experimental subject to a control subject.

Another major conclusion of the author's dissertation was that a measure of serial learning could be used, along with other similar measures, to contribute to the establishment of an objective and differentiated rationale for perceptual learning. In its connected form, speech or spoken language is characterized in part as a series of trains of syllables. Consequently, one of the tasks of speech acquisition is the serial learning of these trains.

Whereas the 18 subjects of the study became effective serial learners, Sanders (1977) indicates that other individuals have difficulty in learning or remembering order. Such persons may recall the components of a pattern but may not be able to relate them temporally and spatially. Sanders notes that sequencing problems may be manifested within words, within sentences, and between sentences. Some individuals may also have difficulty in reproducing prosodic or rhythmic patterns, the suprasegmental components of spoken language. In addition, sequencing is closely related to the structural rules of language processing.

Sensory training may be even more important to clients with combined hearing and perceptual learning problems than to individuals with a basic hearing handicap. The highly structured McGinnis (1963) approach to speech and language remediation, described in chapter 5, includes detailed instructions for training such clients. Commonly called the Association Method, this approach focuses on considerable paired associate learning. Serial learning, described previously, and paired associate learning are two basic forms of educational procedure.

Paired Associate Learning

Gaeth (1960, 1963, 1966, 1971) has used the paired associate format to study the verbal and nonverbal learning of hundreds of hearing-impaired children and thousands of normal-hearing youngsters. In paired associate learning the subject's task is to pair stimuli with responses, notwithstanding serial order. For example, the subject might be required to write or say the letter *M* each time the stimulus *ball* is presented, and *S* each time *chair* is presented. Actual daily examples of paired associate learning are countless. For example, print or writing are associated with spoken words and phonemes during the reading process. In the Association Method a picture or object is associated with writing and with the spoken form of a word. Furthermore the auditory and speech-read forms are associated with articulatory and prosodic patterns.

Gaeth designed equivalent tasks and presented them auditorily (A), visually (V), and auditorily-visually. He prepared and utilized verbal, nonverbal, meaningful, and nonmeaningful auditory and visual signals. His visual stimuli were printed or written rather than spoken. When used as task items, Gaeth discovered that they were more meaningful to hearing-impaired children than auditory stimuli. The visual tasks were learned as fast as the auditory-visual pairs and faster than the auditory tasks. However the Gaeth experiments were not designed to permit a subject to learn many tasks. Therefore the subjects were just beginning to learn by the paired associate method when their inclusion in an experiment was terminated. It can be hypothesized that these hearing-impaired subjects would have improved considerably in learning auditorily if additional tasks or training had been provided.

At least two of Gaeth's findings are relevant to this discussion. One is that a client will utilize meaningful stimuli in learning and will disregard ambiguous stimuli. In the instance of a hearing-impaired child who has not received sensory training with only auditory stimuli, the youngster naturally locks onto the visual modality. A related finding is that even children with mild hearing losses need sensory training or perceptual learning. Notwithstanding the degree of auditory loss, the hearing-impaired youngsters performed better under visual or auditory-visual conditions than under the auditory modality. Gaeth (1960) also noted that severely hearing-impaired children generally learned better visually than auditorily-visually. With this group, auditory stimuli were not just bypassed; they were interfering with paired associate learning.

Prescott, who worked with Gaeth, has since developed a series of 40 auditory training tasks and has administered them to 55 hearing-impaired preschoolers. She discovered that children with profound losses took four times longer to learn the tasks than youngsters with severe losses, and eight times longer than children with moderate hearing impairment. She also noted that some children with profound losses were not progressing satisfactorily for long periods of time and then suddenly made "quantum leaps" in auditory perceptual processing. Further information on Prescott's project and data is presented in chapter 7 (Prescott, 1972; Prescott and Turtz, 1974).

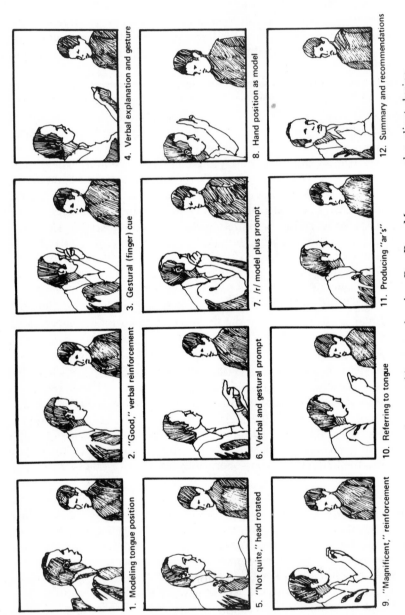

1. Modeling tongue position
2. "Good," verbal reinforcement
3. Gestural (finger) cue
4. Verbal explanation and gesture
5. "Not quite," head rotated
6. Verbal and gestural prompt
7. /r/ model plus prompt
8. Hand position as model
9. "Magnificent," reinforcement
10. Referring to tongue
11. Producing "ar's"
12. Summary and recommendations

Fig. 36. Key scenes from a videotape showing Dr. Don Mowrer and a client during the shaping of /ɝ/. Compliments Arizona State University.

SHAPING AND REFINEMENT

A third part of a remedial speech program for a hearing-impaired client is the shaping and refining of utterance. Shaping and refining are included in articulatory, prosodic, and vocal remediation, and they consist of steps leading through mere target responding to consistent bull's-eye production. By design, shaping and refining should precede habitual production of a correct response, or its transfer into other speech contexts, stimulus conditions, and real life settings. The speech units shaped and refined can be isolated phonemes, syllables, words, phrases, or sentences.

In the shaping and refining process the clinician designs and manages antecedent and subsequent events. Before a client's response, the clinician provides instruction and demonstration. Immediately after the response, he provides the client with reinforcement and feedback about correctness. With antecedent and subsequent management, a client's production is shaped onto the target and refined toward bull's-eye precision.

Reinforcement Techniques

In her design of a speech model, Stoner suggested the use of three graded verbal reinforcers. *That's a try* might be used for a client's first imitation, *good* for an approximation to correct production, and *wonderful* for a closer approximation. These same verbal reinforcers would then be used to convey relatively more precise levels of production, as the client progressed in the shaping and refining process (Rowe, 1974).

One of the current master clinicians, Don Mowrer of Arizona State University, has prepared a videotape that demonstrates important features of the shaping and refining process. Figure 36 includes key scenes from this demonstration. Mowrer is shown assisting a child to articulate the /ɝ/ or /r/ productions. Because of his skill and experience, he is reflexive in his choice of isolated phonemes, syllables, and words while programming speech stimuli. He also spontaneously provides instruction, demonstration, and prompts as facilitative antecedent events. Immediately after the child responds, Mowrer verbally reinforces him.

Three features of Mowrer's reinforcement are noteworthy. One is his appropriate and versatile choice of words. Examples of these words are *no, not quite, good, very good, wonderful,* and *magnificent.* The second reinforcement feature is the vocal inflection utilized by Mowrer. He dynamically varies loudness, pitch, quality, and overall prosodic patterning. Finally, Mowrer also uses his body and his hands to convey gestural reinforcement.

During shaping and refinement, the clinician listens very carefully but responds quickly to each response of the client. He judges progress from incorrect to correct production without hesitation. He also watches the peripheral or visible aspects of the speech organs of the client for supplementary clues. He watches to see, for example, whether the tip of the tongue protrudes for articulation of the /ө/ or /ʒ/, in isolation or in words. Visual perception assists the clinician in many instances, particularly if the client is deaf and has developed many irregular articulatory movements (Stewart, 1968).

Target Format

The author has developed a target format to aid in shaping and refinement processes as well as in evaluation and perceptual learning of speech (Berg, 1976). The basic feature of this format is utilization of an outer ring, an inner ring, and the bull's-eye of a target to record accuracy of speech responses. A target may be used to record data on phonetic, prosodic, or vocal parameters of utterances. Specific speech contexts may include sounds in isolation, words, phrases, or sentences. The author's initial use of the target format has been confined largely to judging the accuracy of 36 critical articulations in isolation, words, and sentences.

The targets of Figure 37 illustrate one application of the use of this format in a speech program. The baseline articulations of three hearing-impaired children were recorded in the upper left, lower left, and lower right quadrants of 36 targets. Circles were used for one client, squares for the second, and triangles for the third. The circles indicate the clinician's judgment of articulatory accuracy for the first client, the squares for the second, and the triangles for the third. Each target provides space for a different one of 36 consonants, vowels, and diphthongs. Isolated phoneme production was measured under the combined echoic-graphemic (imitative-print) condition. For example, the clinician said the /f/ phoneme and a client looked at him, listened to him, and also viewed the symbol or graphemic form of the stimulus before imitating or echoing the stimulus. Depending upon his judgment of the responses's accuracy, the clinician then placed the appropriate symbol in the appropriate quadrant of a circle. Placement of the symbol outside the target indicated that the /f/ was not articulated well enough to be recognized as belonging to that phoneme. A mark in the outer circle indicated a gross distortion, and a mark in the inner circle represented a fine distortion or close approximation. If the mark was

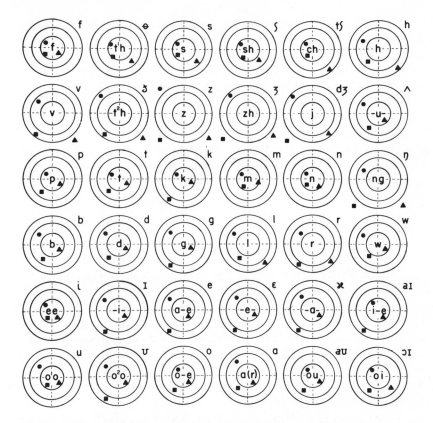

Fig. 37. Articulations and misarticulations of three hearing-impaired children scored as bull's-eye, outer circle, inner circle, and off-target productions of 36 isolated phonemes. ● = first child, ■ = second child, ▲ = third child.

placed within the bull's-eye, the client's response was judged to be an "exact" imitation of the /f/ stimulus.

The responses of each child or client were converted to the numbers one to four. A one indicated bull's-eye production, a two a close approximation to correct production, a three a gross distortion of the phoneme, and a four a production that could not be identified as falling within the phoneme. An overall score was computed for each of the three children. Child number one, for example, accumulated 16 ones, 16 twos, 3 threes, and 1 four, for a total of 61 points. When divided by 36, the child's mean accuracy for isolated production was 1.7—between bull's-eye and close approximation.

Another common design and evaluative procedure is to use quadrants of targets for recording judgments of speech in isolation, releasing a word, arresting a word, or within a sentence. The upper left quadrant might be for marking accuracy of production in isolation, the lower left for releasing a word, the lower right for arresting a word, and the upper right for production in a sentence. Circles might be used for baseline judgments, dots for training sessions, and squares for final measures.

A third target format used by the author is to divide the target into 36 segments rather than quadrants. Each narrow, pie-shaped segment provides sufficient space for recording accuracy of 36 articulations. Circles are used to record baseline responses and squares are used for final measures. Responses between baseline and final measures are recorded as dots.

Target Data

This evaluative procedure has been used in a shaping and refinement program for three young hearing impaired children. Auditory, speechreading, tactile, and electrovisual speech clues were utilized. Time was spent on each of the 36 phonemes during a given training session, whether it was an error sound or not. If a phoneme was already at bull's-eye accuracy, an effort was made to stabilize it. By training both articulated and misarticulated phonemes, a high rate of correct reponse was achieved. However much more time was spent in training the error articulations.

While training a client, a clinician modeled a given misarticulated phoneme, using a facial-auditory-video (electrovisual) condition. The client imitated the clinician and the clinician pointed on or off target to indicate the response's degree of correctness. The clinician also provided token and social reinforcement to reward improvements from off the target to the outer ring, to the inner ring, and into the bull's-eye. Numerous repetitions of this procedure were presented. Before each stimulus presentation, the clinician pointed to the mouth, throat, nose, ear, or video screen to draw the attention of the client to an appropriate clue. All of the client's responses were recorded. The best response for each phoneme provided the basis for affixing a score of four, three, two, or one.

The mean accuracy of articulation at baseline was 2.8—nearly gross distortion. The corresponding post-training measure after 10 blocks or presentations of 36 phonemes was 1.2. Preliminary training was given to condition the client to utilize video clues in addition to other sensory input.

Video Articulator

The electrovisual clues described in this chapter have been patterns of the Video Articulator, a successor to the Voice Visualizer (Pronovost, Yenkin, Anderson, et al., 1967). This device is marketed by Amera Incorporated, Box 627, Logan, Utah. The Video Articulator consists of a modified Sony television set weighing nine pounds. It displays visual patterns that vary in size and configuration as speech input varies. One or more microphones attached to the unit permit a hearing-impaired client to evaluate his speech output by studying it visually. With the Video Articulator the client can perceive features of speech that are difficult or impossible to recognize through audition, visual speech clues (speechreading), or tactile speech clues. The electrovisual or video patterns correspond to the acoustic features of the signal input. Because they are visual, the hearing-impaired person can perceive them as well as a normally-hearing person can.

Video Patterns

When a person says a sentence into the microphone of the Video Articulator, he can view a sequence of visual patterns corresponding to the overall vocal, prosodic, and phonetic content of connected utterance. Specifically, he views a series of loop like patterns that vary in size and configuration. As he slows his rate of speech, smaller circle concentrations and even more concentrated whirls appear within the larger loops. It is not until he articulates single phonemes or words, however, that the client perceives splashes as well. The loops occur when vowels, diphthongs, glides, nasals, and voiced consonants are produced. Whirl concentrations appear when the voiceless fricatives /ɵ/, /f/, /s/, /ʃ/, and /h/ are articulated. Whirl concentrations within loops are generated when the voiced fricatives /ʝ/, /v/, /z/, and /ʒ/ are pronounced. When voiceless stops are articulated, isolated splashes of light appear. Voiced stops appear as splashes that are more concentrated. The voiceless affricative /tʃ/ is a splashlike whirl. The voiced cognate /dʒ/ appears as a whirl and a loop configuration.

Illustrated reproductions of the video patterns of the writer are shown in Figure 38. A pattern can be seen for each of 36 critical articulations. Both visual configuration and relative size are approximated. For example, relative intensities of the voiceless fricatives /ɵ/, /f/, /s/, and /ʃ/ appear as increasingly larger circle concentrations. If another clinician were to draw his or her video patterns, he or she should go through the process twice. On the first trial the configurations might be studied and drawn. Afterwards they should be redrawn according to

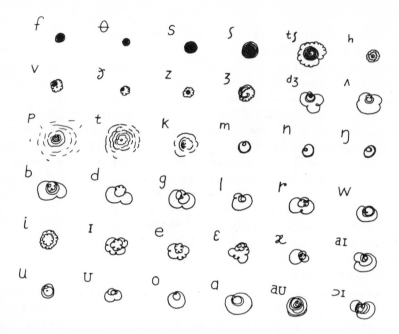

Fig. 38. Freehand drawings of Video Articulator patterns for 36 isolated phonemes articulated by the author. Compliments Utah State University, Logan.

relative size. It is also useful to draw patterns of the client's best productions during the shaping process and to redraw these as speech becomes more and more refined. The drawings serve as models for the
client to duplicate. They can also be placed on transparency material
and positioned on the screen of the Video Articulator.

Each of the 36 video configurations is distinct. The visual patterns
are as unique as the sounds that produce them. If a person articulates a
phoneme repeatedly, the video configurations will be as identical as the
corresponding sounds. If another speaker articulates the same phonemes, the unique loops, circles, whirls, and splashes will be present
but the detail of each configuration will be at least somewhat different,
particularly for voiced phonemes. If the same speaker increases his
intensity or pitch or varies his distance from the microphone, additional
differences in patterns will be evident.

Modeling

A clinician will find that his articulations can be useful models for
most phonemes during initial shaping or when the goal is to move a

production onto target. Afterwards, however, the client's own video "hits" should be the standard he is trying to reproduce. The clinician's task, then, is to listen critically and to indicate how closely the client approaches the desired production. In time the client learns to recognize and monitor his own hits and improvements. During the entire training process, the client utilizes video clues as an adjunct to auditory, speechreading, and tactile speech clues.

The surface or speechreading and tactile speech clues may be particularly helpful in shaping an articulation onto the target. The auditory speech clues may assist in refining speech into outer and even inner rings of the target. The video clues may complete the refinement by prompting the speech response into the bull's-eye.

Stimulus Levels

The Video Articulator has a role in the articulation of sound combinations as well as isolated consonants, vowels, and diphthongs. For example, the client can perceive the video pattern for /s/ in isolated production or in *so, us, nice, listen,* or *Mississippi.* When articulations are shaped and incorporated into syllables, words, and sentences, the corresponding video patterns can be observed on the TV screen, particularly as utterance is slowed down. Once habit patterns are shaped and established, video clues may be of no further use unless the client retrogresses. Ordinarily, however, auditory-tactile-kinesthetic (ATK) feedback provides the client with necessary speech monitoring information after he leaves the therapy session.

Errors Needing Remediation

The Video Articulator is also being applied to evaluation and remediation of other speech problems of hard-of-hearing and deaf clients. Speech errors of the deaf include abnormally slow rate of utterance, insufficient duration distinctions between stressed and unstressed syllables, use of more pauses and pauses of longer durations, incorrect rhythm or prosody, inadequate breath control, excessive duration for certain sounds, inappropriate average pitch, improper intonation, tendency to nasalize sounds that should not be nasalized, failure to develop certain sounds, use of the neutral schwa as a general purpose vowel, distortion in articulating sounds, malarticulation of compound and abutting consonants, difficulties in executing smooth transitions between consonant-vowel combinations, throaty, flat, breathy, and harsh voice quality, too soft or too loud of a voice, and erratic variation in loudness. All of these errors and their corresponding correct productions are included in the patterns appearing on the screen of the Video Articulator. However the number that can be perceived is subject to question and clinicial research. Basically, stress appears as size of pattern, timing as pauses and numbers of patterns, and pitch, nasality, and quality as pattern configuration. Articulatory correlates have been described.

Pitch Feature

Recently, Amera engineers have added an audio oscillator system to the Video Articulator. The oscillator permits the clinician to identify quantitatively the pitch or fundamental frequency of vocalization. Controls on the front of the unit can vary oscillator frequency from 50 to 500 Hz. Whatever the frequency of the tone, it appears as a single circle on the screen. When the client produces speech containing fundamental frequencies at the oscillator frequency, a "beating" or combined pulsating configuration appears on the screen. The clinician can determine this frequency by looking at the numbered oscillator dial.

A pitch shaping and refinement program can also be initiated with the Video Articulator if the client is off target. The client can be encouraged to replicate the beating phenomenon as the clinician systematically changes the oscillator dial in the direction of desired pitch level. During each clinical session, the client might be required to evoke beating a certain number of times, both with sustained vowels and with a core of words and sentences. Targets might be designed so that progress in training is visualized and documented.

Equipment Components

Figure 39 shows six views of the Video Articulator or its component parts. Frame 1 depicts the stripped-down Sony TV set. The high voltage and power supply components remain, as does the TV tube, a cathode ray oscilloscope. The new components to be inserted are shown in frame 2. They include a potentiometer or variable resistor for varying the frequency of the oscillator, which is used to measure and shape pitch. Also shown is a board containing a preamplifier, a mixing amplifier, a brightness control, the audio oscillator, and the signal splitter and phase shifter for articulation display. A second circuit board includes additional power supply and drive circuits for the horizontal and vertical yokes of the oscilloscope. These components are shown in place, together with original components, in frame 3.

Frames 5 and 6 of Figure 40 depict the front of the outside of the completely assembled Video Articulator. Frame 6 shows a single cir-

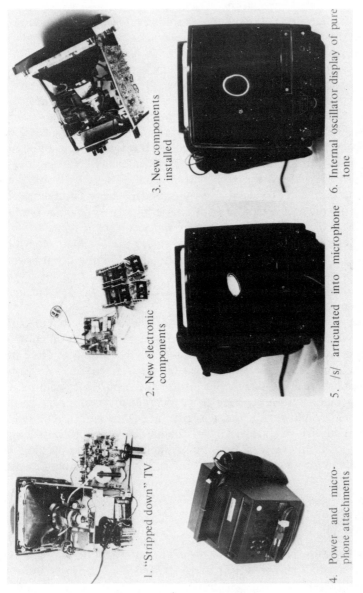

1. "Stripped down" TV

2. New electronic components

3. New components installed

4. Power and microphone attachments

5. /s/ articulated into microphone

6. Internal oscillator display of pure tone

Fig. 39. Six views of the Video Articulator and its component parts. Compliments Amera Incorporated, Logan, Utah.

cle, the basic pattern corresponding to production of a single tone or frequency. In this instance the internal oscillator of the unit is generating the tone. In frame 5 an /s/ articulation is spoken into the microphone of the Video Articulator. Auditorily the /s/ is a white noise composed of many frequencies produced simultaneously. Visually, it appears as many circles, previously called a whirl.

The Video Articulator screen dimensions are 7 inches by 7 inches. Two microphone inputs are shown below the screen and to the right. On the bottom left of the device are on–off, frequency; brightness; and oscillator controls. The switch on the extreme left enables the clinician to turn the power on or off. It also permits variation of oscillator frequency from 50 to 500 Hz. The control to the right of the brightness control turns on the oscillator and varies its intensity. Varying the intensity does not change the size of the visual pattern; it controls the loudness of the tone produced from the loudspeaker. The control between the on–off and oscillator controls permits the clinician to adjust the brightness of the video patterns that appear on the screen.

In a quiet room the screen is blank unless the oscillator control is on or a signal is introduced at the microphone. When a signal appears on the screen, its brightness needs to be controlled so that the pattern can be readily perceived and yet not "burn" the phosphorescent material on the inside of the screen.

Frame 4 shows the back and top of the assembled Video Articulator. When the instrument is not being used, the power cord can be wrapped around holders at the back as shown in frame 4. The carrying handle and the speaker outlet can be seen. A pouch for carrying the microphone is also shown. Because of these portable features, the Video Articulator can be carried from location to location by an itinerant specialist. However, the clinician needs to be careful not to bump or otherwise damage it. If it is damaged, it should be returned to the factory in the original box, which includes suitable packing material. The unit should be shipped by air or by bus to facilitate prompt servicing.

Controls and Patterns

The clinician must take care in providing a precise stimulus at a moderate intensity. Both distance from the microphone and intensity are critical in producing a video pattern. By design, the device does not include circuitry for automatic gain control or intensity compression. If the clinician is too close to the microphone or the speech input is too intense, the video pattern will be too large and extend beyond the boundaries of the TV screen. The clinician must be trained in providing speech models.

Other Economical Devices

Three economical visual indicating devices have been developed by Risberg (1968) of Sweden. They are commercially available in the United States from Special Instruments America, 255 S. 17th St. Philadelphia, Pennsylvania 19103. These units indicate fundamental frequency or pitch, nasality, and presence of the phoneme /s/. Each instrument also includes lights and controls for operant conditioning and shaping of these speech parameters. The clinician can adjust a control to determine whether a light goes on, indicating a desired or improved production. Controls can be readjusted to prompt a client to make further improvements in pitch, reduced nasality, or strength of /s/ production. Calibration adjustments are also included. These devices are particularly applicable to independent work by a client. However the clinician must be available to instruct the client on how to use the equipment and to explain the meaning of the operant adjustment controls.

The pitch, nasality, and /s/ indications on these devices are meter needle deflections. When a needle deflects into a desired area, a speech response is judged acceptable. A limitation of the meter needle display is that it does not respond instantaneously to changes in signal input. The lights of the operant components of the devices, however, do respond reflexively.

The microphones of the three devices are used differently. The standard procedure for speaking into a microphone is used for the /s/ indicator. The microphone of the pitch indicator is placed in contact with the skin of the neck below the larynx. The microphone of the nasality indicator is placed in contact with the nose.

The current prices of the fundamental frequency, nasality, and /s/ indicators are $495, $495, and $395 respectively. The price of the Video Articulator, described in the preceding sections, is $445. In contrast to the /s/ indicator, the Video Articulator displays the other consonants, vowels, and diphthongs of speech. The Video Articulator also includes provision for measuring and shaping the fundamental frequency or pitch. In addition, amounts of nasality in speech can be seen in video patterns by variations in configurations.

Ling (1975) describes the spectrographic features of nasality, a feature common to /m/, /n/, and /ŋ/. He notes that when the nasal cavities are coupled to the oral cavity by lowering the velum, considerable low frequency resonance around 300 Hz results. Immediately above 300 Hz, antiformants or suppression of speech harmonics occur. The antiformants occur at about 1200 Hz for /m/, at 1700 Hz for /n/, and at 2000 Hz for /ŋ/. Further detail on nasality is included in the book *Visible Speech* by Potter, Kopp, and Green (1966). Such nasality features are easily seen in the visual patterns of the Video Articulator for the /m/, /n/, and /ŋ/ and for the other sounds of speech when nasalized.

The comparative advantage of the associated lights of the Special Instruments of America (SIA) devices is presently unknown. As an alternative approach, the Video Articulator utilizes an instantaneous visual pattern change to reveal directly the acoustic content of speech production. The clinician also judges the response of the client and provides reinforcement or feedback. The use of targets in the shaping procedure with the Video Articulator is an extension of the clinician's judgments. The lights on the SIA devices respond to preset physical differences. They do not rely upon the clinician's judgments. Interpretation of SIA lights may require less instruction than perceptual utilization of video patterns and changes. In summary, however, the Video Articulator may be preferred because of its versatility, sensitivity and relatively low cost.

Lucia, VSA, Voice Lite, and the Gallaudet Trainer

Three additional electrovisual aids utilized by some speech clinicians are SIA's Lucia, the Visible Speech Apparatus (VSA) of Precision Acoustics, and Voice Lite I of Behavioral Controls. The first two of these speech analyzing aids display colored spectrums or vertical bar patterns for the consonants, vowels, and diphthongs. On the VSA, for example, the speech signal passes through one or more of 16 bandpass filters between 90 and 8000 Hz. Each bar or light column covers a one-half or one-third octave interval. Whereas frequency is displayed horizontally, intensities within these intervals are displayed vertically. Depending upon interval intensity, one or two lamps behind the translucent front panel can be lit. One lamp is positioned above the other for each frequency interval.

The Lucia display is divided into 20 horizontal bands. Vertical blocks of light within each band convey relative amplitudes of spectral concentrations. Ten lights or steps of 3 dB each appear within each band or interval. The available 30 dB dynamic range permits rather refined differentiation of phonemes and the monitoring of voice quality.

Both the Lucia device and the VSA include freezing circuits. By pressing a button, the clinician can freeze the spectral pattern for a given speech sound on the light panel until the button is released. Outlines of these unique patterns can be traced and placed over the light panels. A client can attempt to duplicate these standards or models by speaking into the microphone.

The cost of either Lucia or the VSA is about three times that of the Video Articulator. The displays, however, do not provide as close tracking of the acoustic input. Furthermore the memory feature of the human brain may negate the advantage of the freeze circuit for shaping and refining speech. In addition, the spectral displays of the Lucia and VSA units may not be as easily identified and learned as the circular and concentrated patterns of the Video Articulator.

The third aid, Voice Lite I, provides a display of loudness and duration of sound. The microphone input is positioned on the surface of the unit, and a translucent dome caps it. The dome lights to varying brightnesses, depending upon signal intensity. The cost of the unit is about one-third to one-half that of the Video Articulator. However it is much less versatile. Its main advantages may be its simplicity, durability, and role for loudness and stress applications with deaf clients. However other speech aids like Lucia, VSA, or the Video Articulator in particular will perform the same role and also display articulatory and pitch information.

Still another speech analyzing device relevant to shaping and refining is the Gallaudet Speech Trainer (Pickett and Constam, 1968). This device presents a single spot of light on an oscilloscope screen. The location of the spot corresponds roughly to an acoustic vowel diagram. For example, the /i/ appears in the upper left corner of the screen, and the /u/ toward the bottom and to the left. This device has been used to assist in the correction of vowel sounds. When diphthongs are produced, the initial and final positions are shown, as well as a trace from one to the other.

Many additional electrosensory aids are included in a recent review by a physicist from Brigham Young University (Strong, 1975). Currently, more than 100 speech and hearing centers, schools, or laboratories are developing or utilizing new devices for displaying speech parameters. The clinician is hard pressed to keep track of the detail of this rapidly developing speech technology.

During the past decade electronic and computer technology have made promising inroads into the practice of speech remediation for the hearing impaired. Some of the more relevant and rigorous of these technological developments, in addition to the Video Articulator and aids just described, will be discussed under the topic of shaping and refinement. The discussion emphasizes speech analyzing aids for evaluation and remediation of pitch, hypernasality, and timing.

Boothroyd Experiment

In a series of three experiments, Boothroyd (1973) studied voice control among profoundly hearing-impaired children by use of a pitch extractor and storage oscilloscope display. In the first experiment the instrument aided in the evaluation of voluntary pitch control. In the second study instrumental and noninstrumental pitch control training were compared. In the third experiment a single subject was trained in complex pitch control skills.

Sixty hearing-impaired students of the Clarke School for the Deaf served as subjects in the first experiment. Twenty each were enrolled in the Upper, Middle, and Lower Schools or departments. They were asked to sustain 200, 300, and 400 Hz tones for 10 seconds apiece. The patterns they produced on the oscilloscope screen were photographed and assessed on a point scale. One subject sustained the three frequencies within or close to targets for six to 10 seconds. Eight sustained three levels somewhat away from the targets. Eleven subjects sustained two of the tones within or close to targets. Seventeen showed some ability to control pitch, and 23 were unable to control pitch.

The data on the 60 students revealed that they generally had poor pitch control. It should be emphasized, however, that none of these children had considerable residual hearing. Previous training and age did have some effect. The children from the Upper School characteristically performed better than those from the Middle School, and the Middle School children generally used better pitch control than those from the Lower School.

In the second experiment the subjects were 20 children from 4 years 10 months to 12 years 11 months. All had hearing losses in excess of 95 dB. Each subject had 10 minutes of training daily for eight weeks. The task was threefold: (1) to sustain vowels at 250 Hz and 350 Hz, (2) to change pitch from 250 Hz to 350 Hz repeatedly, and (3) to vary pitch from 350 Hz to 250 Hz repeatedly.

The 20 children were divided into two groups of 10 subjects each. One group received instrumental support during the first 4 weeks. The other group received it during the second 4 weeks. During the first 4 weeks, both groups of children improved in pitch control. During the second 4 weeks, only the instrumental group made gains. It may be hypothesized that electrovisual feedback is particularly helpful during the refining rather than initial shaping of a speech response.

Deterioration of performance was not significant during a six-week period following training. In fact children with better hearing at 250 and 500 Hz continued to make significant gains during this period.

The subject of the third experiment was a 15-year-old girl with a little residual hearing at low frequencies. Her voice was falsetto and her intonation was abnormal. During a six-month training period she received 15 minutes of instruction each day. She learned to produce a more normal voice, to adjust her pitch to a more suitable range, to intone her pitch up or down, and to change pitch and duration to produce stress. However these improvements in voice and in pitch control were not transferred to her everyday communicative behavior. Boothroyd found the visual display of value to him in objectively judging the temporal and intonation patterns of the student. With prolonged listening he had found it extremely difficult to make judgments based on hearing alone. He had adjusted to accepting defective speech.

Ross Evaluation

Ross (1972) has developed a procedure that assists an evaluator in guarding against changing his standard as he listens to one sample of defective speech after another. This procedure consists of periodically listening to normal speech along with the defective speech that is being rated. Normal speech is interspersed as auditors are rating intelligibility, voice quality, and prosody or rhythm on a bipolar seven-point scale. Specifically, Ross incorporates the procedure in a speech test that includes 20 eight-syllable sentences. Each sentence includes a key word, or rather five alternatives for the key word. As a client reads a sentence, he uses one of the five alternatives. The number of key words that the auditors can identify is scored. The test was introduced at the Willie Ross School for the Deaf.

Second Boothroyd Experiment

In another major investigation of instrumental speech training, Boothroyd and coworkers (1975) are using a digital computer and oscilloscope to provide feedback on loudness, pitch, voicing, nasality, tongue position, aspiration, and selected combinations of these parameters. The speech input is measured and stored by the computer and then converted into oscilloscopic patterns. Four computer programs have been produced: (1) the parameters of speech identified above; (2) a vertical spectrum in which width varies with energy at a given frequency; (3) a cartoon face that can be modified; and (4) a game of transferring balls into a basket to the right of the oscilloscopic screen. A computer-based system has the advantages of simplicity of use as well as versatility in programming and displaying unique but complicated speech parameters.

The digital computer and oscilloscope were utilized by teachers of the deaf for a two-year period. Forty-two students of the Clarke School participated. With few exceptions they were profoundly hearing impaired. Many had little if any residual hearing. The typical student received approximately nine hours of tutoring. Initially and at seven-week intervals, a speech sample from each student was recorded. The

sample included 33 words with broad distribution of phonemic categories, phrases and sentences incorporating the same words, phrases
designed to test velar control and intonation, spontaneous speech elicited from a humorous picture sequence, and a set of six sentences
from a pool of 600 prepared by Magner (1972) for conventional evaluation at the Clarke School. The general format of the tutorial program
included four phases: vocal gymnastics, rehearsed speech, internaliza-
tion, and carry-over. Vocal gymnastics are speech tasks that do not
include meaningful language. Rehearsed speech includes meaningful
language incorporated into the training activities.

A five-point rating scale was developed to evaluate student progress. This ranged from no improvement (0) to considerable progress
and meeting criteria (5). The ratings varied among subjects because
tutoring goals were individualized. The post-training mean ratings for
the 42 students were 2.9 for vocal gymnastics, 2.5 for rehearsed
speech, 1.7 for unrehearsed speech, and 1.4 for spontaneous speech.
Within the context of the overall program, studies were carried out in
areas of rhythm, intonation, and velar control. The data from these
investigations showed that the students reduced faults in rehearsed
speech and to a lesser extent in unrehearsed utterances. Improvements
in overall speech intelligibility, with few exceptions, were not demonstrated. The investigators noted that the instrumental system, however,
was designed to have direct impact upon only imitative speech.

Magner Evaluation

The Magner sets of six sentences are ordinarily administered to
children at the Clarke School for the Deaf in October and in April of
each year. Each child reads four sets or 24 sentences during each of
these times of the year. Each sentence includes 10 syllables and 8 to 10
words. Each set of six sentences is designed to include all consonants,
with the exception of the affricatives /tʃ/ and /tʒ/. The sentences are
simple in construction and include third grade vocabulary words, according to the school curriculum. However, simple modifying phrases
and compound subjects, predicates, and objects are utilized. The sentences are unrelated (Magner, 1972).

Magner states that the test is not designed to evaluate the phonetic
aspect of speech or any other single parameter. She indicates that the
test content, however, provides sufficient stimuli for assessing speech
intelligibility and for identifying specific speech problems.

Each sentence set is tape-recorded while being read by a child.
Later, six adult auditors write down the recorded sentences or the
parts of them which they can perceive. One point is given for each

syllable correctly written down by an auditor. A perfect score is 360 points since six auditors listen to 60 syllables for each six-sentence set. The scores are converted to percentages and plotted on a cumulative speech record kept on each child. The graphs are filed and periodically checked for identification of problems and record of progress.

Boothroyd (1972) states that the Magner Speech Intelligibility Test has never been assessed for reliability. He states that it appears to have poor reliability because of differences in the difficulty of sentences and in listener performance among auditors. He also indicates that caution should be used in interpreting the results of this test, particularly with younger children, because it is an oral reading task. Many of the differences and improvements over time can be attributed to improved reading ability rather than to increased speech competencies. Nevertheless the Clarke School has been unique among special programs for the hearing impaired in that they have systematically conducted speech evaluation among their students.

Snow (1974) utilized 20 sets of Magner sentences and the sentence subtest of the Utley Lipreading Test to determine whether speaking was correlated with lipreading performance. She compared each set of sentences against each other set according to four articulatory or phonetic phenomena: voiced–voiceless, oral–nasal, manner of articulation, and place of articulation. The percentages of these distinctive features among the sentence sets generally correlated closely. Snow also found a 0.75 correlation between speech and lipreading for 20 children in the Utah School for the Deaf who were 14 to 20 years old. However this result must be viewed with caution because factors of language, residual hearing, and age of onset of hearing loss were not controlled.

CCR Equipment

Stewart, Houde, and Larkin (1973) of the Center for Communications Research (CCR) of Rochester, New York, have recently developed two electrovisual analyzing aids for speech remediation with the hearing impaired. One is the Visual Speech Training Aid (VSTA), which displays and stores vocal intensity, voiced–voiceless distinctions, and pitch (if voiced) or frequency of maximum energy concentration (if voiceless). An accelerometer is placed on the nose for nasal intensity and on the larynx for laryngeal intensity. The VSTA enables a therapist to compare visually one or more of these speech parameters with those of his client. Using a specific sequence of syllables as a stimulus, for example, the clinician speaks and a microphone or accelerometer transduces the signal, which in turn is processed by the instrument and displayed and frozen in the upper section of the TV screen. The client can try to match or approximate this trace or pattern by similarly speaking himself. The visual traces of the clinician and client can be compared to indicate the extent to which the matching is accomplished. The client can try to reproduce the pattern of the clinician as many times as he wishes. The clinician's trace stays on the screen until his next trace is produced. Using his memory for the visual traces, the client can also compare his own repeated trials or speech productions.

Houde (1973) described VSTA's ability to support independent speech practice by young adult students at the National Technical Institute for the Deaf. One task was reducing the duration of /tu/ in *to show* through 750 training trials. Initial durations were three times as long as those of the clinician. Final productions were normal or even shorter than those of the model. The data indicated that sensory feedback was effective in modifying speech behavior. It also suggested that considerable practice was necessary before the shaping and refinement task was accomplished.

The question of whether or not this skill was stabilized remains unanswered. Mowrer (1969) uses time delay and distraction activities to stabilize speech production that is shaped and refined. He finds that when a client has received minimal training in shaping and refining a phoneme, he does not continue to produce it correctly when there is an interruption or delay between responses. Using time delay simulation, Mowrer has set up a criterion of 85 percent correct responses in 330 trials. During distraction simulation he requires 90 percent accuracy in 45 responses.

Houde, Stewart, and Larkin (1975) state that the difficulty of reliably detecting the manner and place of articulation features when voiced fricatives are produced with VSTA has led to the development of a real-time speech spectrographic display (SSD). The objective of the SSD is to display time, frequency, and intensity resolution in a manner comparable to the sound spectrograph conventionally used for analysis of speech in a laboratory. Earlier direct translators of spectrographic patterns developed at Bell Telephone Laboratories have had limited resolution (Kopp and Kopp, 1963; Stark, 1971).

The current SSD displays a 100 to 5000 Hz frequency range which is logarithmically scaled to make the speech productions of normally-hearing men, women, and children look more similar. The complete acoustic features of speech are displayed on the screen, in real time, by pressing the record button and using the microphone. The display appears on the screen, from left to right, as the stimulus occurs in time. The pattern is frozen on the screen for several minutes. A new utterance can also be displayed by releasing the record button, pressing the erase button, and speaking into the microphone again. The cost of SSD, approximately $10,000, makes extensive application of the unit prohibitive. The developers, however, are seeking to develop a pool of researchers and clinicians who would invest in the units and facilitate the development of special training methods. In two mini-studies conducted at NTID, one subject independently learned to produce adequate second formants in front vowels, and four additional subjects are being trained in articulation of vowels, voiced fricatives, and a voiceless stop.

Making a Spectrogram

In the past, analysis of the frequency, intensity, and durational features of speech has depended upon use of the sound spectrograph, which costs about half as much as the SSD. Figure 40 shows a six-step procedure for making a spectrogram using the Voice Identification 700 unit. First audio tape is threaded onto a high quality tape recorder. Then the speech sample is recorded by speaking into the microphone. The next step is to adjust the tape manually to catch the signal on playback. In steps four and five, the operator sets a scan level and presses an analysis button. The final step is removal of the completed spectrogram. A push button tape advance also allows the operator to analyze one section of the tape recording after another without erasing previously analyzed speech. Spectrograms produced on this unit exhibit high resolution across the frequency scale to 8000 Hz. An internal oscillator provides reference marks at 1000 Hz intervals. Each spectrogram may take a minute to make. However a permanent record is then available. The spectrograph sheets cost much less than the photographic process used to record similar visible speech patterns on the SSD. This advantage is counterbalanced by the SSD feature of direct translation of speech into spectrographic patterns. The question of whether to purchase a conventional or direct translation spectrograph must be answered in terms of the particular applications needed.

The Boothroyd and CCR developments in speech technology emphasize the use of electrovisual analyzers and displays for independent remediation and drill. Houde, Steward, and Larkin (1975) note, for example, that speech development among the profoundly hearing impaired may be accomplished only after skilled teachers have invested considerable individualized instruction. Similarly, refinement of the speech articulation of children with severe and even moderate hearing impairment requires a considerable investment of clinical time. Economic factors limit the administration of skilled and extensive instruc-

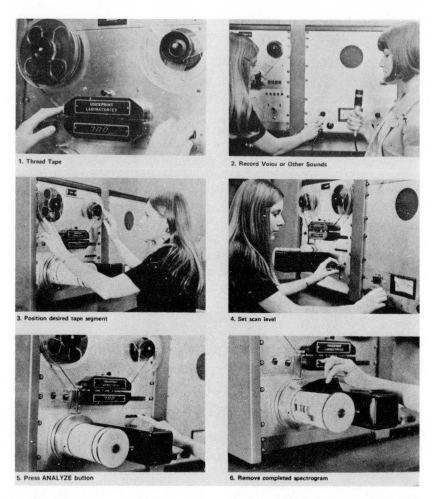

Fig. 40. Six-step procedure for making a spectrogram with the Voice Identification 700 unit. Compliments Bill Hughes.

tion to relatively few hearing-impaired children at this time. Few clinicians or teachers of the hearing impaired are currently using electrovisual speech analyzing aids.

Holbrook Devices

Holbrook (1972) of Florida State University has developed three electronic devices that are relevant to the shaping and refinement of speech production. The first was named FLORIDA (frequency lower-

ing or raising intensity determining apparatus), which was later re-
named FLORIDA I. The second device was called FLORIDA II. It
was designed to measure, shape, and refine the degree of nasality in
speech. The third device developed by Holbrook was named VIC
(voice intensity controller). Each of the two FLORIDA devices utilizes
a computer and measures, stores, and processes information. Digital
displays, meter needles, and lights provide readouts and reinforcers. A
"Charlie Brown" output attachment called REWARD is used with
young children. It advances when the child is meeting criterion in
pitch, intensity, or nasality programming and then kicks over a cup
containing a reinforcer. The VIC device includes a contact throat microphone, a pocket-sized amplifier and oscillator, and an earphone attached to an ear insert. If a client speaks too loudly, he immediately
hears an unpleasant beep. These three speech aids have been produced
commercially by Saber Inc. of Cocoa Beach, Florida.

Holbrook (1972) has used FLORIDA I to lower excessively high
pitch levels among hearing-impaired adults and children including
an infant. In one instance a male adult's fundamental frequency was
reduced from 260 to 130 Hz. During another remedial program, one
woman began with a voice frequency of 470 Hz and came down to a
normal 210 Hz. Two other women reduced their fundamental frequencies from 300 to 225 Hz. During a 10-week program Holbrook conditioned the infant to progressively lower inflectional utterances to activate a feeder. He reported similar successes in reducing hypernasality
with FLORIDA II. He has used a nasal transducer attached to the
nose with FLORIDA II, whereas a conventional microphone has been
employed with FLORIDA I.

With either FLORIDA I or FLORIDA II, a green light on the
console indicates that the client should respond (go), a white light
glows to show correct performance, and a red light glows for two seconds to penalize a client for excessive loudness. Controls on the con-
soles also enable the clinician to set and change criteria for correct
production. When criteria settings are changed systematically, speech
behavior is shaped and refined to desirable performance.

Pitch Conditioning

An early experiment by Holbrook and Crawford (1970) provides
detail on the FLORIDA approach to pitch evaluation. Baseline measures on clients were called habitual pitch levels (HPL); final training
measures were named conditioned pitch levels (CPL); post-training
measures were called extinction pitch levels (EPL); and measures
taken three months after training were referred to as post-experimental

pitch levels (PEPL). Data on four adult deaf subjects revealed dramatic reductions from HPL to CPL, a slight reversal for EPL, and a general maintenance of reduced pitch levels for PEPL. During training, interval schedules of reinforcement varied from 6 to 125 seconds. Withholding the white reinforcement light for variable periods was successful in maintaining CPL for relatively long periods.

Clients participated for eight four-minute trials daily, four days per week, for seven weeks. Baseline stability was established initially by having a client read orally while keeping the white light on and the red light off. Baseline was considered stable when duration of response in an individually adjusted frequency region did not vary on the ninth trial from its average on eight preceding trials.

Conditioning trials then commenced. An appropriate frequency range criterion was set. White and red light feedback corresponded to the extent to which the client's vocal frequencies met this criterion. A 100 percent reinforcement schedule was utilized until the client achieved a high rate of response within the criterion range. This procedure was repeated for narrower and narrower frequency range criteria. After so many days, the client was conditioned to vocalize at a more optimal pitch level. Then extinction trials commenced until stability was established by following the same procedure and criterion utilized during baseline trials. Afterward conditioning was reinstated and a variable interval schedule of reinforcement was utilized to resist extinction. Because the intervals in which lights were unavailable varied during extinction trials, the client learned to respond appropriately without being continually reinforced. At the termination of each interval in which reinforcement was not given, the client had to respond correctly at least once before the lights could again be operational. During the reinstatement of conditioning, a given reinforcement or "lights on" period lasted only 10 seconds. Changes in fundamental vocal frequency were analyzed during each phase of the experiment.

Holbrook (1970) similarly conditioned three school-age children with profound hearing loss to lower their pitch levels. Each child was conditioned for eight 30-second trials daily for six weeks. The pitch of one child was lowered from 450 to 350 Hz, the second from 510 to 310 Hz, and the third from 450 to 370 Hz. The data indicate that each child made considerable progress toward a normal pitch level within a relatively limited time. Holbrook stated that two of the children needed further training.

Differences Between Approaches

Two striking differences between the Holbrook approach to modification of pitch level and that of Boothroyd and CCR are length of stimulus and use of sophisticated conditioning procedures. Holbrook instructs the client to read sentences, whereas Boothroyd and teachers at the Clarke School use shorter imitative speech sequences. The FLORIDA equipment is designed to activate a white light when the average of fundamental frequency during running speech or oral reading is within a preset range of energies. The task of the client is to vocalize while reading or speaking in such a way as to keep the white light on and the red light off. The use of an oscilloscope trace (Boothroyd, 1972), on the other hand, requires the client to monitor pitch by comparing his electrovisual pattern with a previous effort or with a display produced by the clinician. A definite advantage of the Holbrook procedure seems to be incorporation of conditioning and extinction into programming, with consequent generalization or transfer of improved speech into everyday vocal behavior. Clinicians are challenged to extend this technology into all areas of speech remediation.

Daley and Wolff (1970) describe operant conditioning procedures that have been used to develop, maintain, and increase the rate of desired behavior in any educational area. They identify 11 procedures and possible applications used to shape and maintain operant behavior. The serious student is challenged to familiarize himself with various features and procedures of operant conditioning.

Ling and Bennett Study

Ling and Bennett (1974–1975) utilized operant conditioning and baseline and probe measures in a vowel training program for young profoundly hearing-impaired children. In the first of two experiments, two children underwent training in imitating the isolated vowels /a/, /æ/, /o/, /i/, and /u/ using an audiovisual (speechreading) condition. Each subject received training four times a week for 10-minute sessions. During a given session a subject was trained until he could imitate each vowel correctly on 15 of 25 trials or presentations. When this criterion was met for each vowel, a probe was administered to determine generalization among the vowel productions. The probe included 10 presentations of each of the vowels. The training order of vowel imitations required a child to place his tongue anteriorly or posteriorly at successively increasing distances from the neutral or rest position. Before the training the vocalizations of the subjects consisted of bilabial articulations and neutral vowel productions. The children were able to imitate bilabial and lingual movements. An electric train activated by a push button provided consequent reinforcement for correct responses.

At baseline, one child could only occasionally imitate any of the vowels. The other could imitate the /a/ most of the time, and the /u/ on four of ten trials. By the fifth and final probe, the first child was imitating each of the vowels at least half of the time. The second child was echoing each at least eight out of 10 trials. The numbers of trials needed by the first child to reach criterion for /a/, /æ/, /o/, /i/, and /u/ were 75, 150, 50, 500, and 25 respectively. The numbers of trials required by the second child were 75, 25, 50, 225, and 25.

It is evident that the vowel /i/ was the most difficult to train. Its production requires a high front tense placement of the forepart of the tongue. In addition, discrimination of this vowel from /u/ requires auditory perception up to 2290 Hz for male adult production. The first child had no measurable hearing for 2000 Hz or above. The second child's threshold at 2000 Hz was 100 dB. This audiometric evidence suggested that neither child seemed to hear the 2290 Hz second formant. The similar locations of second formants for /a/, /æ/, /o/, and /u/ are 1090, 1720, approximately 800, and 870 (Denes and Pinson, 1973; Fairbanks, 1960). The tongue placement for /a/ and /æ/ is easily seen, but it cannot be seen during imitation of the other three vowels.

Second Experiment

The difficulty that these children had in learning to produce /i/ led to the second experiment. Even after 500 trials the first child produced only 50 percent of the /i/ models correctly when reinforcement was not provided. The second child, who perhaps learned to perceive the second formant of /i/, performed relatively better on this task. In the second experiment two additional profoundly hearing-impaired children, 4½ years of age, underwent similar training with /i/ and /au/ combined with the initial /p/ consonant. The /po/ consonant–vowel combination was also used during baseline and probe tests to determine whether generalization had occurred. The /pa/, already within the repertoire of each subject, was used to provide preliminary training in understanding that tokens would be awarded for correct responses, and that they could be exchanged for trinkets at the end of each session.

Daily training sessions were held for three weeks. During baseline and probe tests, a subject received 10 trials with /pi/, /pau/, and /po/ using the audiovisual (AV) condition. During each of four series of training trials, a child had to reach a criterion of 15 out of 25 correct imitations before probe tests were given. During the first two steps or series of trials, concurrent training was administered with one syllable under AV and the other syllable under a tactile kinesthetic (TK) condition. The third and fourth steps utilized the TK and AV conditions respectively. In the TK condition a child placed a finger of one hand in his mouth and the corresponding finger of the other hand in the experimenter's mouth. These fingers were placed on the tongue to feel position or placement.

During the first step of training, the first child imitated /pi/ in 14 of

25 and 22 of 25 trials under the TK condition. He imitated /pau/ in only 6 of 25 trials on two successive blocks under the AV condition. Similarly, the other child imitated /pi/ 24 of 25 times and /pau/ 6 of 25 times by using TK and AV conditions respectively. As a result of this training, the number of correct imitations by each child on probes for /pi/, /pau/, and /po/ increased from baseline, but the increase was greater for syllables trained under the TK condition. Probes were given by means of AV stimulation.

The AV condition was utilized during the second step of training. The first child imitated /pi/ 19 of 25 times and /pau/ on only 5 of 25 occasions. Similarly, the second child was correct 4 of 25 and 1 of 25 times for /pi/ and 18 of 25 times for /pau/. The evidence indicated that, whatever the syllable, the first step of training under the TK condition generalized to facilitate correct production under the AV condition during the second step. Considerable generalization from TK to AV was similarly evident during the following two AV probes.

During the third or entirely TK step of training, the first child imitated /pau/ in 11 of 25, 12 of 25, and 15 of 25 trials. The second child performed similarly in imitating /pi/. His data showed 10 of 25, 10 of 25, and 16 of 25 correct responses. It should be recalled that these syllables were imitated much less often under AV stimulation during previous AV conditioning and probes.

The fourth and last step of training utilized the AV condition. The first child imitated /pau/ on 10, 11, 10, 10, and 15 of 25 trials. The second child similarly responded correctly to /pau/ on 11, 10, and 16 of 25 occasions. During the following two AV probes, the first child was correct 8 of 10 times on each occasion for /pau/, 10 and 6 of 10 times for /pi/, and 8 and 7 of 10 times on /po/. Similarly, the second child responded correctly 6 and 7 of 10 times for /pi/, 9 of 10 times for /pau/, and 4 and 5 of 10 times for /po/. Correct production had not completely stabilized, but improvement due to training was evident. Considerable generalization among phonemes had also occurred. In contrast to data from the first experiment, imitation of the syllable on which no training had been administered improved as conditioning proceeded.

The results of the second experiment revealed that initial TK training of profoundly hearing-impaired children facilitated progress in learning to imitate high front and high back tongue placement. It seemed that the lip rounding and back elevation of the tongue at the end of /pau/ was specifically generalizing to production of /po/ during probes. It would be interesting to replicate these experiments, using children with varying degrees and slopes of severe and profound hearing impairment, to assess the value and permanence of initial conditioning with tactile–kinesthetic stimulation during the shaping and refinement of consonants, vowels, and diphthongs. Such stimulation may be particularly applicable to guiding a phoneme onto target, whereas AV conditioning may be especially helpful in refining accuracy, and electrovisual feedback in facilitating bull's-eye production.

Sensory Clues in Speech Development

In speech development and correction with deaf or near-deaf children, particular attention is given to visual or speechreading clues, tactile speech clues, and to tactile and kinesthetic feedback information. Calvert and Silverman (1975) detail the production of each consonant, vowel, and diphthong as well as associated internal feedback information, sensory instructional possibilities, suggestions for development, and common errors and suggestions for improvement. The extent to which this information is applicable to hearing-impaired children in general depends upon the degree and extent to which residual hearing is utilized. Even among hard-of-hearing children, the information is applicable for any sound that cannot be heard. Because the clinician is faced with clients with varying degrees of hearing loss, he should have this information at his fingertips. Similar sources of information on development and correction of deaf speech are those of the Clarke School for the Deaf (Magner, 1972) and the Utah School for the Deaf (Seamons, 1972).

Fletcher and TONAR II

Fletcher (1972) combined electronic, computer, and operant technology in the development of TONAR II. This speech analyzing aid enables the clinician to measure precisely and instrumentally modify nasality, fundamental frequency, and intensity of speech during continuous utterance. An initial TONAR (the oral nasal acoustic ratio) aid was developed to measure and modify nasality. The functional capabilities were expanded in TONAR II to permit diagnosis and treatment of fundamental frequency and intensity.

Equipment Components

The components of TONAR II are a sound separation microphone assembly, a control and display console, a reinforcement display panel, an XY recorder and oscillograph, and a stereo tape recorder. The microphone assembly separates the oral and nasal energies of speech and amplifies them prior to transmission to the control console. The control and display console includes a dual channel wave analyzer system, a

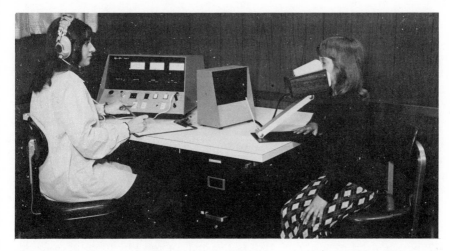

Fig. 41.   Clinician and client using TONAR II. Compliments Quan Tech Industries.

nasality ratio computer, logic and control circuitry for behavioral management, and analog and digital displays to present signal, frequency, and reinforcement information.

Figure 41 shows all components of TONAR II with the exception of the recorders and oscillograph. The client is shown speaking into the sound separation microphone assembly. She can also observe the reinforcement display panel. The clinician operates the controls of the control and display console and records data on a clipboard sheet. This particular staging might be typical of the use of TONAR II for shaping and refining pitch or nasality.

Baseline Readouts

In training, TONAR II is first used to obtain baseline information on the amount of nasality or the pitch levels during a connected speech sample. The client speaks into the oral–nasal sound separator and the instrument provides continuous meter needle displays of oral and nasal output or digital readout of fundamental frequency or pitch. When the oscilloscopic recorder is connected to the system, oral–nasal printouts called "tonagrams" can be obtained, as can amplitude versus frequency graphs. Detailed study of these nasality and frequency readouts enables the clinician to determine the extent and variation of the speech error from moment to moment during continuous utterance. With this information the clinician is better able to design shaping and refinement procedures.

Shaping Features

When the clinician desires to reduce nasality to acceptable amounts, he sets the goal ratio dial of the control panel to an appropriate number between zero and 99. Normal nasal to oral acoustic ratios are between zero and about 20 percent. When speech is so hypernasal that it is essentially unintelligible, the reading may be 100 percent. If the nasal to oral ratio is 40 percent, for example, the goal ratio dial might be set to 38 percent initially. As the client speaks, then, the nasal–oral ratio is computed and compared to 38. If the ratio is equal to or less than 38, the response is a success and a light climbs one step on the reinforcement display panel. Criteria for number of successes are preset and determine when to change the goal ratio dial to a lower percentage. Following this procedure, nasality is systematically reduced within physiological limits. A similar procedure is followed for shaping and refining a pitch that is too high or too low to an acceptable level.

One of the criteria in the design of TONAR II is that the goal ratio be variable in small steps. A variable goal ratio permits success to vary from client to client and from time to time for the same client. Another criterion is the option of success by trial or success by time. In the success by time mode, a success is counted if the goal ratio threshold is crossed at any time. This provision permits the clinician to shape gross errors toward target nasality even though considerable nasality regression occurs. In the success by time mode, TONAR II counts success when the client maintains the nasal–oral acoustic ratio below the goal ratio for selected periods of time. This provision limits the allowable regression and thus maintains improvements that have been achieved. The latter mode may be especially useful in late phases of shaping, refinement, and stabilization.

TONAR II includes a set of criterion level switches that allow the client to vary the schedule of reinforcement. These switches specify the number of consecutive successes needed for making the lights climb on the reinforcement panel. This number can be varied from one to 10.

White, blue, and green lights are positioned on the reinforcement panel. A white light is lit briefly when a spoken response reaches the specified goal ratio level. One of 10 blue lights is lit when the number of successes reaches the number preset on a criterion switch. These 10 lights are positioned diagonally up the panel. If the criterion setting is 2, for example, the blue lights move one space after the white light has blinked twice. When the tenth blue light is lit, one of a series of 10 green lights, serving as decade counters, is triggered. The green lights are positioned along the bottom of the display panel. Together with blue lights, the green lights inform the client of his total successes. Each time a succeeding green light is triggered, the next success is signaled by the first or lower left blue light.

The control and display console of TONAR II also includes four counters: total trials, total successes, criterion trials, and criterion successes. Total reset and separate reset switches permit the clinician to track successes within different criterion settings.

When TONAR II is switched to modify a fundamental frequency or pitch that is too high or too low, the white or success light is similarly triggered. The nasality meter then functions as a sound level meter, and the goal ratio dial specifies an intensity goal. If vocal intensity exceeds the goal ratio, a red warning light is activated on the reinforcement panel. Thus intensity can be controlled while frequency of pitch is shaped and refined. A frequency-raising or lowering switch is also provided. The criterion level switches, the blue and green success lights, and the counters are also used.

The latest version of TONAR, as shown in Figure 41, enables the client to operate the control and display console with ease. The client can also evaluate his progress easily on the reinforcement panel, and with supervision he can be shown how to set his own training goals.

Nasality Data

Fletcher and Daley (1973) utilized TONAR II to gather nasality data on 50 children and young adults at the Alabama School for the Deaf. These students ranged in age from seven to 21 years with a mean of 15.9. The mean hearing loss was 83 dB. A control group of 32 males and 32 females, 7 to 25 years of age with a mean of 13.5, was similarly tested. Fletcher's (1972) zoo passage and a sustained isolated /a/ provided the speech stimuli that were recorded by each subject and played back and processed by TONAR II. The Goldman-Fristoe Speech Articulation Test was also used to determine the articulatory errors of the subjects.

Four nasality percentages were derived from tonagrams of the zoo passage and the /a/ vowel: minimum, maximum, midpoint, and 10-second average. The corresponding mean percentages of the experimental and control groups were 12 and 0, 28 and 0, 20 and 0, and 19 and 6 for the /a/; and 6 and 3, 46 and 18, 26 and 10, and 22 and 8 for the zoo passage. Twenty-two or 44 percent of the hearing-impaired subjects were within normal limits of 15 percent nasality or less while uttering the zoo passage. Sixteen were in the mild hypernasality range of 16 to 30 percent nasality. Twelve had moderate hypernasality of 31 to 45 percent. One hearing-impaired subject exhibited 47 percent nasality and thus was in the moderate to severe hypernasality range. Significant correlations were not found between any of the articulatory classifications and nasality scores for connected speech utterances of the zoo passage. Low negative correlations were found between nasality of the /ɑ/ and errors in sibilants, plosive blends, nasals, and fricative blends.

The TONAR procedure for obtaining objective measures of nasality among the hearing impaired represents an advance in speech technology. Previous investigations among the hearing impaired, based upon perceptual judgments, have reported widely varying data. Colton and Cooker (1968) reported a study in which 26 of 28 adult "deaf" speakers were judged as being more than moderately nasal. In an earlier study of "deaf" speech, Hudgins and Numbers (1942) noted that only 0.8 percent of the vowels of 192 children were judged to be overly nasalized.

Fletcher and Daley (1973) describe at least four different explanations for the excessive nasality of hearing-impaired speakers. One explanation is that such individuals may have difficulty in controlling the velopharyngeal musculature. An alternative is that nasality perceived may be the consequence of reduced speech rate. This perception may be a "halo effect" confusion or a "groping for" correct movement patterns because of incomplete auditory feedback. A third explanation is that the client hypernasalizes in order to hear his own voice. A fourth reason is that refined auditory feedback is absent or is not being utilized to regulate the fine nuances of nasality control. The fourth reason was supported by articulation data from the study. The hearing-impaired subjects misarticulated more than half of the sibilant sounds of the Goldman-Fristoe test. Articulation of sibilant sounds requires rather precise channeling of the air stream through the front of the mouth. The resulting acoustic components include considerable high frequency energies, characteristically difficult for the hearing impaired to hear and particularly to perceive accurately.

Fletcher (1974) notes that when velopharyngeal valving is defective, sound spills into the nose and severely disturbs speech output. The vowels tend to be blurred and the consonants lose their precision and crispness. In addition, certain consonants are frequently omitted or replaced by others that do not require an oral pressure buildup in the mouth. With competing and distracting nasal resonance, verbal communication can be disrupted and personality and behavior deleteriously affected. Consequently, it becomes important to shape and refine the speech of such handicapped individuals to alleviate and even to eliminate hypernasality. TONAR II is particularly suited for such speech remediation. However the cost of the entire system, including training and recording capabilities, is approximately $10,000.

Monitoring Applications

The high cost of TONAR II, the Boothroyd devices, the Holbrook aids, and the Center for Communications Research (CCR) indicators suggests that these sophisticated analyzers may be more useful for monitoring speech remediation than for directly facilitating it. Continuous or periodic monitoring of various parameters of speech can serve to track clinical interaction effectiveness and progress. For example, the Video Articulator and a target format might be utilized for remediation of articulation, pitch, or nasality, whereas the CCR or Boothroyd device and TONAR II might be used to monitor and evaluate progress in shaping and refinement. These data could include baseline information, intervention tracking data, and postintervention information at the end of a 20-week period. Visual graphs could be kept on each tracking parameter. The intervention data could be collected every two weeks.

Continuous instrumental monitoring in the therapeutic management of voice disorders is planned in a project conducted at Utah State University (USU) during 1976 to 1979. Clinical research will be conducted with children and adults with hearing loss, hyperfunctional voice, mental retardation, cleft palate, and dysarthrias. Initial emphasis will be placed upon development of instrumental capability for the generation of voice profiles. Next a measurement package will be developed to monitor continuously the progress of clients during voice therapy. Afterwards voice profiles on the clinical populations will be generated. Finally the findings reached and the technologies achieved will be incorporated into training programs for departmental majors and practicing clinicians. Five data phases are included in the training design: feasibility, pilot, preliminary, replication, and field testing. Additional, materials developed for dissemination will include (1) a general manual of background and instructions, (2) the profile protocol sheets, (3) data collection tables and graphs, and (4) appropriate training tapes and the like. Workshop-skillshop formats will also be developed. Verbal and performance competencies will be specified and appropriate supporting materials will be compiled.

VARP

A Vocal Abuse Reduction Program (VARP) developed by Johnson (1974b) may serve as a model for all intervention programs of the USU project. This program (1) pinpoints vocal abuse behaviors for each client in whom such behaviors have resulted in the formation of laryngeal pathologies, (2) systematically reduces these behaviors in specific high probability situations or time periods, and (3) reduces the size of or eliminates laryngeal pathology, making possible the establishment of normal vocal quality.

The VARP has undergone five years of formative development to combat the specific clinical problems that commonly arise in the remedial process. During the first two years, attempts were made to utilize self-monitoring of the voice problem as a tool in remediation. The final three years were devoted to a series of clinical application studies, resulting in refinements, additions, and modifications of the program concept. Under Johnson's close scrutiny, the clinical studies at USU have demonstrated a success rate of over 95 percent. The program is now being used in many clinic settings throughout the United States. A project by school district clinicians in Montana has just been completed. The success rate with vocal abuse cases exceeded 80 percent (Johnson, 1975).

The VARP program may also be applicable, at least in part, to reduction of the voice problems of hard-of-hearing and especially deaf clients. Calvert and Silverman (1975) indicate that the deaf individual speaks with generalized constriction and tension in both glottal and supraglottal regions. Acoustically, this vocal abnormality is called stridency or harshness. Normally the muscles of articulation and voice production work together with minimal tension. Because the deaf client gropes for feedback and/or places undue emphasis on tactile impressions from the clinician's larynx, his voice is typically strident or harsh. His voice is also typically breathy because of abnormal leakage of air between the vocal folds during vibration or voicing.

Precision Teaching Features

Lindsley (1971) describes features of precision teaching, which underpins the development of the VARP program. He credits Skinner (1953), the developer of operant conditioning, with the innovation of recording frequency of behavior, which he called rate. Lindsley states that every behavior has a frequency and that any two behaviors can be compared on the basis of frequency. He also found that changes in frequency over weeks, called acceleration if positive or deceleration if negative, are universal and easily read from a daily behavior chart. The data for the chart are counted by the client, so there is no problem of observer reliability. The response that is being counted and graphed is the same behavior that is being manipulated or reinforced.

Another feature of the Skinner-Lindsley strategy is that the client is free to behave at any moment. The client is not responding to the trial by trial, or block by block stimuli presented by the clinician. He is, however, keeping track of the number of precise or specific behaviors he is emitting during a given time period. Synthetic or extrinsic consequences are not involved either.

Daily Behavior Chart

Using the counting and charting procedure, Lindsley has discovered that an extrinsic reward may initially accelerate correct responses but later decelerates them. The chart itself, notwithstanding the collection of data, is logarithmically scaled to enable plotting of a considerable number of responses per unit of time. Clients call this feature a *multiply divide scale.* Going up the left of the chart by equal distances is equivalent to multiplying numbers by equal amounts. Going down by equal distances is the same as dividing them by equal factors. The label for these numbers of distances is *movements per minute.* The base of the chart is labeled *successive calendar days,* and there are 140 up and down or day lines. The dark blue lines that go up and down are Sunday lines. Figure 42 illustrates Lindsley's chart. The plot points give examples of how counted data may be converted to the chart.

Since the charts provide feedback to clients, other terminology has been simplified also. The term *pinpoint* refers to the "things" selected for counting in behavior improvement projects. "Things" used for the modification of behavior are simply called *procedures* or *changes.* Conditions are termed *tries,* private events *inner behavior,* public events *outer behavior,* and self-control *personal management.* The four steps to success are *pinpoint, chart daily, change something,* and *try, try again—with love.* Because one chart format can be used universally, the data from all behavior improvement projects can be stored in behavior bank computers.

Johnson (1971) noted that the single most important feature of the Lindsley applications of Skinner's principles is discovering procedures for accurately and reliably measuring behaviors that may need remediation. Traditionally, clinicians and teachers have not utilized precise, continuous monitoring systems in conjunction with remediation. Until recently they have relied on pre- and post-testing or subjective impressions instead.

Figure 43 demonstrates how the Lindsley chart can be utilized to graph the correct and incorrect production of a desirable articulatory, prosodic, or vocal behavior during the training process. The chart shows acceleration and deceleration data for the phoneme /s/, produced in isolation, in monosyllabic words, in polysyllabic words, and in phrases and sentences. The data result from 10-minute probes given during each remedial session (Johnson, 1971).

Diedrich (1973) has developed a program designed to teach a clinician how to utilize the Lindsley chart to record data on progress in speech remediation. Six steps are followed in counting and charting

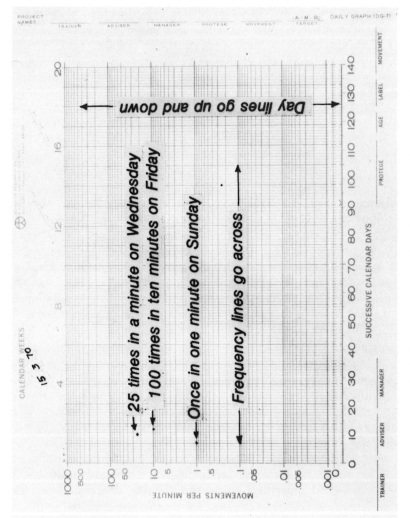

Fig. 42. The daily behavior chart developed by Ogden Lindsley (1971, p 8).

226

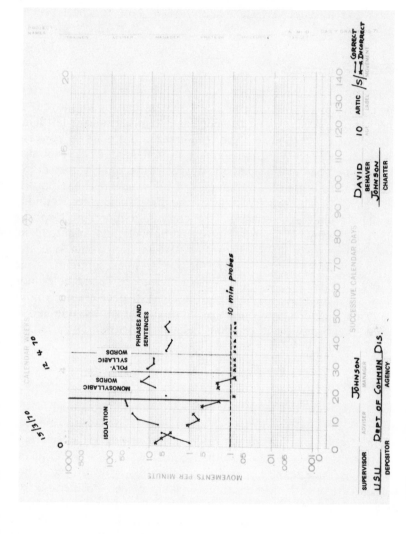

Fig. 43. Charting correct and incorrect phonemes in isolation, words, phrases, and sentences (Johnson, 1971, p 43). Compliments Utah State University, Logan.

target behaviors: (1) Define the critical behaviors to be charted. (2) Define what is to be accepted as right and wrong. (3) Decide the time base. (4) Decide how often the behavior will be charted. (5) Decide by what means the responses will be elicited. (6) Decide in what environment the sample will be taken. Detailed printed materials supplement a 16 mm film and a slide cassette description of how to chart speech behavior.

Counting Responses

In counting behavior a paper can be utilized for tallying correct and incorrect responses, or mechanical counters can be employed. A right-hand counter is suggested for correct responses, and a left-hand counter for incorrect responses. The completed count must be converted from the time sample used into one-minute rates. Correct responses are plotted with dots and joined by a green line, and incorrect responses are plotted with x's and connected by a red line. The floor is drawn in black. It tells the duration of the time sample for counting behavior. The floor line represents one correct or incorrect response during the time sampled. Dashes are placed between plot points to indicate therapy sessions that are missed. When more than one frequency dot is plotted on the chart, the joined lines summarize and evaluate progress or the lack of it. Such lines are called celeration lines. They can accelerate or move up the chart or decelerate or move down the chart. The celeration line should be drawn so that one-half of the plot points are above and one-half below it (Diedrich, 1973; Koorland and Martin, 1975).

Celeration

Celeration or numerical values can be computed to quantify the upward of downward slope of the celeration line. These values indicate how fast the frequencies of correct or incorrect responses are increasing or decreasing each week. When the frequency value is higher at the end of the week than at the beginning, acceleration is occurring. When the values are reversed, deceleration is taking place. Acceleration or deceleration values are computed by dividing the larger frequency by the smaller frequency. A multiplication sign, for example $\times 2$, is placed before the value to indicate acceleration. A division sign, for example $\div 2$, would indicate a deceleration of the same degree. A special tool called a celeration finder has been developed to eliminate hand division (Koorland and Martin, 1975).

It is desirable in counting, plotting, and measuring behavior to track both appropriate and inappropriate responding. For example, information on total behavior in articulating /s/ is available when both correct and incorrect productions are plotted. It is possible to plot additional categories of response as well. For example, off target, gross distortion, fine distortion or close approximation, and bull's-eye productions might be counted, plotted, and measured. A complete glossary of terms related to the Lindsley behavior chart is included in Koorland and Martin's (1975) program or instructional manual describing the system.

TRANSFER AND GENERALIZATION

The precision teaching approach of Lindsley can be used to monitor progress during any stage of speech remediation. This section of the chapter describes transfer or generalization of a desirable speech performance once it has been shaped and refined to an acceptable degree. Such carry-over programming is indispensable to effective interpersonal communication. Often the hearing-impaired client can produce a speech response, for example an /s/ phoneme in a few words or a stress pattern, and not be able to incorporate these features into other contexts.

Currently, the extent to which a shaped response transfers or generalizes into other speech contexts without carry-over programming is not fully documented. Evidence suggests, however, that the amount of carry-over may be minimal. Without transfer training, the hearing-impaired client also finds overall speech work to be less meaningful and functional.

Pure Oralism

The oral philosophy of education of the hearing impaired emphasizes the utilization of speech outside of remedial sessions (Calvert and Silverman, 1975). Once a speech response is acquired, its use is required in all situations during school or after school. In an oral setting the teacher does not limit training or application to specific settings and high probability situations but fosters good speech continually. Once a child has completed school, he is encouraged to seek further education in an environment in which speech is utilized for interpersonal communication. In order to speak well, the graduate is prompted to monitor his utterances carefully and to learn to pronounce new words. There are few data, however, that detail and clarify the effect of this oral approach. In addition, data-based speech technology is just now beginning to be incorporated into special programs for hearing-impaired children. A strong argument can be advanced for implementation of the new speech technology, even within the finest oral schools for the hearing impaired, because the speech of typical graduates of even these programs includes substantial articulatory, prosodic, and vocal errors. These uncorrected errors interfere significantly with interpersonal communication, even when the hearing-impaired person is committed to use of speech rather than signs and finger spelling.

S-Pack

One recent approach to speech transfer programming is the one developed by Mowrer, Baker, and Schutz (1970). The original program, called the S-Pack or S Programmed Articulation Control Kit, is designed to shape the consonant phoneme but particularly to transfer its correct articulation into word, sentence, and story contexts. The entire kit includes 269 verbal and picture stimuli for the /s/ phoneme and to some extent for /z/. It is subdivided into three parts.

The first part of the S-Pack is designed to shape the /s/ in isolation and then to incorporate it into consonant-vowel combinations and into words of sentences. In the second part the previous responses are strengthened, and the /s/ is incorporated into initial, medial, and final positions of polysyllabic words. The /s/ is also included in sentences and the cognate /z/ is introduced. Part three of the program is designed to strengthen the responses of the previous parts and to extend the production of /s/ into the connected speech of stories. Each part requires about 30 minutes to administer, after the /s/ is initially shaped and refined. A criterion test is administered at the termination of each of these subprograms to determine whether the client should pass on to the next part or repeat the same items. On a given criterion test, at least 80 percent of the items must be correct for passing.

During the administration of S-Pack stimuli, the clinician faces the client. A bound set of pages including verbal directions and picture stimuli are utilized. The clinician can read the directions while the client views the picture and/or printed stimuli that incorporate the /s/. Particularly during the initial 20 to 30 shaping items, the clinician provides an audiovisual model for the client to imitate.

Hearing-Impaired Application

The S-Pack has been utilized by Rouzer (1972) to train two hearing-impaired children to articulate the /s/ phoneme. The children met all criteria for completion of the program in fifteen and sixteen 15-

to 20-minute sessions respectively. Rouzer utilized auditory, visual or speechreading, tactile, and video speech clues. At the end of each session she probed progress in transferring correct production from training items to one of three /s/ forms of the 30-item sound production tasks of Shelton and his associates (Elbert, Shelton, and Arndt, 1967; Shelton, Elbert, and Arndt, 1967; Wright, Shelton, and Arndt, 1969).

Sound Production Task

Each of the three /s/ forms of the sound production task includes a different order of the 30 items. The orders shown below includes five different articulatory contexts: isolation, nonsense syllables, monosyllabic words, polysyllabic words, and phrases and sentences. The items are presented by the clinician, using an AV condition, and the client imitates them. The clinician counts the number of correct and incorrect responses. The task provides a sensitive measure of articulatory progress on an imitative level.

1.	/u*s*/	16.	cla*ss*day
2.	mu*st*y	17.	Please brea*the* *s*oftly.
3.	/*s*ae/	18.	He has on a clea*n* *s*uit.
4.	hou*seh*old	19.	pa*ss* *th*at
5.	gla*ss* *z*oo	20.	i*ce* *r*oom
6.	I'm on you*r* *s*ide.	21.	Will he be ho*me* *s*oon?
7.	pla*cem*at	22.	hu*sk*y
8.	mi*ss*ing	23.	/i*s*/
9.	The do*g* *s*its up.	24.	Will you be u*p* *S*unday?
10.	hou*sekn*ife	25.	a*sl*eep
11.	/*s*/	26.	Who took hi*s* *s*eat?
12.	I will ge*t* *s*ome.	27.	I li*ke* *s*oup.
13.	Bo*b* *s*ent me.	28.	The dress is a*ll* *s*ilk.
14.	/*s*a/	29.	I*cew*ater
15.	bu*sb*oy	30.	I lost my re*d* *s*ocks.

(Shelton, Elbert, and Arndt, 1967)

Figure 44 shows the number of correct responses on successive presentation of the three orders of 30 items by Rouzer. The first child progressed from four correct items during the first session to 27 correct /s/ articulations by the end of the sixteenth session. The second child similarly improved in transferring articulation from the S-Pack training items to the Shelton sound production task. He did not articulate any of the transfer items correctly on the first probe. By the end of the fifteenth session, however, he scored correctly with 23 of 30 items.

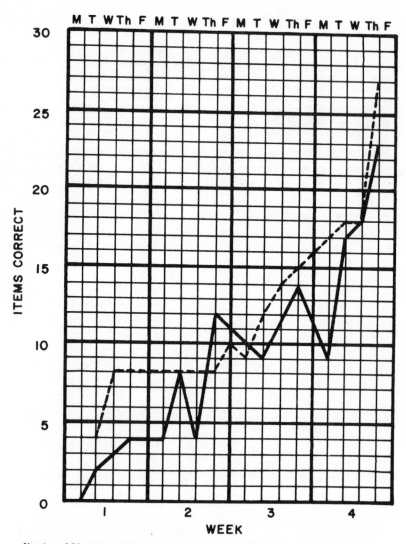

Number of 30-item transfer tasks articulated correctly by each of two hearing impaired children at the end of 15 and 16 training sessions respectively.

Fig. 44. Number of Sound Production Task items articulated correctly by two young hearing-impaired children at the completion of each of 15 and 16 training sessions respectively (Rouzer, 1972, pp 60, 67). Compliments Utah State University, Logan.

Kansas Project

Diedrich (1971) and associates participated in a major project to train speech clinicians to record and analyze articulatory behavior. Twenty clinicians from the greater Kansas City area participated together with staff from the University of Kansas. Specifically, data on /s/ and /r/ error sounds were obtained by means of the Screening Deep Test of Articulation by McDonald (1964), which samples each of nine difficult-to-produce consonants in 10 syllable contexts, the Sound Production Task (SPT) format of Shelton, Elbert, and Arndt (1967), and a three-minute sample of conversation or talk. The SPT included 30 /s/ items and 30 /z/ items, as well as a new set of 60 /r/ items developed by Wright, a member of the project staff. A pool of 320 /s/ children and 280 /r/ children received remediation during the year. Therapy was conducted once or twice a week, or under a block system of four times a week for eight weeks, then no therapy, then resumption of remediation, and so forth.

The McDonald test and the /z/ SPT were administered to all children in September, January, and May. The other tests were given more often and constituted probes of progress. It took 2½ minutes to administer the /s/ items of the SPT and 5 minutes to administer the /r/ items. Data was recorded on IBM porta-punch cards and processed by a computation center. The average time per child taken by a clinician to keep computer records and to chart client progress was 15 minutes. This average was considerably less than the time typically spent in keeping progress logs and checking files.

The computation center printouts provided both individual and group data on the progress of the children receiving /s/ and /r/ remediation. Some clinicians regrouped their children according to similar patterns of learning on the SPT and talk or conversation charts. A series of studies were conducted within the overall project.

Error Type Considerations

Elbert (Diedrich, 1971) studied the effects of remediation on distortion, substitution, and omission errors. Using /s/ and /r/ data from the McDonald test, she noted that fewer than one percent of the errors were omissions. Most of the errors were substitutions, but a significant number were distortions. Elbert discovered that clients did not shift from one category of error to another during remediation. A substitution error, unless remediated, typically remained a substitution error. The same held true for distortions. Elbert concluded that determining whether the /s/ or /r/ was in error was diagnostically more important then identifying the type or error.

Elbert also noted that the clients made considerable progress in correction of error sounds from September to January, and even more by May. A similar control group, who did not receive remediation, showed considerably less improvement during the year. The children were in grades one through six, with an average grade level of 2.3.

Ranking Phoneme Difficulty

Another associate, Wright, (Diedrich, 1971) analyzed the error patterns of the clients in order to determine the effect of context. She ranked the stimuli of the SPT according to the mean number of correct responses made by clients in producing the items. She noted that the /r/ items could be categorized into consonant /r/ stimuli, unstressed vocalic /ɚ/ items, and vocalic /ɝ/ stimuli. Analysis of the means indicated generally that the /r/ items were the easiest to articulate, followed by /ɚ/ and /ɝ/ in that order. Neither these categories of difficulty nor the ranking of the /s/ items altered because of therapy.

Criteria for Termination

A third study conducted by Denes (Diedrich, 1971) is particularly relevant to the topic of transfer and generalization of speech responses. Although remediation is often programmed or sequenced when training is for sounds in isolation or in syllables, words, and phrases or sentences, it is seldom designed systematically into everyday conversation. In the Diedrich project, three-minute conversational samples were recorded in the therapy session, in the classroom, and at home. Fifty-eight children were encouraged individually to talk about topics of interest. Clinicians scored tape recordings of this conversational speech according to correct and incorrect /s/ and /r/ phonemes. No significant differences were observed in mean correct scores when analyzed by age, grade, sex, or speaking condition. Denes concluded that the correct/wrong count for a three-minute conversational sample in the therapy room could be a useful tool in predicting the client's articulation in other settings at school and at home.

Denes also noted that such prediction would not hold true for all children. She admitted that some clients will behave differently and revert to error productions once they leave the therapy session. However these individuals can be identified. Further data suggest that when clients receive therapy for /r/ or /s/ and have maintained correct responses at 70 percent or above for an average of 12 weeks, they are demonstrating that their speech has generalized to the same degree outside of therapy.

A major problem facing the clinician is when to terminate a client from speech remediation. Denes suggested using an SPT score of 28/30 for /s/, 56/60 for /r/, and 70 percent or more correct target productions in two successive, three-minute talk periods. Diedrich (1973) stated that their preliminary data indicated that when 80 percent of public school children, without hearing losses, reach 75 percent correct target responding in conversation, they need no further remediation on those sounds. Similar criteria have not as yet been established for hearing-impaired clients, who typically exhibit a great many more speech errors. In addition, deaf and hard-of-hearing children are subject to speech deterioration when remediation is terminated or when they do not use the oral skills they have developed. We are also well aware that when a person becomes deaf adventitiously, speech remediation should be initiated immediately to limit the amount of vocal disorder that will develop because of lack of auditory feedback.

In spite of these factors, criteria must be developed for termination of speech remediation. Currently, most hearing-impaired children do not receive individualized speech correction after they have completed elementary schooling. In most schools for the deaf, for example, emphasis on language and academic training at the secondary level in place of individualized speech training is considered desirable by school administrators. The development of the newer speech technology and accountability in education may lead to a change in such policy. The task of developing, refining, and transferring speech into life situations for the deaf client is a particular long-range goal of remediation.

Phoneme Kits

The American Book Company at 300 Pike St., Cincinnati, Ohio 45202, publishes speech articulation kits for /s/, /l/, /r/, and /th/. Each kit or program includes material and procedures for up to fifteen 20-minute therapy sessions. Each also includes a school or home program of similar length. The kits are designed to enable clients to produce a target phoneme correctly and consistently in a variety of natural speech situations. The criterion for moving from the initial program to the extension program is 80 percent correct responses on a 36-item test. A type of conversational transfer test is also administered. A client who uses the target phoneme correctly in at least 90 percent of the specified locations in the transfer test has met the criterion for completion of the program. This commercial development follows the Mowrer S-Pack format, with some modifications and improvements, including assessment and recording of progress from session to session.

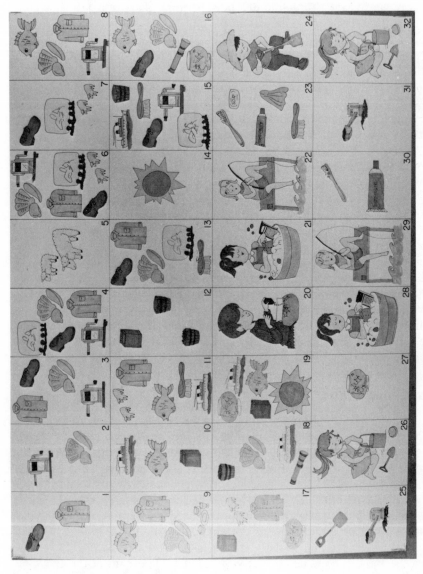

Fig. 45. Picture stimuli for a /ʃ/ kit developed by Snow (1974). Compliments Utah State University, Logan.

Students of the author have developed similar kits designed to shape and extend the production of other phonemes in connected speech contexts. Picture stimuli for a /ʃ/ program developed by Snow (1974) are shown in Figure 45. These pictures are used to elicit speech responses during both the subprogram and the criterion tests. The situational pictures are utilized with the stories.

Iowa Project

Comprehensive articulation programs for 10 phonemes have been developed for aides of speech clinicians in Allamakee, Howard, and Winneshiek counties of Iowa (Lubbert, Johnson, Brenner, et al., 1973). Initial, carry-over, and home program phases are included for /s/, /z/, /ɵ/, /ʝ/, /f/, /ʃ/, /tʃ/, /k/, /r/, and /l/. The use of qualified aides frees the clinicians for other tasks and increases the coverage and depth of the overall program. The aides assist speech cases on an individual basis, 15 minutes per day, three to four times a week. The children are scheduled into three available blocks, each eight to 10 weeks long. During preliminary instruction, the aides are trained in the administration of the Behavior Modification Articulation Program and in improving auditory discrimination competencies.

Terminology

Terminology used by the project staff specifies the features and tasks of the Lubbert program. For example, *establishment* refers to learning the target phoneme and producing it consistently. *Transfer* means learning to use the sound consistently outside the clinic room. During *maintenance* the client learns to produce the target phoneme habitually. *Carry-over* includes steps in which he moves from structured sentences into conversation. When the client fails to meet criteria and misses a certain number of consecutive items, the aide is required to *branch*. A *conversion chart* is included to facilitate the computation of rates or frequency.

Initial Program

In the initial program aides assist clients in producing a target phoneme in a series of steps or contexts: isolation, syllables, words, phrases, and sentences. Criteria are met in moving from one step to the next. To meet the terminal objective the client must respond to 15 pictures, which contain the target phoneme in initial, medial, and final positions. The client must also correctly articulate 24 of 30 sound production items. By this time he is beginning to generalize to other words and should be moved into the carry-over program.

Carry-Over Program

The aide follows additional specific steps in the carry-over program. Five stages are included: reading phrases and sentences, responding to a story, activities with action pictures and conversation, reading combinations of sentences, and conversing outside the clinic. To complete the program the client must produce the target phoneme in 100 percent of the 30 items of the SPT and 95 percent of the time in each of a 30-minute conversation sample and in the three-minute reading sample. If the client meets these criteria, he moves on to the home program.

Home Program

The home program is designed to extend the transfer and maintenance of the target phoneme into the home environment. The target phoneme is incorporated in seven stages: isolation, syllables, words and syllables, sentences, reading, structured conversation, and regular conversation. In each of 19 steps, an activity is continued until a criterion is reached. For example, the child must produce 30 consecutive correct responses in saying the words of 15 pictures. By the end of the program, he must correctly articulate the target phoneme in five-minute talks for three consecutive days.

Reinforcement

Three schedules of reinforcement are utilized in the Lubbert program. One is 100 percent, or a reinforcer after every response. The second is 50 percent, or a reinforcer for two consecutive correct articulations. The third schedule is 10 percent, or a reinforcer after 10 consecutive correct responses. Token reinforcers and social reinforcers are also provided. Within each of the subprograms, the steps specify each schedule of reinforcement to be used. Initially, 100 percent reinforcement is provided. Later, steps often specify 50 percent. By the end of each subprogram, the schedule of reinforcement is 10 percent.

Recording and Charting

The aides also record and chart data. A daily information sheet provides space for up to 900 responses. This record-keeping includes identifying information, dates, the time therapy begins and ends, total time, the initial step, the step number for the next session, total number of responses divided by total number of errors, and response rate and error rate. On another recording sheet, each correct and reinforced response is marked with X, each correct unreinforced response with /, and each incorrect response with O. Lindsley charts and accompanying forms are also kept on each client.

The appendices of the Lubbert program include stimulus words and a story for each target phoneme. Similarly, they include phrase lists, sentence lists, and SPT stimuli. Data on project clients include grade, number of children, total time, sessions, total responses, errors, and correct articulations.

Nevada Project

Speech aides are also utilized by Bokelmann (1973) and her associates in the Clark County School District of Las Vegas, Nevada. A training aide manual (Wallace, 1972–1973) and six instructional material manuals have been developed for teaching the TH sound, the L sound, the S and Z sounds, the SH and ZH sounds, the CH and J sounds, and the R sound. Each program is designed to transfer correct production of a target phoneme from the therapy room to the principal's office in 15 steps. The training aide is the primary facilitator in this transfer.

The training aide manual details procedures for the preparation of the overall program. It also specifies steps for recruiting prospective aides and for selecting volunteers. An outline of an introductory lecture for aides is also provided. Then the manual describes training in discriminating or identifying the target sounds and in using the transfer programs. An outline for observation and supervision is also presented. The final and major portion of the manual includes several levels of stimulus material to help training aides discriminate target phonemes from error sounds; these levels are isolation, words, phrases, unrelated sentences, and related sentences. Behavioral goals and accompanying procedures are also discussed.

The criterion for introduction into a transfer program is correct production of the target or corrected sound in a five-minute conversational speech sample structured in the therapy room. During the program itself, the client must correctly produce 48 of 50 items before progressing to the next of the 15 steps. If he fails on more than two items, he is referred back to the speech clinician for further preliminary training.

Table 20

Bokelmann Transfer Program for the /r/ Phoneme

Step	Setting	Personnel	Activities
1	Therapy room	Aide, therapist	Name, fill in, make up
2	Therapy room	Aide	Name, answer
3	Therapy room	Aide, adult, or peer	Answer, fill in, tell story, repeat
4	Therapy room, quiet outside setting	Aide, one person	Tell me about picture, say, repeat, make up
5	Therapy room	Aide, one peer	Answer, fill in, tell story, say from memory
6	Therapy room, quiet outside setting	Aide, two peers	Tell story, answer, say, name pictures
7	Quiet outside setting	Aide	Name picture, make up sentence, answer, say from memory
8	Therapy room, hallway	Aide	Say, answer, make up story, complete story
9	Therapy room, classroom	Aide, teacher, therapist	Fill in, tell story, say
10	Busy outside area	Aide	Answer, say word and make up sentences from pictures, name
11	Busy outside area	Aide	Repeat words and evaluate, answer, fill in, tell story
12	Therapy room	Aide, five peers	Tell story, choose student to repeat, repeat
13	Classroom	Aide, teacher, classmates, therapist	Tell story
14	Therapy room, office	Aide, office staff or adult	Tell stories, reproduce words from stories
15	Principal's office	Aide, principal, therapist	Tell story, repeat words

Generalization Format

Table 20 outlines the steps, settings, personnel, and activities for one of these transfer or generalization programs. It can be seen that the client generally progresses from speech activities in the therapy room to a quiet outside setting and hallway. Afterwards the setting is a classroom and a busy outside area. Finally the client is in the school office and then the office of the principal, who awards a certificate of program completion. The aide is always present, whatever the setting. The therapist or clinician, the classroom teacher, the peers, the classmates, the office staff or an adult, and the principal also interact at various points of the program. The general format of activities include (1) naming pictures, (2) making up sentences, (3) recalling pictures, (4) telling stories, and (5) answering questions.

In each of the instructional materials manuals, preliminary instructions are outlined for the speech clinician. The clinician is informed that the program is structured to fade reinforcement. Two tangible reinforcers are provided. The clinician decides if additional reinforcers are needed and provides a two- or three-item menu of activities. Clients exchange reinforcers for items from this menu. A scoring sheet records correct (+) and incorrect (0) responses for each step. Retention tasks are also administered weekly for one month after completion of the program, and for six weeks after completion of the transfer program. Such a task requires utterance of the target phoneme in five to 10 words of a spontaneous speech sample. This sample is derived from a conversation between three to five students who have been dismissed as clients.

The transfer programs of Bokelmann and her associates were utilized by 95 speech aides and over 1000 students in speech therapy during the 1972–1973 school year (Bokelmann, 1973). The students were formerly in the case loads of practicing clinicians in the Clark country school district. The utilization of lay personnel as speech aides seems particularly appropriate at this stage of speech remediation. Such programming should also be beneficial to hearing-impaired children who are enrolled in the regular schools or in special schools and classes.

McLean Transfer Format

During the past decade McLean (1967) has developed a program for transferring correct articulation from one stimulus condition to another. The clinician presents 10 words containing the target phoneme under each condition. First they are presented in echoic condition, then as pictures, then as print, and finally as words used to complete printed sentences. The words are presented under each condition until a criterion is reached. The target phoneme appears initially in each word. For example, the target phoneme might be /tʃ/, and the ten words might be *chair, check, cheek, cheese, cherry, child, chimney, chin, chip,* and *chocolate* (White, 1972).

Stimulus Conditions

During the echoic condition the clinician says a word and the client repeats it. Each of the 10 words is said so that the client can look and listen before he responds. The clinician records the number of correct responses on each series or block of 10 words. When the client responds correctly 50 percent of the time during four successive blocks, he is ready for the picture condition.

The clinician then presents pictures of the 10 words, one by one. First he also says the words, so that the client can view the picture and look for speechreading clues and listen for auditory clues. When he responds correctly to each word two consecutive times, the echoic condition is withdrawn. The clinician then presents the pictures again but does not say them. The client says what they are. When he achieves 38 of 40 correct responses, he moves to the graphemic condition.

The graphemic condition first employs the words in print and as pictures. The client must be able to respond to this combined condition without making errors during presentation of 20 consecutive items —twice for each of the 10 words. When this criterion is reached, the 10 words in print are presented one by one, without the pictures. A criterion of 38 of 40 correct responses must be met before the graphemic condition is completed.

During the final or intraverbal condition, the clinician presents a series of 10 incomplete sentences to the client. These sentences are printed so that the final words are missing. Each final word is one of the 10 target words. In this intraverbal condition, the graphemes are first presented with the printed words and the incomplete sentences. The client must respond to this combined presentation of 10 words by articulating the target phoneme correctly 20 consecutive times. Meeting this criterion, the client then responds to the same stimuli under the intraverbal condition only. He sees the first words of the sentences in print and completes them orally. This condition is completed when the client responds correctly 38 of 40 times.

White Experiment

In brief, the four conditions are echoic or S^1; echoic-picture or S^1S^2 and picture or S^2; picture-graphemic or S^2S^3 and graphemic or S^3; graphemic-intraverbal or S^3S^4 and intraverbal or S^4. In simplified form, the conditions are S^1, S^2, S^3, and S^4.

Figure 46 presents data on a fourth grade boy who learned to articulate the /tʃ/ phoneme in 10 words of the McLean program. He required 30 blocks to complete the program. Each block was one presentation of the 10 target words (White, 1972). The criteria he had to meet in moving from one condition to the next are also indicated. The boy had a severe to profound bilateral hearing loss.

Before the program the subject typically substituted the /ʃ/ phoneme for the /tʃ/ phoneme. However he could articulate the /tʃ/ in isolation and in some words. By the end of the program he was articulating the /tʃ/ consistently in all target words. The data of Figure 46 in chapter 6 show that once the boy articulated the /tʃ/ consistently under the echoic condition, correct responding transferred quickly to the picture, graphemic, and intraverbal conditions.

Guarding Against Overgeneralization

Before this single subject experiment was conducted, White was concerned that the boy might overgeneralize in using the /tʃ/ phoneme. Whereas the boy had been substituting /ʃ/ for /tʃ/, White predicted that after training he might substitute /tʃ/ for /ʃ/. Therefore he designed his experiment to guard against overgeneralization. Specifically, he included two /ʃ/ words with the 10 /tʃ/ words during all training blocks. By doing this, White prompted the boy to discriminate continually between the target and the substituted phoneme as he moved through the program.

Immediately after the boy had met the final criterion, White presented 15 additional words. Five words included the /tʃ/ in the initial position, and five words ended with the /tʃ/ phoneme. The other five words included the /ʃ/ in the initial position. These words were *chain, chalk, chart, chest, chick; catch, hatch, latch, patch, watch;* and *shark, sharp, ship, shoot,* and *shower.* These three series were used to measure new item generalization, across-position generalization, and overgeneralization respectively. White's subject responded correctly to all of these items during both the post-test and a retention test given a week later. White later became the boy's teacher. He noted that the target phoneme generalized also to other /tʃ/ words. It is interesting however, that at least on one occasion the boy substituted /ʃ/ for /tʃ/

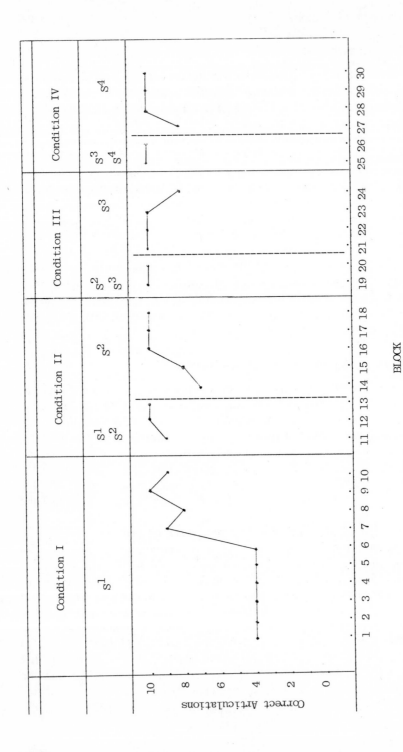

Fig. 46. Number of correct /tʃ/ articulations produced by a hearing-impaired boy during each of 30 training blocks (White, 1972, p 35). Compliments Utah State University, Logan.

when a different teacher was present. This occasional substitution suggests that further generalization training was perhaps necessary. One approach to providing such training is the Bokelmann program, which was described in a preceding section of this chapter.

White's training program lasted three to four hours. Half-hour sessions were conducted on consecutive weekdays. The generalization tests were conducted one day and then one week afterwards. Throughout training, each correct response was immediately reinforced by presentation of a poker chip in a shallow box. At the end of each training session, the boy redeemed poker chips for money. One penny was given for every five poker chips.

Rationale for Format

The rationale for the McLean format used by White can be clarified. Once a response becomes functional under a wide range of stimulus conditions, it generalizes to similar conditions outside of therapy. McLean's (1967, 1970) initial studies with his format successfully used mentally retarded children as subjects. Later McLean and Raymore (1972) utilized the program for normal-learning public school children. Many speech clinicians in selected school districts have found the program valuable, especially for substitution errors. Often they have omitted the combined conditions.

Programs on Notecards

The author utilizes a series of 51 notecards to present the stimuli of a McLean program. Thirty-six notecards include 10 target words and two substituted words, each in picture, graphemic, and intraverbal conditions. The other 15 notecards present the three types of generalization items. These latter items can be presented as pictures or as printed words. Twelve programs have been developed. Each includes items for a substitution common in the speech of the hearing impaired. Some of the substituted sounds are rather unique to this population, particularly voice–voiceless distinctions. One program, for example, is designed to eliminate the s/z substitution.

Similar sets of cards could be developed for each phoneme. They would not necessarily have to be used for substitution applications. Each set could provide simply the stimuli for the incorporation of a target phoneme into 10 words and four stimulus conditions. A set would be used once a target phoneme is shaped, refined, and stabilized in isolation, in syllables, and in a few words. A criterion would have to be established for moving from the initial program into a McLean program. Sets of cards could incorporate target phonemes in initial, final, and medial positions of words.

Currently, much of the stimulus material for speech remediation exists as pictures that are not incorporated into specific programs. Two companies producing such materials are Modern Education Corporation of Tulsa, Oklahoma, and Word Making Productions of Salt Lake City, Utah. Many school and clinic centers have extensive collections of commercial and homemade pictures. They comprise a rich source of stimuli for the development of specific speech programs. Copyright laws prevent exact duplication of these pictures. However the pictures can provide easily accessible referents for the development of further stimuli needed in modern speech technology. New graphic, photographic, and duplication techniques facilitate such development. Instructional media specialists are being trained to provide professional assistance to teachers and clinicians faced with the task of program development.

Fading Experiment

Another consideration in presentation of a McLean program is whether or not to utilize the fading of stimuli in paired conditions. Fading can be defined as the gradual removal of discriminative stimuli, such as prompts and cues. Evidence shows that it facilitates errorless transfer from a learned situation or condition to an unlearned task (Sidman and Stoddard, 1967).

Stokes (1974) designed a case study experiment to determine the effects of fading upon the learning of correct articulation by two hearing-impaired children. One subject was a seven-year-old girl with a 98 dB loss in the better ear. She responded to the Templin-Darley Test of Articulation by misarticulating 83 of 141 items. Analysis of the errors revealed 44 omissions, 23 substitutions, one addition, and 15 distortions. The most consistent substitution appeared to be k/t in the initial position of words. Her expressive vocabulary was estimated to include at least 600 words.

The other subject was an eight-year-old boy with a 73 dB bilateral hearing loss. He made 66 errors out of 141 items on the Templin-Darley test. The errors included 42 omissions, 18 substitutions, one addition, and five distortions. A frequent substitution was t/s or ts/s.

Two McLean programs were developed by Stokes. A /t/ program with additional /k/ items was selected for the girl. An /s/ program with both /t/ and /ts/ stimuli was developed for the boy.

Fading with First Subject

Each of the two subjects proceeded through the same type of McLean program that White's subject had undergone: S^1; S^1S^2 and S^2; S^2S^3 and S^3; S^3S^4 and S^4. With the first subject, fading was utilized during each of the S^1S^2, S^2S^3, and S^3S^4 conditions. As described previously, the criterion for each of these combined conditions was 20 of 20 items correct within two consecutive blocks of 10 target words each.

Figure 47 clarifies the fading used by Stokes with her first subject. It can be seen that specific blocks included 20 percent, 40 percent, 60 percent, 80 percent, and 100 percent fading. For these blocks, 2 of 10, 4 of 10, 6 of 10, 8 of 10, and 10 of 10 words, respectively, did not include the carry-over condition. For example, when 20 percent fading occurred during Condition IIa, the S^1S^2 condition was used for 8 of 10 words and pictures or the S^2 condition was used for only two words. The same percentage of fading was employed, block by block, until the two faded words were articulated correctly. The same procedure was followed to determine discontinuation of 40 percent, 60 percent, and 80 percent fading.

The data of Figure 47 reveal that the seven-year-old girl completed the /t/ program in 75 blocks. Nearly half of these blocks were used during the S^1S^2 condition. Relatively fewer blocks were required for completion of the program.

Fading with Second Subject

Figure 47 also shows data for the second subject. It can be seen that Stokes did not introduce fading with the eight-year-old boy until block 45. This was the point in a combined condition at which he had arrived at the same performance as the first subject. Fading was then utilized in the same way it had been used for the girl. It is of interest that fading was primarily used in Condition IIa. During S^2S^3 the second subject required fewer blocks than the girl. Therefore fading was not used. During S^3S^4 only 20 percent fading was used. Soon afterwards, the boy met the criterion. The second subject met the final criterion on block 101. Comparison of data between the two graphs indicates that fading seemed to be an effective operant conditioning technique for assisting these two hearing-impaired children to develop correct articulation of phonemes.

Implications and Designs

Both the White (1972) and Stokes (1974) investigations indicated that once a high stable level of correct responding under one stimulus

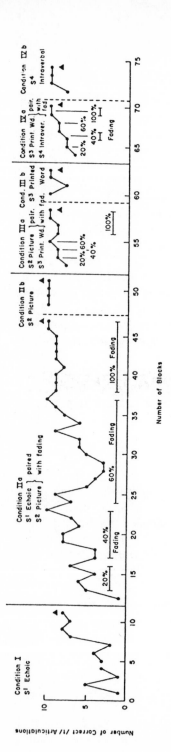
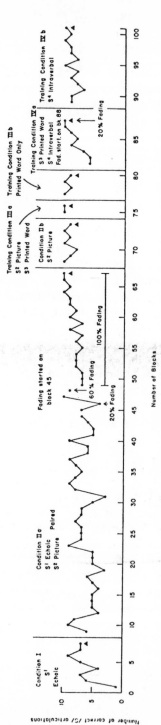

Fig. 47. Comparison of progress of two hearing-impaired children during a modified McLean-White transfer program incorporating fading. The first child was learning to articulate /t/ with fading. The second was learning to articulate /s/ with fading only when he fell behind the first child. Compliments Utah State University, Logan. (Stokes, 1974, pp 62, 71).

condition was reached, this level of performance tended to be transferred to the remaining stimulus conditions. It may be hypothesized, however, that a higher criterion should have been employed for the echoic or first condition. McLean (1967) designed a 50 percent criterion into this initial stage of the program. White's subject, however, achieved a 90 percent level during four consecutive blocks of Condition I. Perhaps because of reaching a high correct response in Condition I, his 11-year-old boy required only 30 blocks to complete the program. In contrast, Stokes's subjects reached only a 70–75 percent correct response rate at the same point of the training program. They required 75 and 101 blocks—considerably more time.

Additional designs for speech training are also now available to the teacher or clinician. For example, Irwin and Weston (1971) have developed a paired stimuli technique of articulatory modification that facilitates the process of moving from a correctly produced word to a string of incorrectly articulated words. The communicative disorders specialist must study out this advancing technology and employ the techniques that contribute to effective speech remediation. A new book by Winitz (1975) entitled *From Syllable to Conversation* exemplifies the advancing knowledge in theory and clinical applications.

SUMMARY

This chapter on the new speech technology details procedures for evaluation, experiments in perceptual learning, features of shaping and refinement including the utilization of electrovisual analyzing aids, the monitoring of progress, and programs of transfer and generalization. Particular focus has been given to the evaluation, design, and implementation of procedures for articulatory remediation. Emphasis, however, has also been placed upon similar technology with prosodic and voice parameters of speech.

REFERENCES

Berg F: Serial Learning: An Approach to a Rationale for Auditory Training. PhD Dissertation. Carbondale, Southern Illinois University, 1960

Berg F: Serial learning: An approach to a rationale for auditory training. Report on the Proceedings of the International Congress on Education of the Deaf and of the 41st Meeting of the Convention of American Instructors of the Deaf. Washington, DC, Gallaudet College, 1963, pp 946–954

Berg F: Educational audiology, in Berg F, Fletcher S (eds): The Hard of Hearing Child. New York and London, Grune & Stratton, 1970, pp 275–318

Berg F: Sensory Aids in Speech Remediation for the Hearing Impaired. Logan, Utah State University, 1972

Berg F: Acceptance of the Video Articulator. Logan, Utah State University, 1974

Berg F: Educational audiology. Aud Hear Educ 1:24–25, 28, 58, 1975

Berg F: Educational audiology, in Bradford L (ed): Audiology: An Audio Journal for Continuing Education. New York, Grune & Stratton, 1:7, 1976

Bokelmann D: Training Aides to Administer Transfer Programs and Discrimination Booklet. Las Vegas, Clark County School District, 1973

Boothroyd A: Personal communication. Northampton, Massachusetts, Clarke School for the Deaf, November 9, 1972

Boothroyd A: Some experiments on the control of voice in the profoundly deaf using a pitch extractor and storage oscilloscope display. IEEE Trans Aud Electroac 21: 274–278, 1973

Boothroyd A: Theoretical aspects of auditory training. Proceedings of International Conference on Oral Education of the Deaf, Vol 1. Washington, DC, AG Bell Assn Deaf, pp 705–729, 1967

Boothroyd A, Archambault P, Adams R, et al: Use of a computer based system of speech training aids for deaf persons. Vol Rev 77:178–193, 1975

Calvert D, Silverman SR: Speech and Deafness. Washington, DC, AG Bell Assn Deaf, 1975

Chomsky N, Halle M: The sound pattern of English. New York, Harper and Row, 1968

Colton R, Cooker H: Perceived nasality in the speech of the deaf. J Speech Hear Res 11:553–559, 1968

Daley M, Wolff P: A functional analysis of behavior, in Berg F, Fletcher S (eds): The Hard of Hearing Child. New York and London, Grune & Stratton, 1970, pp 125–153

Denes P, Pinson E: The speech chain. Murray Hill, N.J., Bell Telephone Labs, 1963

DiCarlo L: Some relationships between frequency discrimination and speech reception performance. J Audiol Res 2:47–59, 1962

Diedrich W: Training Speech Clinicians in the Recording and Analysis of Articulatory Behavior. Year II Summary. OEG 261293 3402 (031). Kansas City, University of Kansas Medical Center, 1971

Diedrich W: Charting Speech Behavior. Kansas City, University of Kansas Medical Center, 1973

Elbert M, Shelton R, Arndt W: A task for evaluation of articulation change. I. Development of methodology. J Speech Hear Res 10:281–288, 1967

Fairbanks G: Voice and Articulation Drillbook. New York, Harper & Row, 1960

Faircloth S, Faircloth M: Phonetic Science. A Program of Instruction. Englewood Cliffs, New Jersey, Prentice Hall, 1973

Fletcher S: Tonar II: An instrument for use in management of nasality. Ala J Med Sci 9:333–338, 1972

Fletcher S: Detection, Measurement, and Modification of Nasality. Whippany, New Jersey, KMS Industries, 1974

Fletcher S, Daley D: Nasality in Utterances of Deaf Speakers. Birmingham, University of Alabama, 1973

French N, Steinberg J: Factors governing the intelligibility of speech sounds. J Acoust Soc Am 19:90–119, 1947

Gaeth J: Verbal Learning Among Children with Reduced Auditory Acuity. Office of Education Project 289. Final Report. Detroit, Wayne State University, 1960

Gaeth J: Verbal and Nonverbal Learning in Children Including Those with Hearing Loss. Office of Education Cooperative Research Project 1001. Detroit, Wayne State University, 1963

Gaeth J: Verbal and Nonverbal Learning in Children Including Those with Hearing
   Loss. Part II. Office of Education Project 2207. Detroit, Wayne State University,
   1966
Gaeth J: Management of the Hard of Hearing Child. Workshop. Salt Lake City, Utah
   Speech and Hearing Association, 1971
Gardner J: Evaluation of preschool children through radio telemetry. J Speech Hear
   Disord 33:48–50, 1973
Goldman R, Fristoe M: Goldman-Fristoe Test of Articulation. Examiner's Manual. Cir-
   cle Pines, Minnesota, American Guidance Service, 1972
Goldstein M: The Acoustic Method for the Training of the Deaf and Hard of Hearing
   Child. St. Louis, Laryngoscope Press, 1939
Holbrook A: Modification of speech behavior with preschool deaf children by means of
   spectrum control. AOEHI Bull 1, No. 3, 1970
Holbrook A: A teaching machine approach to speech problems. Res Rev Flor St U 3:
   1–4, 1972
Holbrook A, Crawford G: Modifications of vocal frequency and intensity in the speech
   of the deaf. Vol Rev 72:492–497, 1970
Hoshiko M, Holloway G: Radio telemetry for the monitoring of verbal behavior. J
   Speech Hear Disord 33:48–50, 1968
Houde R: Instantaneous Visual Feedback in Speech Training for the Deaf. Detroit,
   Convention of American Speech and Hearing Association, 1973
Houde R, Stewart L, Larkin W: Speech Training for the Deaf with a Real Time Speech
   Spectrographic Display. Scientific Exhibit. Washington, DC, American Speech and
   Hearing Association Convention, 1975
Hudgins C, Numbers R: An investigation of the intelligibility of the speech of the deaf.
   Genet Psychol Monogr 25:289–392, 1942
Irwin O: Infant speech: Variability and the problem of diagnosis. J Speech Hear Disord
   12:287–289, 1947
Irwin J, Weston A: Manual for the Clinicial Utilization of the Paired Stimuli Technique,
   Articulatory Modification. Memphis, Tennessee, National Educator Services, 1971
Jacobson R, Fant G, Halle M: Preliminaries to Speech Analysis. Cambridge, Massachu-
   setts, MIT Press, 1952
James V: Informational letter. Witchita, Kansas, Institute of Logopedics, September 19,
   1975
Johnson T: Precision therapy is the way to go, in Jordan J, Robbins L (eds): Let's Try
   Doing Something Else Kind of Thing. Arlington, Virginia, The Council for Excep-
   tional Children, 1971
Johnson T: A Precision Approach to Hyperfunctional Voice Disorders. Logan, Utah
   State University, 1974a
Johnson T: Vocal Abuse Reduction Program. Logan, Utah State University, 1974b
Johnson T: Vocal Abuse Reduction Program. A Montana Pilot Project for the Manage-
   ment of Children's Voice Disorders. Helena, Montana, Office of Superintendent of
   Public Instruction, 1975
Koorland M, Martin M: Elementary Principles and Procedures of the Standard Behavior
   Chart. Gainesville, Florida, Learning Environments, 1975
Kopp G, Kopp H: Visible Speech for the Deaf. Final Report. Social and Rehabilitation
   Services RD 526. Detroit, Wayne State University, 1963
Lewis M: Infant Speech: A Study of the Beginnings of Language. New York, Human-
   ities Press, 1951
Lieberman P: Intonation, Perception, and Language. Research Monograph No. 38.
   Cambridge, Massachusetts, MIT Press, 1967

Lindsley O: From Skinner to precision teaching; the child knows best, in Jordan J, Robbins L (eds): Let's Try Doing Something Else Kind of Thing. Arlington, Virginia, the Council for Exceptional Children, 1971

Ling D: Amplification for speech, in Calvert D, Silverman SR (eds): Speech and Deafness. Washington, DC, AG Bell Assn Deaf, 1975

Ling D, Bennett C: Training severely hearing impaired children in vowel imitation. Hum Communication, Winter, pp 5–18, 1974–1975

Longhurst T, Grubb S: A comparison of language samples collected in four situations. Language, Speech, and Hearing Services in Schools 5:71–77, 1974

Lubbert L, Johnson K, Brenner C, et al: Behavior Modification Articulation Program. Decorah, Iowa, Joint County School System of Allamakee, Howard, and Winneshiek Counties, 1973

McCroskey R: Summary of the Perdoncini Method Research Project. Wichita, Kansas, Wichita State University, 1975

McDonald E: Articulation Testing and Treatment: A Sensory Motor Approach. Pittsburgh, Stanwix House, 1964

McGinnis M: Aphasic Children. Identification and Education by the Association Method. Washington, DC, AG Bell Assn Deaf, 1963

McLean J: Shifting Stimulus Control of Articulation Responses by Operant Techniques. Parsons Demonstration Project. Report No. 82. Lawrence, Kansas, Parsons Research Center, 1967

McLean J: Extending stimulus control of phoneme articulation by operant techniques. Am Speech Hear Assoc Monogr No. 14, pp 24–27, 1970

McLean J, Raymore S: Programmatic Research on a Systematic Articulation Therapy Program: Carryover of Phoneme Responses to Untrained Situations for Normal Learning Public School Children. Lawrence, Kansas, Kansas Center for Research in Mental Retardation and Human Development, 1972

McReynolds L, Engmann D: Distinctive Feature Analysis of Misarticulations. Baltimore, University Park Press, 1975

Magner M: Speech Development. Northampton, Massachusetts, Clarke School for the Deaf, 1971

Magner M: A Speech Intelligibility Test for Deaf Children. Northampton, Massachusetts, Clarke School for the Deaf, 1972

Mowrer D: Working Papers on the Management of Articulation. Tempe, Arizona State University, 1969

Mowrer D: Shaping the /ɝ/. Video Tape Demonstration. Tempe, Arizona State University, 1973

Mowrer D, Baker R, Schutz R: Modification of the Frontal Lisp Programmed Articulation Control Kit. Palos Verdes Estates, California, Educational Psychological Research Associates, 1970

Nickerson R: Characteristics of the speech of deaf persons. Vol Rev 77:342–362, 1975

Pickett J, Constam A: A visual speech trainer with simplified indication of vowel spectrum. Am Ann Deaf 113:253–258, 1968

Pike K: The Intonation of American English. Ann Arbor, University of Michigan Press, 1945

Potter R, Kopp G, Green H: Visible Speech. New York, Dover, 1966

Prescott R: Auditory Patterning Abilities of Young Hearing Impaired Children. Convention of the Alexander Graham Bell Association for the Deaf. Chicago, Illinois, June 30, 1972

Prescott R, Turtz M: Auditory Pattern Recognition by Young Hearing Impaired Children. Washington, DC, Federal City College, 1974

Pronovost W, Yenkin D, Anderson D, et al: The voice visualizer. Am Ann Deaf 113:230–238, 1968

Risberg A: Visual aids for speech correction. Am Ann Deaf 113:178–194, 1968

Ross M: Personal Communication. Longmeadow, Massachusetts, Willie Ross School for the Deaf, November 9, 1972

Rouzer J: Use of the Video Articulator in a Speech Correction Program for the Hearing Impaired. MS Thesis. Logan, Utah State University, 1972

Rowe L: The speech model. Vol Rev 76:107–112, 1974

Sanders D: Auditory Perception of Speech. Englewood Cliffs, New Jersey, Prentice Hall, 1977

Seamons B: Speech Curriculum. Ogden, Utah School for the Deaf, 1972

Shelton R, Elbert M, Arndt W: A task for evaluation of articulation change. II. Comparison of task scores during baseline and lesson series testing. J Speech Hear Res 10:549–557, 1967

Sidman M, Stoddard L: The effectiveness of fading in programming a simultaneous form discrimination for retarded children. J Exp Anal Behav 10:3–15, 1967

Singh S: Distinctive Features: Theory and Validation. Baltimore, University Park Press, 1976

Skinner BF: Science and Human Behavior. New York, Macmillan, 1953

Snow P: SH Kit. Logan, Utah State University, 1974

Snow P: A Comparison of Speaking Abilities and Lipreading Abilities in Hearing Impaired Children. MS Thesis. Logan, Utah State University, 1974

Special Education Catalog. Tulsa, Oklahoma, Modern Education, 1974

Stark R: The use of real time visual displays of speech in the training of a profoundly deaf, nonspeaking child: A case report. J Speech Hear Disord 36:397–409, 1971

Stetson R: Motor Phonetics. Amsterdam, North Holland Publishing, 1951

Stewart L, Houde R, Larkin W: The VSTA: An Approach to the Speech Training Problem. Record of Carhahan Conference on Electronic Prosthetics. Lexington, Kentucky, 1973 pp 10–14

Stewart R: By ear alone. Am Ann Deaf 113:147–155, 1968

Stokes A: The Correction of Phoneme Misarticulation by Stimulus Fading Procedures with the Hearing Impaired. MS Thesis. Logan, Utah State University, 1974

Stokes A: Speech Shaping of Young Hearing Impaired Children. Logan, Utah State University, 1974

Strong W: Speech aids for the profoundly/severely hearing impaired: Requirements, overview, and projections. Vol Rev 77:536–556, 1975

SWRL Speech Articulation Kits Sampler. Cincinnati, Ohio, American Book Company, 1974

Templin: Certain language skills in children. Institute of Child Welfare Monograph No. 26. Minneapolis, University of Minnesota Press, 1957

Templin M, Darley R: The Templin-Darley Tests of Articulation (ed 2). Iowa City, University of Iowa, 1969

Wallace E: Training Aids to Administer Transfer Programs and Discrimination Training Booklet. Las Vegas, Clark County School District, 1972–1973

White W: Stimulus Manipulation in Articulation Therapy with a Hearing Impaired Child. MS Thesis, Logan, Utah State University, 1972

Winitz H: From Syllable to Conversation. Baltimore, University Park Press, 1975

Woodward H: Intonation and the teaching of speech. Proceedings of International Conference on Oral Education of the Deaf. Washington, DC, AG Bell Assn Deaf, 1967, pp 886–907

A World of Words. Salt Lake City, Word Making Productions, 1975

Wright V, Shelton R, Arndt W: A task for evaluation of articulation change. III. Imitative task scores compared with scores for more spontaneous tasks. J Speech Hear Res 12:875–884, 1969

7

Technology in Listening Training

During the past decade innovations in learning and instruction have begun to have impact upon listening training for hearing-impaired clients. These technological advances include stimulus control and programmed conditioning, specification of behavior objectives, prescriptive training, self-instruction, and self-monitoring in high probability situations. Basic to these innovative advances are the concepts and processes of behavioral engineering and instructional technology. Even more basic is the development and refinement of the fundamental principles of a branch of psychology called operant conditioning.

Basic Considerations

Skinner (1953) can be credited with describing the parameters of operant conditioning. He viewed operant conditioning as the relationship between stimulus, response, and consequence. The three-term contingency he developed is symbolized as S^D—R—S^r. S^D is the discriminative stimulus which occasions or prompts the response, R is the response, and S^r is the reinforcing stimulus which immediately follows the response. When positive reinforcement is given, the frequency of the response increases. If negative reinforcement is provided instead, the frequency of response will decrease. Neutral reinforcement will result in no change of response rate or probability. Thus the consequent event contributes to acceleration or deceleration of response.

The antecedent event also determines the response rate. The manipulation of the antecedent event is called stimulus control. When the stimulus is varied, the probability of a desirable or undesirable response can change. The term *behavioral engineering* refers to arranging the environment so that desirable responses are achieved. It is a blend of two technologies: the control of events immediately preceding the response and the management of events immediately following it. It includes both the development of a needed repertoire of behaviors and, with conditioning, reflexive differentiation in the use of these responses.

Behavioral engineering frequently entails design, implementation, and continuing evaluation applied to one observable behavior at a time. It specifies the interrelated antecedents, the behaviors needing development and correction, and the subsequent events. It can graph this information to indicate progress from a baseline, or it can bank the data for convenient retrieval and generalization by means of computer technology.

The related term *instructional technology* is a systematic way of designing, carrying out, and evaluating the total process of learning and teaching. Its specific objectives are based on research in human learning and communication. It employs a combination of human and nonhuman resources to bring about more effective instruction.

Early Studies

Prior to systematic utilization of operant conditioning, very few careful studies of listening instruction had been described. In 1802 Itard devised specific training procedures to develop auditory awareness and discrimination and systematically observed the effects of these methods (Wedenberg, 1951). He utilized a variety of sound stimuli, beginning with a church bell. After a year of training, two of his six clients understood words auditorily. Before training, they had not been able to recognize them. The specific methodology he utilized is not clarified.

A century later Goldstein introduced the auditory training methodology of Urbantschitsch from Vienna to the United States (Wedenberg, 1951). Although the training methodology was not specified carefully, the results were impressive. Before a six-month training period, 54 of 60 hearing-impaired children could only perceive the presence of sound or identify vowels. Afterwards half of the children could also discriminate words or sentences.

Kelly (1954, 1974) conducted six-week remedial programs for hard-of-hearing children which included daily auditory training. Auditory (A) stimuli were presented, children responded, and the clinician or other children provided feedback on the correctness of the response. In addition, discrimination training between the error choice and the correct stimulus was provided. Speech perception scores improved about 20 percent. The gains were revealed unisensorily (A) using alphabet letter sequences, words, and sentences similar to the training stimuli. The stimuli of the six-week programs are included in a handbook for auditory training recently reprinted by the Alexander Graham Bell Association for the Deaf. Utilization of the extensive materials can lead to greater attention to sound stimuli, improved speech discrimination, and increased auditory memory span. These stimuli could be incorporated, at least in part, into the more advanced auditory training programs currently being developed. Derived from listening and telecommunications research conducted during World War II, the stimuli begin with number sequences, progress to letter sequences or "coined words," move on to words, and finally advance to messages.

Bode and Oyer Study

In a chapter of the classic *Handbook of Experimental Psychology,* Wolfle (1951) specified five features that facilitated training or learning: distributed rather than massed practice, active participation by the learner, representative and varied stimuli, monitoring of progress, and, most importantly, immediate knowledge of correctness of performance. Except for distributed practice, Bode and Oyer (1970) incorporated these features into a short-term auditory training program using 32 adults with mild sensorineural hearing loss. Four listening conditions were simulated: constant signal to noise (S/N) ratio of 5 dB with signal decreasing from 79 to 67 dB during five training sessions; varied S/N ratios of 10 to 8 to 6 to 4 to 2 dB, with the signal at 72 dB during each of five sessions; 500 closed-set stimulus words from Larsen's drill items or Kelly's collections in multiple-choice format; and 500 common monosyllabic words developed for intelligibility testing (Petersen and Lehiste, 1962) in an open-set format. The open-set format requires the subject simply to imitate one of a large number of words uttered by a speaker. The noise used for the experiment was recorded speech babble or 20 simultaneous talkers.

Each of the four listening conditions were used with eight of the 32 subjects. Before and after the five training sessions, speech discrimination tests were administered individually. The discrimination tests simulated the training stimuli. They consisted of CID W-22 lists 3 and 4, rhyme lists 1 and 2 of Fairbanks (1958), and Hutton, Curry, and Armstrong's (1964) semidiagnostic form A and B. The Hutton test was specifically developed to assess candidacy for rehabilitation and progress through auditory training. Subjects responded to the W-22 stimuli by repeating verbally the monosyllables in the noise background. For the rhyme test they filled in missing letters in word-initial positions of monosyllables. On the semidiagnostic test the subjects circled correct monosyllables in closed-set format. The semidiagnostic test included 50 ensembles, each containing four words differing only in vowels or consonants.

Two-way communication and observation existed during testing and training. Both the testing and training stimuli were prerecorded. Between the training sessions, each lasting 25 minutes, rest and reinforcement periods were provided. They enabled the trainer to inform a subject of progress and of the types of errors he was making, and they provided the opportunity to encourage more careful listening. Training was being conducted for two subjects at a time. They were listening 56 inches from a loudspeaker.

During this short-term training experiment, the total discrimination change was 4.2 percent. No significant differences were found between listening conditions, between type of training material, or between interaction effects. Persons trained on closed-set material improved somewhat more on the closed-set test than on the open-set tests. Subjects trained with the open-set format demonstrated the opposite tendency. These trends suggest that hearing-impaired persons should receive training using material similar to the stimuli of actual listening situations. The results also revealed that subjects listening to stimuli 15 to 25 dB above speech reception thresholds (SRT) improved as much as those responding to signals 25 to 30 dB above SRTs. Subjects listening at 35 to 40 dB SRTs improved about half as much.

During training itself the five tasks increased in difficulty due to worsened S/N ratios or lowered signal intensities. The mean percentage of stimuli discriminated by subjects generally reflected this increased difficulty, except during the fourth and fifth training sessions on closed-set material. The authors noted that subjects were inhibiting initial noise distractions by learning to concentrate selectively on the training stimuli. They also indicated that noise or competing speech should be a part of an auditory training program. The data also seem to indicate that within an individual's auditory area, the specific dB level above SRT may not be critical. In addition, training should utilize both closed-set and open-set stimuli because both types of tasks are required in practical listening situations. The authors concluded by emphasizing the need for operational research on objectives, procedures, and effects of auditory training methodologies.

Doehring and Ling Experiment

Doehring and Ling (1971) also indicate the necessity of developing auditory training programs for acquisition and generalization of verbal discrimination skills. They conducted an experiment in programmed instruction of vowel discrimination using eight children with severe, severe-to-profound, and profound hearing losses. They utilized a Uher tape system to record and present training items and to drive a projector programmer. The stimuli were words, and each response was made by pushing one of three translucent windows behind which pictures were positioned. If the correct window was pressed following stimulus presentation, both the tape recorder and slide projector quickly advanced. If an incorrect choice was selected, the projected pictures were covered, the tape was rewound, and the trial was repeated. If the stimulus had been presented and no response was made after four seconds, the trial was also repeated. Six sets of three pictures were presented in six different arrangements—a total of 36 sets. Only a vowel differed in each set, for example, *bin, bean, bone*. Similar stimuli were used for pre-post tests and for retraining items. The tests were 13-choice word recognition tasks.

Before presentation of test or training stimuli, optimal listening levels were individually determined. These levels were the sound pressure levels at which each subject best repeated several prerecorded consonant-vowel syllables. Each subject participated in four training series. A subject proceeded from one series to the next after meeting a learning criterion. Retraining took place after one month. A subject could complete from one to three training series in 15 minutes. The sessions were scheduled three to five times per week for two months. Retraining lasted 3½ weeks. Preliminary practice in naming pictures was individually administered. Testing and training were conducted in a sound-damped, distraction-free classroom.

The data indicated that individual children improved steadily with practice. During training and retraining the proportion of correct responses increased and the number of sessions required for meeting criterion decreased. A "learning to learn" effect was noted from session to session. Generalization also occurred from the one speaker in the training series to another speaker employed during retraining. There were no significant differences, however, between pre- and post-test scores. Doehring and Ling (1971) indicated that the step from the three-choice training format to the 13-choice tests was probably too large. Holland (1967) noted that new material in programmed instruction must be introduced in small steps.

Brown Training Format

Brown (1974) has designed a stimulus control, programmed conditioning format for listening training. The program format includes four stages: $S^1S^2S^3$, S^2S^3, S^3S^4, and S^5. S^1 is the graphemic condition; S^2 is speechreading; S^3 is auditory in quiet; S^4 is auditory in 26 dB S/N, 22 dB S/N, and 18 dB S/N; and S^5 is auditory in 14 dB S/N, 10 dB S/N, and 6 dB S/N. Within each stage or stimulus condition, clues are faded or noise is introduced in steps. The stimuli are Magner sentences.

Condition I or $S^1S^2S^3$ is subdivided into six steps. Six sentences are included in each step. Words of sentences are faded 20 percent, 40 percent, 60 percent, 80 percent, and 100 percent from step 2 to step 6 respectively. Full lipreading and auditory clues are available throughout.

In Condition II, S^2S^3, five steps are included. Six sentences are used for each step. More and more speechreading or S^2 clues are faded from step 2 through step 5. In step 1 the clinician faces the client. In step 2 his face is turned at a 45 degree angle from front view. The facial angle is 60, 90, and 110 degrees for steps 3, 4 and 5 respectively. By the fifth or last step of Condition II, the client cannot see the lips of the clinician. Thus the last step leaves only S^3 or auditory clues operational.

Condition III, S^3S^4, includes 12 sentences in each of its four steps. S/N ratios of 26 dB, 22, and 18 dB are introduced in steps 2, 3, and 4 respectively. Condition IV similarly has 12 sentences for each of three steps: 14 dB S/N, 10 dB, and 6 dB S/N respectively. White noise is filtered 12 dB per octave above 1000 Hz. Its masking effects are similar to those of four persons speaking simultaneously (Viehweg, 1968).

During each of the four stages, the training format specifies the step, stimulus condition, stimuli, response instruction, consequence for correct and incorrect responses, schedule of reinforcement, criteria, and branches. The first step of Condition I, for example, indicates that full cues will be utilized and that six sentences will be used as $S^1S^2S^3$ stimuli. The client is to respond to each sentence presented by listening and lipreading it, reading it from a card, and repeating it aloud. If he is correct, the "right" light of a cumulative response counter is turned on, and social reinforcement is provided. If he is incorrect, the "wrong" light is turned on. The clinician also points to a sentence feedback chart to indicate the positions of omitted or incorrect words. The schedule of reinforcement is 100 percent. All six sentences have to be repeated correctly. No branch is specified in this step of the Brown program. A branch is additional instruction or steps that facilitate progress.

The sentence feedback chart devised by Brown is shaped like a ruler. It is subdivided by nine vertical lines into 10 sections. The numbers 1 to 10 are successively placed at the top of each section. Thus sentences with up to 10 words can be represented. If a part of a sentence is not repeated correctly, the serial locations of the word(s) in error can be identified by pointing. For example, in the sentence

Father got a long letter from a boy, the client might repeat *Father got a letter* on the initial presentation. The clinician could then refer to the chart and say, "You got it right, except for omitting a word here [fourth space] and three words here [sixth, seventh, and eighth spaces]."

Brown (1974) specifies three branch conditions for her listening program. One branch provides additional practice with sentences on a previously passed step. The second enables a subject to read sentences before they are presented again with the S^3 condition—auditory in quiet. This second branch is utilized if a subject does not reach criterion under the S^3 step. The third branch enables a subject who does not meet S^3 criterion to practice lipreading five key words from each of a series of additional Magner sentences. A branch is utilized when a sentence is not repeated back in its entirety after 10 consecutive presentations. Each of these sentence presentations is designed to be identical to the previous one.

Brown has followed the progress of two subjects in utilizing her listening program. The first subject had a 60 dB loss and a 74 percent speech discrimination score. The second had a 95 dB loss and could not repeat correctly all of the parts of words of a speech discrimination test. The first was a 22-year-old female, and the second a 21-year-old male. Both were students at Utah State University.

The first subject moved through each stage without requiring a branch. No errors were made in the first condition. She was correct with 86 percent, 87 percent, and 72 percent of the items under the second, third, and fourth conditions. She had most difficulty with the final step of the program. At this point the 12 sentences had to be presented 23 times before she could repeat them correctly. It would have been interesting to determine further progress by extending the program to include higher and higher increments of noise. This extension would more closely simulate the noisy conditions under which we frequently have to distinguish the signal from the noise. With this subject it would also have been interesting to determine how well she would have performed if the sentences had been taken from the pool of 200 C.I.D. sentences rather than the pool of 600 Magner sentences. The Magner sentences are described in the previous chapter. They are not representative of everyday speech to the extent that the C.I.D. sentences are (Fairbanks, 1970).

The C.I.D. sentences are arranged in 20 sets of 10 each. Fairbanks explains that each set of sentences is designed to meet the following criteria.

1. The vocabulary is appropriate to adults.
2. The words appear with high frequency in one or more of the well-known word counts of the English language.

3. Proper names and proper nouns are not used.
4. Common nonslang idioms and contractions are used freely.
5. Phonetic loading and tongue-twisting are avoided.
6. Redundancy is high.
7. The level of abstraction is low.
8. Grammatical structure varies freely.
9. Sentence length varies in the following proportion: two to four words—1, five to nine words—2, ten to twelve words—1.
10. Sentence forms are in the following proportion: declarative—6, rising interrogative—1, falling interrogative—1, and imperative —2.

Brown's male subject, who had a profound hearing loss, progressed rapidly through the sentences of the first condition of the program. He made many more errors during the second condition, before meeting the criteria of its steps. The three branches were utilized to assist the subject in completing the fifth step of this condition. At this point S^2S^3, S^2 or speechreading clues were faded out at the 110 degree angle and the subject was relying upon auditory clues only for perceiving and repeating sentences. Five training sessions were utilized during this step. Because of time constraints, Brown terminated this subject after the next training session. The subject was unable to meet criterion on the first step of the third condition, S^3S^4.

Three features of the Brown program may contribute to listening training. One is the stimulus control format which enables the clinician to determine precisely the baseline of the client in perceiving graphemic, speechreading, and auditory stimuli. The second contribution is the presentation of stimuli under decreasing increments of clue redundancy. The stimuli are initially highly redundant. As a client proceeded through the program, there are fewer and fewer clues in the pool for perceiving sentences. Thus the client is gradually required to perceive speech under more and more difficult stimulus conditions. The third contributory feature of the program is the utilization of branching procedures to assist the client in learning to perceive stimuli under a difficult stimulus condition. This client had received fourteen hours of training.

Another possible contribution of the Brown study is the use of a sentence feedback chart and repeated trials before changing procedure or proceeding to another stimulus. Conventionally, clinicians change stimulus condition or paraphrase error words when a client is unable to repeat the entire sentence after a few solely visual or solely auditory presentations. Brown's procedure is to permit the client to try and try again without any stimulus modifications. However the client apparently did not get discouraged, because precise feedback via the chart was telling him that he was making progress from trial to trial. The client was permitted to respond as many as 10 times before a branch procedure was utilized. Careful study of the conventional procedure and Brown's approach should be made to determine comparative efficacy.

Sanders (1971) cautions the clinician about using an imitative procedure during listening training. He states that the listener ordinarily responds to the message of the speaker by responding to it rather than by imitating the words incorporated. He indicates that imitative training may be more detrimental than helpful. This hypothesis must be tested by experimental or case study. It may be that listening sessions should incorporate procedures that provide opportunity for both imitative and natural responses. For example, the client might respond to the stimulus, *The Mississippi River is the longest river in the United States,* by repeating it, and he might respond to a similar statement by saying, *I know that's true.* The correctness of the second type of response is more difficult to evaluate.

During Brown's training program, each of 150 sentences provided stimuli requiring imitative responses. Additional sentences as well as words were administered before training, immediately afterwards, and one week later to test for generalization of perceptual learning. Some generalization occurred, as indicated by quantitative improvements. Furthermore the second subject made qualitative gains. During the pre-test he typically did not respond. After training he responded to test items by imitating much of the word and sentence stimuli content. However the program had not enabled him to identify consistently the entirety of words and sentences by use of audition. As mentioned previously, he had a 95 dB hearing loss.

Case Study by Larsen

Larsen (1972) conducted auditory training with an eight-year-old boy with a 97 dB loss. This subject, however, began training with 55 percent word discrimination. Since he was two years of age, he had been subjected to an auditory approach to education.

During Larsen's training program, the boy spent approximately eight hours discriminating between members of pairs of isolated phonemes. Another 10 hours was spent in identifying monosyllabic words in a five-choice format. There were fifty training sessions during 10 weeks. Larsen provided immediate feedback to indicate the correctness of each response. During the sixth through ninth weeks, he also gave token reinforcement. Tokens were exchanged for desired activities at the end of each training session.

Larsen's subject discriminated 97 percent of the vowels, 92 percent of the plosives, and 83 percent of the fricatives utilized in the isolated phoneme training. His word discrimination percentages during each of six weeks of further training were: 43, 58, 64, 69, 77, and 57 percent. His best performance occurred during the middle four weeks, during which time he was receiving reinforcers in addition to knowing whether he was right or wrong.

The speech perception improvements of Larsen's subject were accompanied generally by similar gains in speech production of the 100 training words. Tape recordings were made of the experimenter and the subject articulating these stimuli before and after the word discrimination training. Spectrograms were made of each of these recorded words. After training, the subject articulated the 100 words better in 60 instances, the same on 27 occasions, and poorer in 13 instances. These data were established by judging pairs of spectrograms, without knowing which was a pre-training articulation and which was a post-training utterance. This finding provided strong evidence that auditory training resulted in speech production improvements.

Berg Case Study

In a discussion of perceptual learning in the previous chapter, the author described a sensory training experiment with a young adult with an even greater hearing loss. This older "deaf" subject learned to identify auditorily each of 36 consonants, vowels, and diphthongs within the context of a 4½ hour training program. Afterwards he also learned to identify auditorily each of 30 consonant-vowel-consonant (CVC) words within 2 hours of additional training. In contrast to Larsen's subject, the author's subject was at first unable to perceive any of the isolated phonemes by use of audition. He was also unable to repeat any of the PB words used during a speech discrimination test administered prior to any auditory training. His learned perception for isolated phonemes, however, transferred to the word identification training. His baseline for the CVC words was approximately 40 percent.

The author also trained the young "deaf" adult to reiterate series of words in sentences by use of auditory stimulation. Because this subject had not learned the morpho-syntactic code of English, he relied on his memory to repeat words. Even when the sentences were articulated carefully and slowly, he could not repeat more than four words in correct succession. If permitted to speechread also, he typically repeated more of the words of the sentence. However their sequence was often out of order. The subject's responses to sentences demonstrated his need for morpho-syntactic training in language, including perceptual learning of prosodic patterns of stress if not intonation.

Asp Developmental Program

Asp and coworkers (1973) describe a six-level program to facilitate the development of auditory and language competencies among children with hearing impairment. During the first level the child is encouraged to vocalize. This vocalization is monitored primarily by tactile-kinesthetic feedback. No attempt is made to alter his output, but multisensory stimulation is provided.

The child enters the second level of this developmental program when he utilizes audition as the primary reinforcer of his vocal output. At this point the teacher imitates the child's babbling in such a way that he provides a model for expanding and lengthening prosodic patterns. Notwithstanding the input, however, the child's vocalizations or verbalizations are accepted with little or minimal correction.

The third level is reached when the child incorporates words into his vocal play. Expansion modeling is continued, with little or no correction in group remediation. During individual work, however, the teacher corrects the child's perceptual and production errors. Body movements and rhythmic stimulation as well as syllable and word drills are utilized to facilitate this individual remediation. The child might be four years of age.

During the fourth level of the Asp program, remediation focuses on the remaining errors in perception and production of speech prosody and rhythm. Vocal play or babbling continues to be the medium through which the child learns to perceive speech features in error, extending from low-pitched consonants (*p, b, m, n, l,* etc.) and words, to middle-pitched sounds (*t, d, f, v, k, g, j, sh,* etc.). Emphasis is also placed upon increasing auditory memory span beyond three or four elements. The child is instructed to imitate rhythmic stimuli like *tap, tap, tap my nose, tap, tap, tap my toe, tap, tap, tap the floor,* and *tap, tap, tap the door,* and to clap his hands. The voice achieved during this level should be normal or close to it. The articulation of words and phrases should be smooth.

The fifth level is attained when phonemes of all pitches included in speech and voice and prosody are almost normal. The auditory memory span is between four and six units in length. Spoken language is spontaneous and includes questions and statements. Situational and individual teaching are continued. The teacher introduces new sounds, vocabulary, and morpho-syntactic structures, and makes corrections. Normal linguistic progression is followed in stimulation and imitation: pivot open class, kernel sentences, and transforms (Lee, 1966).

During the sixth level perceptual training focuses upon phonemes at the highest pitches and upon auditory memory span. The child is learning linguistic structure through auditory input. His voice is near normal, and his prosodic patterns are more complicated. Auditory training is continually reinforced by use of broad band amplification. Academic instruction in reading, writing, mathematics, and social studies has begun. Visual perceptual training is also employed, as well as musical and rhythmic stimulation. The child receives regular kindergarten training for a half day, and individual and group special instruction for the other half. He receives daily 30- to 40-minute auditory training sessions. Selective frequency amplification, perception and production of sounds in error, and correlated body movements are utilized. The child's hearing aid is reevaluated periodically.

Upon completion of the six-level program of Asp et al., the hearing-impaired child is integrated into the regular public school but receives therapy three times a week. The child with a moderate hearing loss may complete the program in one or two years. The youngster with severe or profound impairment may complete or level off in the progression in three to five years or more. If a child plateaus at level three or four, he is placed in a special class for the hearing impaired.

The reader should compare the features and levels of this program with the State of Utah SKI-HI program for young hearing-impaired children described in chapter 4. In the SKI-HI program a child's linguistic development is facilitated by introducing a combined use of signs and audition when he does not progress by use of hearing only. The shift to a total communication optional input would be made if the child did not enter the second level of the Asp program.

Prescott Puzzles and Experiment

Prescott and Turtz (1975) have studied the perceptual learning of verbal, vocal, and nonvocal stimuli by 55 young hearing-impaired children. Thirty-four of the auditory stimuli are verbal signals from a child, mother, and father. They express emotions such as a warning, a scolding, or a command. Another group of 16 stimuli are vocalizations including a baby cooing, a dog barking, and playground noises. A third group of 14 stimuli are nonvocal sounds, for example, a car horn, people clapping, and a glass breaking. These 64 stimuli are incorporated into 40 acoustic puzzles or forced-choice tasks. Each puzzle includes three to eight pictures. A subject listens to a stimulus and responds by pointing to one of these pictures. Each auditory stimulus is a four-second tape recording.

Originally these acoustic puzzles were incorporated into a teaching machine which required the child to make a visual-motor response to sound (Prescott, 1971). The auditory stimuli in each puzzle were arranged in many random orders, and thus a child could "play the game" indefinitely without order affecting correctness of response. The specific response was pushing a button next to a line drawing. If the correct button was pushed, a light came on next to that button. A simplified modification of the program incorporates the auditory and visual stimuli into a series of tape cassettes and pages of a booklet for home use (Prescott, 1974).

Prescott (1972) calls her model a program in auditory pattern recognition. It facilitates perceptual learning by systematic presentation of auditory stimuli and immediate feedback. It prompts the child to engage in spontaneous matching and sorting activity, an ingredient of intellectual development. A prerequisite to training is the child's ability to match pictures to appropriate objects.

Within the experimental group of 55 children, 28 had hearing losses of 92 dB or greater, 16 had impairment of 70 to 88 dB, five had losses from 50 to 62 dB, and six had impairment from 30 to 48 dB. Among those with profound or greater losses, three did not respond to audiometric stimuli of 110 dB, one did not respond except at 250 Hz, 10 responded at only 250 and 500 Hz, five at only to 750 Hz, and the other 9 at higher frequencies too. Sixteen of the children were three to four years old, 11 were four to five, 16 were five to six, 10 were six to seven, and the other two were seven and eight years old. The mean age was 4.7 years. All but three had worn hearing aids before the experiment for from 0.5 years to 6.0 years. Five children seemed to have neurological deficit in addition to hearing loss. Etiologies of loss were identified in 20 cases and included genetic factors, maternal rubella, RH factor, anoxia, and otoxia.

Training was continued until the subject met criterion or failed to meet it. The criterion was 100 percent correct identification of auditory stimuli of a set or task, for two consecutive presentations. Then the next of the 40 tasks was presented. This procedure was repeated for additional tasks or sets of signals. If a child did not meet criterion on the first five tasks in eight successive sessions, he was considered to have failed. If the child reached criterion on 10 or more successive tasks, he had succeeded. At this point he had identified a minimum of 16 different auditory stimuli in closed sets of four signals apiece. Each session lasted five to twenty minutes. An auditory stimulus was presented during four seconds, with six seconds between each signal of a task. Each stimulus or signal had a distinctive prosodic pattern or pitch contour. An observer recorded trials to criterion, error matrices, and response latency times.

All of the children with mild, moderate, and severe (to 88 dB) hearing losses were successful. Of the 24 children with losses of 92 dB and greater, 10 succeeded. The median average hearing level of the failures was 110 dB. Factors associated with failure were a hearing loss of 92 dB or greater, no response to audiometric signals of 500 Hz or beyond, central nervous system deficit, male sex, and late initiation of language programming. A child with 92 dB or greater loss who succeeded had acquired a hearing aid and begun formal education by 1.8 years. Only hearing threshold level was significantly related to criterion. This finding supports other experimental results that indicate that the audiogram is the single most powerful predictor of speech perception and speech production. However, in and of itself, it does not determine whether or not a child with a hearing loss can perceive and produce speech. Prescott's (1972) findings suggest that her program of auditory pattern recognition should be included with pure tone audiometry to facilitate early identification of children lacking cochlear response.

The Prescott program enables the child to repeat a task as many times as desirable before moving on to the next task. A few subjects spent as long as six months to meet criterion on the first task. Before training, one of these subjects had not responded to the human voice. Eventually he identified all task voices except the bird. Such perceptual reorganization supports the findings of Gengel (1971), who reported that a quantum leap can occur in auditory perceptual learning. After training, a number of Prescott's subjects responded for the first time to life situational analogs of the experimental stimuli. It is interesting that with the exception of one auditory stimulus (the bird song), pitch was not a determinant of correctness of response. During the first 10 tasks, for example, infant and child voices were identified as often as those of the male adult, notwithstanding the hearing loss of the subject.

The speed with which audiometric groups of subjects learned the auditory tasks varied exponentially with mean hearing threshold level. A child with a 100 dB loss learned four times slower than one with an 80 dB loss, and eight times slower than one with a 50 dB hearing level. Given sufficient practice, this profoundly hearing-impaired youngster learned to identify speaker differences and broad outlines of acoustic correlates of emotions such as soothing, warning, and calling. Notwithstanding hearing loss among the experimental successes, stimulus generalization was reported among all such subjects in one form or another.

The auditory stimuli of the 40 tasks of the Prescott program were recorded and played back with an audio tape recorder. At the completion of each series of three to eight auditory signals, the tape had to be rewound to its original position so that the task could be repeated. An easier procedure for repeated presentation of task stimuli is use of an audio flashcard unit. An example of such a device is the Bell and

Howell Language Master. An auditory stimulus can be recorded on a strip of audio tape, which is positioned near the bottom edge of a long card. The machine will play back the stimulus as many times as the clinician desires, without any rewinding of tape. Visual correlates of the auditory stimulus can be drawn or inscribed onto the card to identify and detail prosodic and/or phonetic correlates. A newly developed VOXCOM unit doubles as an audio flashcard system and cassette unit. Its stimulus capacity is five words per inch of tape. Strips of tape can be cut and stuck to varying lengths of paper (Tapecon, 1975).

The Conkey Program

Conkey (1973), Peck (1975), and Smith (1975) have detailed a stimulus control and programmed conditioning format of auditory training developed at the Oregon School for the Deaf. Originally, Conkey (1973) specified in some detail 10 prescriptive programs for auditory training, beginning with recognition of presence of sound and ending with discrimination of acoustically similar words in 5 dB S/N ratios. Intermediate programs focused on auditory localization, discrimination of environmental sounds, and discrimination of acoustically dissimilar words.

Within a given program, Conkey specifies an overall behavioral objective and a series of more detailed steps or behavioral objectives. He also lists several additional instructions. Peck (1975) and Smith (1975) go into even greater detail in sentence and word discrimination programs respectively. Peck, for example, additionally specifies materials, details of stimulus presentation and of consequences, criterion levels for acceptable and unacceptable performance, a series of alternate or branching procedures, selection of stimuli, baseline procedures, and schedules of reinforcement. She also indicates the locations of visual correlates of the auditory stimuli within forced-choice sets. Both the Peck and Smith programs incorporate procedures and criteria for the training of teacher aides.

In Peck's sentence program the overall objective is for the client to point to the printed form of each auditory stimulus five consecutive times. Before training, he must understand the meanings, signs or finger spelling, and words of the sentences. He uses a wearable hearing aid or an auditory trainer. The clinician presents live rather than recorded stimuli at a signal level of at least 60 dB. She faces the client, covering her mouth only when presenting a target sentence. The client responds by pointing rather than by repeating or imitating the utterance of the clinician.

Consequences for both correct and incorrect responses are detailed. When the client is correct, the aide communicates this and provides a reinforcer, following a predetermined schedule of reinforcement. If the client is wrong, the aide says and signs, "No, I said point to (sentence)." She then repeats the trial. The aide also indicates correct and incorrect responses on the data sheet.

At each step of the sentence program, the criterion of acceptable performance is five consecutive correct responses. The corresponding criterion for unacceptable performance is two consecutive incorrect responses. When the acceptable criterion is met, the next step in the program is presented. If an unacceptable criterion is reached, the aide uses a branch procedure. Four branches are designed into the program in the following order: speechreading clues with audition, further addition of signs and finger spelling, pointing by the clinician as well, and finally assisting the client to point to the printed form of the sentence as well. At the completion of any branch in which acceptable performance is met, the aide returns to the original condition of the step.

Conkey (1973) reports a case study on a sample auditory discrimination program. The clinician utilized a series of audio flashcards to present 15 spondaic words like *airplane* and *toothbrush*. The criterion for completion of the task was 90 percent correct responses for two consecutive blocks of items. The schedule of reinforcement shifted from 1:1 to 1:2 and 1:3 during training. The reinforcer was food. During 16 sessions the 15 stimuli were presented 21 times. The number of items correct during the first four presentations of all stimuli were six, three, five, and four. Between the tenth and fifteenth blocks, at least 14 of 15 items were discriminated. Up to this time, stimuli had been presented through earphones. When a wearable hearing aid was utilized instead, criterion was not met again until the twentieth and twenty-first blocks.

In such a program a client responds by pointing to pictures. If he points correctly, the clinician inserts the next audio flashcard into the machine. If not, the previous stimulus is used until a correct pointing response is made. The client is not asked to imitate verbally the stimuli of the program.

Berg Listening Test

In contrast, the author utilizes speech responding in a listening test and training format he has developed (Berg, 1975). The auditory stimuli for both test and training include isolated phonemes for 36 critical articulations, consonant-vowel-consonant (CVC) words, increasing lengths of unrelated sequences, and series of related sentences in messages. Equivalent forms of test stimuli are presented under auditory only (A), visual (speechreading) only (V), and auditory-visual (AV) conditions. The same as well as similar stimuli can be utilized for perceptual learning or listening training.

Specifically, each of the A, V, and AV sections of the listening test includes 36 isolated phonemes, 10 CVC words, 10 unrelated sequences with 55 words, and seven related sentences with 45 words. The isolated phonemes are the same from section to section, but they are scrambled into different orders. Each word list includes a different set of 10 CVC words. However each includes the same phonemes except for two of four voiced fricatives. Also, the phonemes /w/, /aɪ/, /ɔɪ/, and /aʊ/ are not included in any of the CVC lists. However their articulations are approximated in the other phonemes utilized. One order of the 36 isolated phonemes and three CVC lists follow.

Isolated phonemes. f, ŋ, b, w, h, i, v, o, z, ɛ, k, e, ɵ, aɪ, ʃ, ʊ, t, ɔɪ, s, n, p, r, g, aʊ, dʒ, m, tʃ, ɑ, ʒ, ɪ, d, u, l, æ, ð, ʌ.

CVC word lists. (1) fame, thick, salve, bell, cheap, hood, judge, note, range, shoes; (2) food, bath, then, jar, gate, cheese, kill, sung, push, home; (3) foam, rouge, jade, has, thin, tong, beach, sell, pug, shook.

Each set of 10 unrelated sequences meets three criteria: (1) incremental increase in number of words from item to item; (2) inclusion of each of 36 critical articulations except for /ʒ/; and (3) item-to-item equivalence in prosodic patterns of phrases from the first item to the tenth or last item. The A, V, and AV lists of unrelated sequences are arranged in left, middle, and right columns below.

1.	toothbrush	1.	thumbtack	1.	armchair
2.	two boys	2.	five noises	2.	one toy
3.	four white chairs	3.	six blue balls	3.	nine red rugs
4.	How do you do?	4.	What is his name?	4.	Where are they from?
5.	He ran home from school.	5.	I went back to bed.	5.	You came here to play.
6.	Bill goes to college next year.	6.	Bob plans to sing this week.	6.	Tom went to town last month.
7.	Betty practices piano before work every morning.	7.	Peggy washes dishes after meals each day.	7.	Janet has dreams during sleep some nights.
8.	If you go home, I will give up.	8.	When he comes here, they can change off.	8.	While we stay there, she can find out.

9. I often observe birds flying up in the air.

9. We seldom notice bugs crawling along on the ground.

9. He never sees fish swimming down in the water.

10. The dogs ran through the woods and played in the field.

10. The horses jumped over the fence and ran to the barn.

10. The boats sailed under the bridge and raced out to sea.

Each of the seven sentences of a message also has a prosodic pattern equivalent or highly similar to corresponding sentences of the other two messages. Oral–nasal, voiced–voiceless, restriction of articulation, place of articulation, and the other distinctive phonetic features are also present in each message. The A, V, and AV messages appear in order below.

Message. Just before dawn, Penny woke up. She looked out of the cave. Suddenly, she caught the scent of a bear. She didn't like the smell. It was a strange odor. She had never been where there were wild animals before. She hated to be there.

Message. Soon after dark, Kittie got tired. She laid down on the floor. Carefully, she moved her paw along the rug. She couldn't feel a thing. She took a deep breath. She could not remember when rest seemed quite so welcome. She slept a long time.

Message. Along about noon, Starlight came home. She ran over to the barn. Quickly, she grabbed the latch of the door. It wouldn't move at all. She tried again and failed. She did not know why people closed places at all. She wanted to eat lunch.

During the listening test the clinician presents the stimuli and records the responses of the client. She uses checks for correct responses, IPA symbols or written words for substitutions, and dashes or lines for omissions. Before the test she evaluates the articulatory proficiency of the client and shapes sounds in error onto phonemic targets as necessary. However it is not necessary that the client speak precisely, in the bull's-eyes of targets, before the listening test is administered. If the client hesitates before responding, the clinician places a dot before the corresponding item on the recording form.

The distance between clinician and client for A, V, or AV test stagings is approximately four feet. The clinician covers her mouth or faces away from the client during auditory presentation. The client's hearing aid is optimally set to receive maximum auditory clues. Under the visual condition the aid is turned off or down and the client faces the clinician. With AV presentation the client still faces the clinician but utilizes auditory clues again.

Eight scores are obtained for each of the A, V, and AV conditions. These scores include number and percentage of (1) isolated phonemes, (2) phonemes in CVC words, (3) CVC words, (4) words in unrelated sequences, (5) unrelated sequences, (6) words in messages, (7) sentences in messages, and (8) key ideas from messages. Each message includes five ideas. Corresponding questions for the first message are exemplified as follows: When did Penny wake up? Where was she? What did she smell? Did she like the smell? Did she like where she was?

Careful administration of this listening test enables the clinician to identify the baseline of the client in the unisensory and multisensory perception of different lengths of speech stimuli. With these data the clinician is able to predict specific areas and extents of sensory training needed. These data can be utilized together with other information on the client in the design of individualized listening training. A percentage format derived from raw scores is shown in a hypothetical example of a client with profound hearing loss.

	A	V	AV
Isolated phonemes	40	60	80
Phonemes in CVC words	45	62	86
CVC words	20	30	40
Words in unrelated sequences	30	40	50
Unrelated sequences	30	50	70
Words in messages	36	42	54
Sentences in messages	29	43	57
Ideas in messages	40	60	80

The hypothetical data provide valuable interpretative and predictive information. It can be seen immediately that the client is perceiving visual or speechreading clues better than auditory clues.

It is also clear that neither of these sensory modalities is providing sufficient perceptual clues. Even under the AV condition, the client consistently misidentifies speech stimuli.

The listening test data suggest that such a client receive A and V sensory training. When an auditory area of a client reveals that residual hearing exists, tentative precedence should be given to auditory training. Initially, training stimuli might include isolated phonemes and/or CVC words. Later on, unrelated sentences and messages could be incorporated. As training proceeds, the clinician presents stimuli and records each response of the client. She also continually provides feedback on the correctness of responses. In addition, she stops after each error response to provide discrimination training, contrasting the correct and error sounds. At the end of each block or series, the clinician tallys the number of correct responses and converts this to a percentage score. She and the client then compare this score with previous scores including the baseline measure, using the same sensory condition and the same type of stimuli. On CVC words, for example, the baseline measure under the A condition was 20 percent. Succeeding measures under the same condition might be 30, 40, 60, and 80 percent at the point of measurement. In time the client might score 100 percent of these items correctly. Whatever the sensory condition or length of stimulus, the terminal goal is 100 percent correct.

Training with isolated phonemes and/or CVC words may facilitate progress in using longer stimulus materials. The perceptual clues increasingly incorporated during successive training blocks, and the perceptual set and mobilization developed are contributors to sentence and message perception. Other contributors include familiarity with vocabulary, knowledge of morpho-syntactic structure, auditory and visual memory span, intelligence, and motivation.

During the listening test the clinician compares the client's responses to different lengths of stimulus materials. If the client has not developed the linguistic code or structure, he will be much more dependent upon memory span for repeating a series of stimuli in an item. He may be successful in auditory or visual discrimination but unsuccessful in imitating a stimulus longer than three or four syllables. Specifically, he may break down when item four or five in an unrelated sequence serves as the stimulus. Training in the auditory perception of prosodic features of speech is then suggested.

Berg Auditory Training Program

The author has also developed a basic auditory training program that includes prosodic stimuli as well as phonetic stimuli. The program consists of 500 training items and 50 test items. The training items are subdivided into 10 tasks of equal length. Thus there are 11 50-item programs. The test program is given initially to determine which training tasks a client needs. It includes a representative sample of the stimuli of the 500 training items.

Introductory and forced-choice formats of program items are exemplified in Figure 48. The auditory stimulus, *He ducked around the*

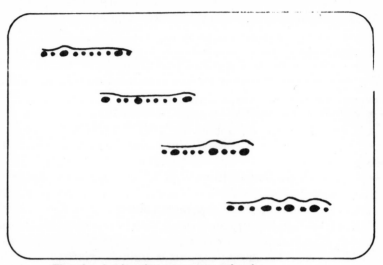

There's a bridge that goes across the river.
Drive over here and pick up the boat.
He ducked around the corner and hid.
He has the strength to move a mountain.

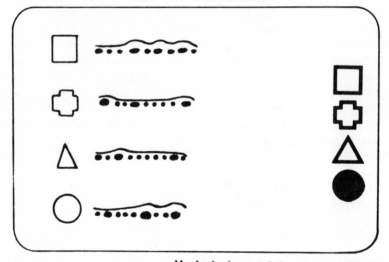

He ducked around the corner and hid.

Fig. 48. Sample frames from prosodic subprogram of Berg listening program. Compliments Utah State University, Logan.

corner and hid, matches the bottom notation of the lower frame. The clinician or a teaching machine presents the auditory stimulus so that it incorporates the stress and intonation features of this pattern. The client should repeat the stimulus and/or press the circle symbol. He only sees the four symbols and corresponding visual patterns on the left side of the bottom frame. The blocked-in circle is a key for the programmer of the machine software or the clinician making a live presentation. It is not seen by the client.

One teaching machine designed for the presentation of such stimuli is the AVS-10 system developed by Peter Goldmark of the Columbia Broadcasting System and marketed by Basic Education Computers, 2772 South Randolph, Arlington, Virginia 22206. Figure 49 depicts videotape views of the hardware and software. The heart of the system is a cartridge that includes one of the 11 programs or tests. The auditory stimuli are recorded on the inner disk. The 50 corresponding visual stimuli appear as photographs or slides on the encircling frames of the cartridge. A loudspeaker or earphones are used to present auditory stimuli. The visual stimuli are projected onto a pop-up screen. The square, cross, triangle, and circle for four-choice closed-set responding can be seen also.

The client inserts the cartridge into the machine and starts it. He listens with his hearing aid or through earphones while he looks at the screen for visual options. As soon as he hears an auditory stimulus, he presses the appropriate symbol: square, cross, triangle, or circle. If correct, the cartridge advances and the next stimulus and pattern are presented. If the client pushes an incorrect symbol, the cartridge does not rotate and the counter tallies the error. A green light also appears for a correct response and a red light for an error. After the client completes one block of 50 items, he removes the cartridge. This procedure can be repeated block after block, using the same cartridge or different cartridges. The progress of the client and monitoring by the clinician determine the utilization of cartridges.

The training and test items can also be presented by the clinician without using a machine. The square, cross, triangle, and circle and corresponding visual options are on the front of a notecard. Visual notes used by the clinician for producing the auditory stimulus are on the back of the card. The clinician holds a stack of 50 notecards in one hand. He presents one card at a time while covering his mouth with his free hand. He must be very careful to present the stimulus precisely. This requires considerable preliminary practice and familiarization with the stimuli of the listening program. During live presentation the clinician also tallys errors. He can also stop at any point to provide dis-

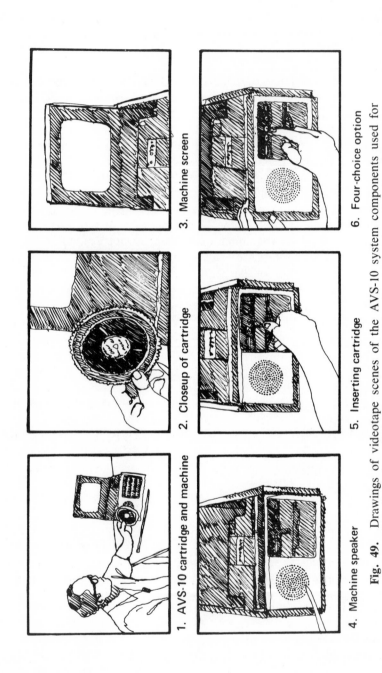

1. AVS-10 cartridge and machine

2. Closeup of cartridge

3. Machine screen

4. Machine speaker

5. Inserting cartridge

6. Four-choice option

Fig. 49. Drawings of videotape scenes of the AVS-10 system components used for presentation of the Berg listening program. Compliments Basic Education Computers Incorporated.

Table 21
Summary of the Berg Listening Programs I–XI

Program	Discrimination Content
I	Number (21 frames) and stress patterns
II	Intonation contours
III	Combined stress patterns and intonation contours
IV	36 isolated phonemes
V	Front and back vowels in CV, VC, and CVC syllables
VI	Back and central vowels and diphthongs in CV, VC, and CVC syllables
VII	Vowels and diphthongs in picturable words
VIII	Vowels, diphthongs, and consonants in additional words
IX	Words in sentences
X	Words and sentences in brief dialogues
XI	Test items drawn from I–X above

crimination practice, and he can correlate errors with specific stimulus items.

Approximately one out of each four items of a program is used to introduce stimulus options. For example, the auditory stimuli *pum*, *pum pum*, and *pum pum pum* are repeated three times in the first frame of the first program. Corresponding dot patterns could be on a screen or on the front of a notecard. The client listens and watches. The clinician may prompt him to correlate the auditory and visual stimuli and to vocalize what he hears. However the client does not respond by pushing a square, cross, triangle, or circle. After listening and viewing this frame, he is presented with a series of response frames as described previously. This alteration of stimulus frame and response frames is repeated throughout a program.

Table 21 identifies the prosodic and phonetic content of the test and training programs. Prosodic discrimination is featured in Programs I, II, and III. Phonetic discrimination is developed in Programs IV to IX. The discriminations of dialogues or conversations of Program X utilize both prosodic and phonetic clues. Program XI is the test. The detail of the 500 different frames is not indicated. The reader should contact the author for further information on the program.

Tobin Device

Lately, Tobin (1975) has developed a sophisticated response device that can be utilized in listening testing or training. The device provides the client with immediate and detailed feedback of information on responses. A trial counter indicates the number of items that have been presented. A percent correct indicator provides a cumulative measure of progress on a program. As many as eight choices can be opposed on any one trial or as few as two in a minimal pair condition. Items are assigned class and number categories while a program is being written and tape recorded. Uniquely different tones are correlated with the choices of the testing or training material. They are also recorded on the same channel or a parallel one. A light comes on when a correct choice is selected, or the light is activated according to a preset intermittent reinforcement schedule.

The Tobin device also provides a readout of stimuli that sound alike to the client. If the client initially selects an incorrect option, he can get credit for second or third best responses. Stimuli that are confused are displayed on an 8×8 matrix. The clinician can use this information to develop a branch program to meet individual needs.

Still another advantage of the Tobin device is a readout of confidence of response. Before the client pushes a button that indicates his choice of response, he pushes one of two other buttons. The one indicates that he is positive of his choice. Pushing the other button means he is uncertain and is guessing. A four-celled decision matrix provides a readout of his confidence. The options are a hit, a miss, a false alarm, and a correct rejection. With training, the client can use the matrix information to assess, and if necessary, to modify his confidence upwards or downwards.

Tobin believes that clients prefer to monitor their own progress and to assess their own capabilities. The development of listening programs that can be incorporated into teaching machines, such as the Acoustic puzzle and AVS-10 systems and Tobin unit, will provide this option for clients. However the clinician will need to be available as a learning mentor, a guide, a counselor, and a director of listening experience (Stepp, 1970).

SUMMARY

Technology in listening training is advancing rapidly. Stimulus control, programmed conditioning formats are being developed. Behavioral objectives are also being incorporated into the design of programs. In addition, perceptual learning data are emerging that indicate that most hearing-impaired children and adults can be trained to mobilize audition. They can also learn to discriminate many prosodic and phonetic features of speech, an ability that contributes to the development of communication skills. A newly devised listening test and listening program provides a useful package for obtaining predictive baseline information and facilitating the acquisition of listening skills. Machine approaches to learning are also described.

REFERENCES

Asp C, Berry J, Berry C, et al: Auditory Training Procedures for Children and Adults. Knoxville, University of Tennessee, 1973

BECI AVS–10 System. Arlington, Virginia, Basic Education Computers, 1976

Berg F: Home Study in Listening and Speech Training. Washington, DC, American Speech and Hearing Association Convention, 1975

Bode D, Oyer H: Auditory training and speech discrimination. J Speech Hear Res 13: 839–855, 1970

Brown K: A Stimulus Control, Programmed Conditioning Format for Auditory Training. MS Thesis. Logan, Utah State University, 1974

Conkey H: Auditory Discrimination Program. Corvallis, Oregon State University, 1973

Doehring D, Ling D: Programmed instruction of hearing impaired children in the auditory discrimination of vowels. J Speech Hear Res 14:746–753, 1971

Fairbanks G: Test of phonemic differentiation: The rhyme test. J Acoust Soc Am 30: 596–600, 1958

Fairbanks G: Everyday speech. In Davis H, Silverman S (eds): Hearing and Deafness. New York, Holt, Rinehart & Winston, 1970, pp 492–495

Gengel R: Acceptable speech to noise ratios for aided speech discrimination by the hearing impaired. J Audiol Res 11:219–222, 1971

Holland A: Some applications of behavioral principles to clinical speech problems. J Speech Hear Disord 32:11–18, 1967

Hutton C, Curry E, Armstrong M: Semi-diagnostic test materials for aural rehabilitation. J Speech Hear Disord 29:215–230, 1964

Kelly J: A summer residential program in hearing education. J Speech Hear Disord 19:17–27, 1954

Kelly J: Clinician's Handbook for Auditory Training. Washington, D.C., AG Bell Assn Deaf, 1974

Larsen D: Operant and Nonoperant Tasks in Auditory Training. MS Thesis. Logan, Utah State University, 1972

Lee L: Developmental sentence types: A method for comparing normal and deviant syntactical development. J Speech Hear Disord 31:311–330, 1966

Peck M: Auditory Training Program. Sentence Discrimination. Salem, Oregon School for the Deaf, 1975

Petersen G, Lehiste I: Revised CNC lists for auditory tests. J Speech Hear Disord 27: 62–70, 1962

Prescott R: Acoustic puzzles: Auditory training games. Vol Rev 73:51–53, 1971

Prescott R: Auditory Patterning Abilities of Young Hearing Impaired Children. Chicago, AG Bell Assn Convention, 1972

Prescott R: Acoustic Puzzles. Listening Games to Play at Home. Washington, DC, Federal City College, 1974

Prescott R, Turtz M: Auditory Pattern Recognition by Young Hearing Impaired Children. Washington, DC, Federal City College, 1975

Sanders D: Aural Rehabilitation. Englewood Cliffs, New Jersey, Prentice Hall, 1971

Skinner BF: Science and Human Behavior. New York, Macmillan, 1953

Smith N: Auditory Training Program. Salem, Oregon School for the Deaf, 1975

Stepp R: Utilization of educational media in the education of the acoustically handi-capped student. In Berg F, Fletcher S (eds): The Hard of Hearing Child. New York and London, Grune & Stratton, 1970, pp 217–231

Tapecon. Introducing Voxcom. Rochester, New York, 1975

Tobin H: The Programming for Audiologic Habilitation. Scientific Exhibit. Washington, DC, ASHA Convention, 1975

Viehweg S: Differential Effects of Signal and Noise Filtering on Speech Intelligibility in Sensorineural Hypacusis. Ph.D. Dissertation. Evanston, Illinois, Northwestern University, 1968

Wedenberg E: Auditory training of deaf and hard of hearing children. Acta Otolaryngol [Suppl] (Stockh), 1951

Wolfle B: Training. In Stevens S (ed): Handbook of Experimental Psychology. New York, Wiley, 1951

8

Supportive Services for the Hearing Impaired

In the United States hard-of-hearing children are typically not being educationally managed well enough to permit them to compete satisfactorily in society. In the relatively few school systems where services for these youngsters are established, the critical resources that do exist generally are not being utilized effectively. In the great majority of school systems, supportive services for the hearing impaired are minimal or nonexistent, and administrative personnel often seem unaware of the need for special programming and adjustments for these children. Many hard-of-hearing children are referred to schools for the deaf; but in these facilities their unique needs are also characteristically neglected (Berg, 1974; Fricke, 1969).

Goals and Plans

A goal of the Bureau of Education for the Handicapped, United States Office of Education, is to stimulate the establishment of full services for children with communicative handicaps by 1980. The providing of comprehensive quality services for this population is also the concern of the American Speech and Hearing Association (ASHA), which claims as members 19,000 of the 32,000 audiologists and speech pathologists of this country. Improvement of the quality and quantity of services is made possible by ASHA's school affairs program, and is endorsed by state consultants, school personnel, and university supervisors. William Healey (1971), ASHA Associate Secretary for School Affairs, has recommended that a National Work Force for Hearing

Clinician Programs be established. The reader is referred to the American Speech and Hearing Association, 9030 Old Georgetown Road, Washington, DC 20014, for updated information on this development. "Standards and Guidelines for Comprehensive Language, Speech, and Hearing Programs in the Schools," a recent ASHA publication, indicates that only 17 percent of an estimated 260,981 hard of hearing children of the United States are receiving special education services.

Since 1966 an Academy of Rehabilitative Audiology (ARA) has emerged within the membership of ASHA. A main concern of ARA is to provide optimal habilitative and rehabilitative services to the entire hearing-impaired population. Committees have been established within this 150 to 200 member group to develop guidelines for the development of services and standards for programs. Members of this group also participate on an ASHA committee that is charged with the responsibility of developing similar guidelines and standards for coordinating audiological and educational activities among the hearing impaired.

Program Guidelines

A relatively small professional subdivision of the Alexander Graham Bell Association for the Deaf is also actively seeking to improve aural rehabilitative services. Called the American Organization for the Education of the Hearing Impaired (AOEHI), this group of communicative disorders specialists was established in 1969. A list of their "Guidelines for Oral Programs for Hearing Impaired Children" (AOEHI, 1971) appears below.

1. Willingness of parents to complement the school program with home experiences and activities.
2. Existence of coordinated programs that provide for the needs of hearing impaired from birth through placement in gainful employment.
3. A state plan of organization of educational programs.
4. Provision for separate programming of the educationally hard of hearing.
5. Acoustically treated classrooms, instructional media, and tutorial rooms for individualized instruction and/or independent study.
6. Amplification units in each classroom.
7. Formalized curriculum outlines stated in terms of observable behaviors that stress speech and auditory training skills.
8. Faculty members participate in a yearly critique of the total school program.

9. Infant programs should train children to make maximum use of their residual hearing and to develop aural and oral language through the use of residual hearing and speech reading.
10. Preschool (three to six years) programs should provide appropriate oral–aural stimulation.
11. A hearing-impaired child eligible for a preschool program is any child with a hearing loss that is educationally handicapping from the standpoint of language development. This term includes those who may later function as hard-of-hearing children as well as those who may later function as deaf children.
12. The aim of each level of a special educational facility should be to leave the hearing impaired child less dependent upon special provisions for his educational progress.

Mainstreaming

Lately, increasing numbers of hearing-impaired children are being educated in regular classrooms rather than in special classrooms. Such integration, called "mainstreaming," is taking place not only in high school but at various elementary grade levels. Northcott (1973) states that candidates for admission to or continuation in regular classes have certain characteristics in common: (1) active utilization of residual hearing; (2) full-time hearing aid use if prescribed; (3) social, academic, cognitive, and aural–oral communicative skills within the normal range of behaviors; (4) competence in understanding and exchanging ideas with others by use of speech, reading, and writing; and (5) self-direction in completing tasks at hand.

According to Northcott (1973) at least six current educational trends mandate mainstreaming: (1) benefits derived from an infant-preschool start; (2) public school advantages for coordinating programming; (3) general preference for a normal rather than special educational environment; (4) a shift from a medical model of intervention to an educational one; (5) interpersonal utilization of residual hearing; and (6) development of a new specialty for initiating and coordinating supportive services.

Cascade Model

In 1973 a cascade system of special supportive services was adopted by the Council for Exceptional Children. The cascade concept specifies that a continuum of educational services and program alternatives should be utilized for exceptional children, including the hearing

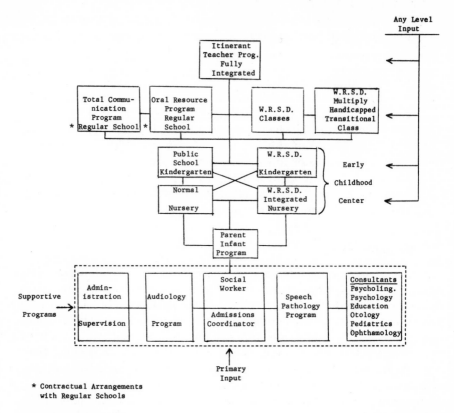

Fig. 50. Program flow chart model of the Willie Ross School. From Ross, 1976, p. 229.

impaired. Figure 50 presents a program flow chart model of the Willie Ross School, which utilizes a cascade of services and alternatives (Ross, 1976).

Ross (1976) states that the viability of his cascade program depends upon the competencies of an evaluation and placement team, representing the supportive and academic services. Success is also facilitated by central administration of all facets of the program. Finally, the staff must be committed to children rather than to methods or economics.

A hearing-impaired child can enter the Willie Ross program during infancy. At this time he is fitted with binaural aids and his parents receive counseling, instruction, and training through home visits. At the age of three the child can be enrolled in a regular nursery, or in a special nursery at the school, depending upon communicative readiness. At the kindergarten level the child then enters an auditory–oral class or a total communication class. Afterwards his educational options are threefold: (1) continuation of total communication, (2) partial integration, or (3) full integration. Provisions are also made through the school or by referral to meet the needs of multiply handicapped children and oral youngsters with profound hearing impairment. Day school options are preferred, but residential placements are legitimate alternatives. Criteria are utilized at each decision point of programming.

The Willie Ross School currently enrolls 98 children. Ten are in the parent-infant program, 28 in the itinerant program, and 60 in the special class programs. The ultimate aim is full integration of those hearing-impaired children who can benefit from it. In addition to classroom specialists, three audiologists and four speech pathologists are employed on a full-time basis. Social, psychological, and other supportive services are provided as well. All of the children are under 13 years of age because the program emerged from the rubella epidemic of 1964–1965.

AURAL HABILITATION MODEL

Currently, each state and community is faced with the task of developing a cascade system for hearing-impaired children. The scope of this task can be clarified by referring to Figure 51, which depicts the author's aural habilitative program model for kindergarten through the twelfth grade. This model identifies six main areas of necessary programming: (1) identification audiometry, (2) otological assistance and audiological consultation, (3) hearing aid fitting, (4) parent-home programs, (5) community programs, and (6) school programs.

Identification Audiometry

A comprehensive program of identification audiometry should be conducted in each school district on a continuing basis. Such a program includes use of conventional and/or impedance audiometers to identify ear pathology and hearing loss among children. In Illinois new laws mandate that this service must be provided annually for children in kindergarten and grades 1, 2, 3, 5, 7, 9, and 11. It is also to be administered to children receiving special supportive services, those with a history of hearing loss, youngsters new to a school, and pre-school children enrolled for educational programming (Shattuck, 1973).

The implementation of the new Illinois program should require the

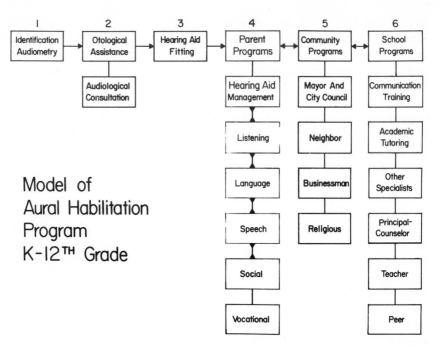

Fig. 51. Model of aural habilitation program, kindergarten through high school. Compliments Utah State University, Logan.

hiring of school audiologists throughout the state. If other states follow Illinois, audiometric information will be available on nearly all children with hearing loss throughout the country. Currently, comprehensive identification audiometry is utilized in relatively few places in the United States (Dyer, 1969; Fricke, 1969).

The hearing conservation services of the Muscatine-Scott County School System of Iowa (Huddleston, 1971) provide an exemplary identification program. During 1969–1970 a team of school audiologists and assistants served a total elementary and secondary school population of 47,897. Using audiometers they screened 35,306 children. More than 4,411 follow-up evaluations were performed on screening failures, high risk and regular referrals, and known losses. Afterwards 2,173 youngsters were referred to otolaryngologists and/or clinical audiologists and school personnel.

A similar program of identification audiometry was conducted during 1972–1975 in Roane County, West Virginia, under an ESEA Title III project support. A mobile unit housing audiometric equipment and facilities was driven from one rural school to another. Audiometric information was obtained on nearly all of the 3,000 children of the county. Of the first 1,200 tested, 227 were referred for medical diagnosis of ear pathology. More than half of these children received otological diagnoses. Most of these received medical treatment and many benefited from surgical treatment or recommendation to purchase a hearing aid. Audiometric data obtained before and after medical and/or surgical treatment revealed an average lessening of hearing loss from 25 dB to 11 dB. A special resource classroom and a mobile itinerant therapy program was established to provide educational and communicative assistance for the children with more serious hearing losses (Johnson, 1974a, 1974b).

Otology and Audiology

Otological assistance and audiological consultation constitute the second main area in the aural habilitative model developed by the author. Examples of cases of ear pathology and hearing loss, and corresponding medical and surgical assistance, are detailed in chapter 1. It is important to emphasize here that the audiologist utilizes audiological tests to assist the otologist in determing the presence and location of pathology within the ear. He also evaluates the degree of auditory insensitivity before and after medical or surgical intervention. With the recent advent of impedance audiometry, the audiologist is able to provide additional objective measurements, which are not dependent upon the availability of a quiet testing environment.

Impedance audiometry coupled with conventional audiometry is being utilized increasingly in school districts to identify and diagnose children with hearing impairment and ear pathology. Figure 52 illustrates the American Electromedics Model 81 impedance audiometer, which is manufactured by the same company that has published the *Handbook of Clinical Impedance Audiometry* (Jerger, 1975) and has sponsored a regular series of impedance workshops throughout the country. The basic impedance audiometry test battery consists of tympanometry, static compliance, and acoustic reflex measurement. McCandless (1975) predicts that with technological progress this battery will permit the audiologist to assist the otologist in providing a more precise description of ear pathology and an exact method for recording the progress of various disease processes.

In a study of 730 children three to 15 years of age, McCandless and Thomas (1974) compared the effectiveness of impedance audiometry and pure tone screening in identifying middle ear disorders. They used the otoscopic examination as the validating criterion. The agreement between impedance results and otoscopy was 93 percent, but between pure tone screening and otoscopy it was only 66 percent.

A similar investigation was conducted by Fox-Buckley and As-

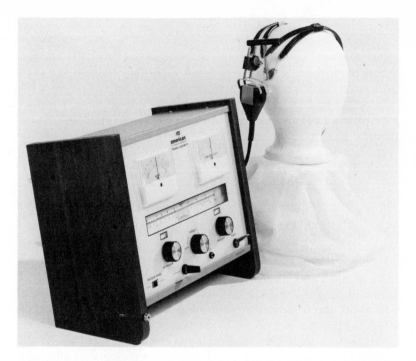

Fig. 52.   American Electromedics Model 81 Impedance Audiometer.

sociates (1974) using the well-accepted air-bone pure tone audiometric relationship as the criterion of a conductive disorder. With 341 elementary school children, they found a 33 percent relationship between otoscopy and impedance results and a nine percent agreement between otoscopy and pure tone results. According to the validating criterion, 65 or 19 percent of the 341 children had a conductive problem. Impedance identified the highest percentage (35 percent), otoscopy the next highest (22 percent), and pure tone screening the least (eight percent). Those who advocate the use of impedance audiometry for screening school populations for hearing loss or ear pathology note that this technique is particularly helpful in detecting conductive problems, whereas pure tone screening is effective in identifying impairment of the sensorineural hearing mechanism.

Hearing Aid Fitting

The third main area of aural programming needed in the schools is hearing aid fitting. The proper fitting of a child with a wearable hearing aid is a professional task. In each instance audiological information

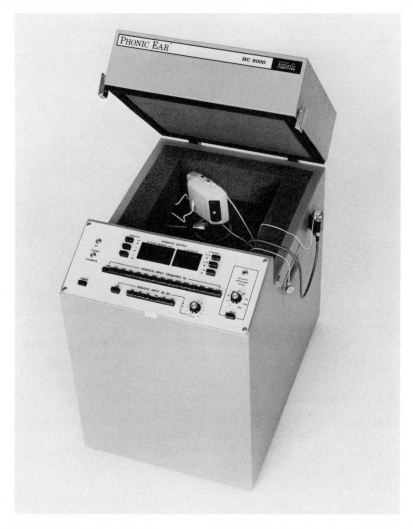

Fig. 53. Phonic Ear HC 2000 acoustic computer utilized for evaluation of amplification units. Compliments of HC Electronics, Tiburon, California

should be obtained to describe hearing loss, the type of hearing aid needed, and the physical characteristics of the aid being considered for purchase. An impression of the ear should be carefully made, an individually molded earpiece fashioned, and minor comfort adjustments conducted to ensure that incoming amplified sound is being effectively delivered to the ear rather than leaking out and causing a squeal. In addition, both the hearing aid and the earpiece must sooner or later be replaced. The average life of a wearable aid is three to five years, and of a useful earpiece little more than one year for a school-age child.

The selection and fitting of an auditory training system for a regular or special class is also a complex problem. As described in chapter
4, wireless systems of amplification are preferable to other group auditory training systems. As many as eight companies are now manufacturing wireless systems. In many instances representatives of these
companies are not audiologically oriented. They are not sophisticated
in converting the capabilities of equipment to the listening needs of
hard-of-hearing individuals. The comparative chart of Table 9 in chapter 3 suggests that many acoustic and technical details must be weighed
in the selection and fitting of an auditory trainer.

Devices for the acoustic analysis of amplification systems are now
available for use in the schools. The HC 2000 Phonic Ear system can
be seen in Figure 53. Using this acoustic computer, the clinician can
quickly measure the acoustic output, frequency response, and harmonic distortion of a wearable hearing aid or a wireless receiver unit.
These data can be compared with manufacturers' specifications and
with previous information on the same unit. Frequent measures of
amplification equipment will provide the school system with a powerful
evaluative tool. Such information should facilitate improvements in
manufacturing and maintenance standards, audiological consultation,
and technical assistance.

Parent Programs

The fourth main area of the aural habilitative model is programming for parents of the hearing impaired. Six subprogram areas for
parents and siblings are identified: (1) hearing aid mangement, (2) listening, (3) language, (4) speech, (5) social training, and (6) vocational
training. Each of these unique areas can assist the hearing-impaired
individual in his development and education. For example, parents
need to be trained in adjusting, troubleshooting, and making minor
hearing aid repairs. They must also learn how to teach listening and
language skills and to chart and monitor speech. Parents also need
counseling in accepting themselves and handicapped children, and they
should be oriented in social and vocational considerations.

Increasing numbers of mediated materials are becoming available
to assist parents. For example, the author has developed a booklet and
record entitled "Breakthrough for the Hard of Hearing Child," that
includes specific information and suggestions for the home (Berg,
1971). He has also prepared extensive home study coursework and
modules in educational audiology (Berg, 1975). As an outgrowth of
Project NEED (Normal Educational Environment for the Deaf), Bitter

(1975) has developed a series of nine sound-filmstrip presentations on topics of integrated education. His kit, called Systems ONE (Orientation to Normal Environment), includes information on family orientation, hearing aids, language, reading, and other topics. A similar kit of four sound-filmstrip presentations has been prepared by Pauls (1974). It is entitled "Management Guide for the Hearing Impaired Child in the Regular Classroom," but it is adaptable for home use.

Notwithstanding the availability of home study materials, a parent program is incomplete without direct contact from a hearing specialist. Ideally, home visits should be set up to provide counseling and training. Such a home visit program could be similar to the SKI-HI project described in chapter 4. However, much of the content would be at more advanced levels. It is critically necessary to develop specific materials and procedures for parents of hearing-impaired children enrolled in the regular schools.

Community Programs

Community programs are the fifth main area of the model. Figure 51 identifies four subareas: (1) major and city council, (2) neighbors, (3) businessmen, and (4) church. A specific need exists to develop materials and procedures for mobilizing community members and groups to assist in making communicative adjustments for hearing-impaired individuals. For too long, members of the community outside of the home and the school have had little to do with the hearing impaired. They have tended to ostracize the handicapped from the mainstream of community activities, opportunities, and responsibilities. The development of community facilitative programs remains the untapped area of aural habilitation.

School Programs

The last main area of the aural habilitative model encompasses school programs, which can be divided into subprograms of communication training, academic tutoring, and supportive specialists. All educational personnel who have direct or indirect contact with the hearing-impaired child can facilitate or inhibit his success. Key responsibilities are assigned to the clinician or audiologist, the regular classroom teacher, and the school principal. Backup staff includes the psychologist and social worker, the school guidance counselor, the nurse, the otologist, remedial personnel, and media specialists. The aural rehabilitative functions to be conducted are evaluation, design, remediation, facilitation, and counseling (Yater, 1971).

Four job titles can be identified among hearing specialists working in the school systems of the country: (1) teacher of a segregated classroom, (2) resource classroom teacher, (3) hearing clinician, and (4) school or educational audiologist. The segregated classroom has been the conventional model of delivery of services in schools or programs for the deaf. The resource classroom provides less than full-time special assistance to hearing-impaired children, who are typically bussed to one school. The hearing clinician is an itinerant therapist who serves hard-of-hearing and deaf youngsters in several schools. The audiologist fulfills one or more of three main tasks: audiometry, hearing aid management, and consultation on room acoustics.

All four jobs can be a part of a special program for the hearing impaired in a highly populated school area. In a smaller school district one educational hearing specialist might combine the tasks of two or more of these jobs. He becomes primarily the coordinator or catalyst of the "good things" that can happen to hearing-impaired children when an aural habilitation program is mounted in a school district or in a combination of them. Naturally, he has to define his job task within the constraints of his time and energies. He must mobilize other personnel and aides and resources to implement the plan he develops.

In Iowa a state plan has been designed to employ one hearing specialist for each 5,000 children in the general school population (Dublinskie, 1971). According to Iowa guidelines, the job task is to identify children with hearing impairment and to plan and provide special education as needed. This role is more that of the school audiologist than of the hearing clinician.

The job task of the hearing clinician in the exemplary St. Louis Special School District of Missouri is multifaceted. It includes evaluation, reevaluation, and remediation in skill areas. It also encompasses observing children and teachers in their classrooms, and conferring with teachers, principals, counselors, and other concerned professionals. The hearing clinician also prepares curriculum and materials, keeps records, conducts research, and participates in meetings. He interacts with the coordinating clinician, interfaces with the social worker and psychologist, and confers with the director of audiological services. The clinician continually upgrades his competencies through in-service training (Yater, 1971).

The number of hearing-impaired children served by one hearing specialist in the regular schools can be considerable. In a school district of 5,000, it can be estimated that 10 children have bilateral losses of 46 dB or greater, 25 have 26 to 45 dB bilateral impairment, and 15 have 46 to 100 dB unilateral loss (Willeford, 1971). These three subgroups of hearing-impaired children need decreasing amounts of supportive services or educational adjustments. In one way or another, each contributes to the case load.

A hearing specialist thus coordinates services for perhaps 50 hearing-impaired children in a school district of 5,000. It can be estimated that the 50 million school-age children in the United States require the services of least 10,000 hearing specialists. Currently, it appears that no more than 1,000 communicative disorders specialists are employed as hearing clinicians or school audiologists in our nation's schools, and relatively few of these have had the advantage of sufficient professional preparation in this newly mobilized area of education (Sommers, 1968).

The Principal

The school principal is perhaps the "make-or-break" member of the school aural rehabilitative team. As administrator and coodinator of the total education and rehabilitative program of a school, he has at least four responsibilities in the area of aural habilitation: conservation of hearing, reduction of noise level, educational adjustments, and staff meetings focusing on hearing-impaired students.

A hearing conservation program in a school should include ongoing identification of all children suspected of having unilateral or bilateral hearing loss. Whether or not audiometric screening and follow-up hearing threshold testing is available in a district, the principal can instruct his staff to use a check sheet of characteristics that may indicate the presence of hearing loss in a particular child. The principal can then recommend that the parents obtain audiological and otological assistance and prompt them until this help is secured or hearing loss and ear pathology are shown to be nonexistent.

The principal may recognize that his school is too noisy and reverberant for any child who is using a hearing aid. Therefore he might consult with an acoustical engineer who can advise him on the sound conditions in classrooms and other spaces. In all probability at least minor modifications of the school plant are necessary. An expenditure of funds for this purpose, however, benefits not only the hearing-impaired child but also all the other youngsters. Attention should be given to reducing reverberance from sound bouncing between hard-surfaced walls, and to alleviating noise from footsteps on hard floors, from the moving of desks or chairs, and from the opening and closing of doors. Noise reducers and alleviators include sound absorbent tiling, heavy drapes, carpet, cork, or rubberized floor coverings, rubber caps on chair and table legs, tightly sealed solid-core doors, and sneakers in kindergartens (Sanders, 1965). It is particularly critical that the classroom and the clinical teaching and tutoring spaces have low noise and reverberance levels.

The principal should also take the lead in developing a program to orient his or her entire staff to the characteristics and needs of a youngster with hearing loss. Currently, an in-service program is needed because colleges and universities generally do not provide preservice education based on the understandings and competencies required for work with the hard-of-hearing child. Topics of importance include the hearing aid, noise in the classroom, curricular modifications, instructional adjustments, monitoring performance, special evaluative tools, use of tutors and notetakers, and counseling. A hearing clinician can be called upon to provide explanations and demonstrations. However the principal has to work with his staff, particularly the regular teachers, to give them the continuing and long-range support and assurance they need to make headway with the hard-of-hearing child.

Perhaps the last major responsibility of the principal toward the hearing-impaired child is the administration or coordination of at least one staff meeting each year. The meeting should be announced long before it is to be held so that all pertinent reports from parents, outside specialists, and school district staff are available. Particular attention should be given to medical considerations, hearing aids, communicative skills, academic competencies, and adjustment considerations. Progress or lack of it as well as further recommendations should be offered, and responsibilities for implementation should be identified. Informal follow-up meetings or communications should be conducted with all members of the aural rehabilitative team of a given child.

An excellent approach to such staff conferences is described by an elementary school principal. Every Wednesday afternoon between 2:30 and 5:00 PM this principal meets with his teachers, outside resource personnel, and parents when appropriate. He uses a strategy sheet to record problems, hypotheses, suggested solutions, and assignment of roles for implementation. This individualized educational program is then put into effect. A reevaluation is conducted at another staff meeting two or three weeks later. By this procedure the special needs of each child in his school are given careful consideration each year (Berg, 1971).

The Classroom Teacher

A classroom teacher is perhaps the most critical component of an aural rehabilitative program in the schools. Generally, she has a multifaceted role that includes evaluation of the individual needs of all pupils, selection of appropriate teaching materials for her class, preparation, presentation, and evaluation of lessons and activities, and classroom control. With the hard-of-hearing child, she also faces additional challenges: monitoring hearing aid use, keeping the room relatively free from unnecessary noise, speaking so as to be heard and lip-read, permitting special seating, using visual aids as much as possible, selecting class members as backup helpers, and counseling.

The teacher must realize that many hearing-impaired children who own hearing aids reject them or use them ineffectively. The problem usually stems from one or more of the following reasons: the aid itself is defective, the child is not oriented to its use and care, or the environment in which it is used is either overstimulating or impoverished. The teacher must become familiar with the hearing aid and should notify the parents when it is not operating correctly. Orientation to and care of a hearing aid are as serious as driver education. The child may require help in using controls, changing batteries, and troubleshooting a problem. The youngster may not have learned as yet the "rules" of the hearing aid "road," including when to wear the aid and what to expect from it. Unless a hearing specialist is available, it is the role of the regular teacher to monitor hearing aid use until the child becomes trained to do it for himself.

As mentioned before, the environment in which a hearing aid is used should be relatively quiet. Whereas a normal-hearing child can understand speech when it is no more intense than the competing noise, a youngster wearing a hearing aid ordinarily requires a speech input 10 dB louder than background sound (Gengel, 1971). In addition, the classroom should be a stimulating and meaningful place. It should combine order and quiet with action and explanation. Language acquisition by the young hearing-impaired child requires frequently repeated association of experience and speech stimulation. Oral communication with all hard-of-hearing youngsters requires attention to the listening and lipreading processes.

A classroom teacher can help the child to hear and to lip-read by speaking normally, naturally, rather slowly, with continual eye contact, and with sufficient volume. She should avoid exaggerating speech movements, turning to the chalkboard, looking at notes, looking down, or covering her mouth as she speaks. She should also speak in phrases or sentences, and rephrase a statement that is not understood. To further facilitate use of lipreading clues, the teacher should allow the hard-of-hearing child to sit with his back to the windows, near the front, and not too close to the speaker. During class discussion, he should be permitted to have a roving seat so that he can more easily follow the various speakers. Other suggestions for the classroom teacher include delaying presentation of information until the hard-of-hearing child is looking, interpreting the remarks of other children if necessary, frequently checking for understanding, and making sure the child knows the subject under discussion (Thomas, 1971). An invaluable aid to a classroom teacher is an overhead tranparency projector for maintaining continuity of communication during lecture presentation.

A classroom teacher also may need to adjust her curriculum itself to facilitate the educational progress of a hard-of-hearing child. Self-instructional materials partially alleviate this problem. For the most part, however, she must adapt her regular materials and procedures. Evaluations of instructional reading level, academic achievement, and written compositional proficiency are particularly valuable baseline data. With this information, she can design or select media and modifications that will benefit this youngster. The teacher should also try to obtain a tutoring assistant.

In the advanced grades the teacher must periodically remind herself that the hearing-impaired child may not be able to take notes and look at her at the same time. Therefore she should help the child to select a classmate who is willing to take duplicate notes by use of carbon or pressure-sensitive paper. Legibility and detail in note taking are important considerations (Stuckless, 1969).

The teacher must also be prepared to face conflicts that might arise between herself, the hard-of-hearing child, and other children in the class. For example, she might become annoyed when a child does not readily accept help. Then again, the child might become upset when a notetaker has neglected his special assignment. Or classmates might resent the special considerations and adjustments being made for the hard-of-hearing child.

The teacher should be aware that many hearing-impaired children have become masters of the neutral response in order to appear to be like other children. They may smile, say "yes," and periodically nod their heads in the affirmative when they do not understand at all. Also they may either keep quiet or try to dominate conversation to avoid revealing their misunderstanding. The teacher must continually be prepared to counsel the child to eliminate this type of undesirable behavior. She must also ward off a tendency by others as well as herself to label such a child as uncooperative, mentally defective, or emotionally disturbed. Together with the principal she must be willing to use all the evaluative, remedial, designing, facilitative, and counseling expertise available in the community.

Postsecondary Programming

Once hearing-impaired students complete elementary and high school programs, postsecondary schooling should be available to them. The first such program, Gallaudet College, was established in Washing-

ton, DC, in 1864. Other postsecondary programs for the hearing impaired did not emerge until 1960, when the program at Riverside City
College was founded in California. The National Technical Institute
for the Deaf (NTID) was created in 1967 and established at the
Rochester Institute of Technology in New York. During the last five
years, at least 28 additional postsecondary or college programs have
been established. Currently, 43 are described in a recent publication
entitled *A Guide To College/Career Programs for Deaf Students*
(Rawlings, Trybus, Delgado, et al., 1975), including a rather large program at California State University in Northridge (Jones and Murphy,
1972).

Since 1968 college facilitative services for hard-of-hearing and oral
deaf college students have been uniquely provided at Utah State University (Berg, 1972; Ivory, 1975). A feature of this postsecondary program is the reliance by students on utilization of listening and speech
skills. In contrast to other facilitative programs for the hearing impaired at the postsecondary level, the Utah program does not utilize
signs and finger spelling for instructional support (Rawlings, Trybus,
Delgado, et al., 1975). Three levels of programming—remedial, facilitative, and independent—accommodate students at varying points of
educational progress. Initial focus is given to upgrading the listening,
speech, language, and remedial reading and mathematical skills of the
special students. Later emphasis is placed on providing backup support
in notetaking, tutoring, and classroom adjustments. Admission requirements tend to require a tenth grade reading level in addition to an
aural–oral rather than a manual background.

The USU facilitative program is administered by the Head of
the Department of Communicative Disorders. The campus Speech and
Hearing Center houses both audiology and speech pathology programs
of professional preparation and offices the supportive program for
hearing-impaired college students. The audiological and remedial spaces of the Center are used for audiometric testing, hearing aid evaluation, tutoring, and communication training. A full-time coordinator-
counselor is hired to direct the facilitative program. The course offer-
ings and supportive services of the entire university, with its 9000 students and 500 faculty members, are at his fingertips.

The coordinator-counselor has a multifaceted role. He recruits,
processes special records, and works closely with the admissions,
housing, and testing and placement offices. He assists with registration
and secures and maintains tutors and notetakers. He orients professors
and functions as an ombudsman. He secures audiological and communication training support and interfaces with the administrator of the
department. He also coordinates the raising of funds and works closely
with parents and vocational rehabilitation counselors from many states.

The program has maintained itself without continuing grant support. It is a visible and viable campus entity. Currently, approximately 25 hearing-impaired young adults from throughout the country are enrolled at USU. Twelve students have graduated to date (Rawlings, Trybus, Delgado, et al., 1975). The graduates include both hard-of-hearing and deaf individuals. Their associations have been with the normally hearing and among themselves.

Instructional development advances are having a positive effect upon the suitability of regular institutions of higher learning for facilitating the schooling of hearing impaired individuals. At Utah State University, for example, a major program has been instituted to encourage and assist professors to improve their respective courses. Course objectives are being pinpointed, mediated materials developed, and evaluation procedures updated. A campus-wide media center has been established, and increasing amounts of self-instructional materials are being located there. The professors are subjected to periodic evaluation on all course work. The evaluation of teaching performance is affecting continual upgrading of course quality, because professor salary increases are related to it. These improvements are in addition to the educational adjustment that has been stimulated through the facilitative program for hearing-impaired college students.

Services Index

Fellendorf (1975) recently developed an instrument designed to predict the effectiveness of education and health care services for the hearing impaired. Called an EDUHEALTH Delivery Service Index, its use is currently limited to young hearing-impaired children and their parents. However it provides a model that could be adapted for use with older children and young adults. At least four procedures must be followed: (1) creation of an instrument, (2) establishment of procedures for using it, (3) identification of the critical predictors, and (4) development of a prediction equation. Sixteen predictors are identified for young hearing-impaired children. They are classified in five areas: hearing aid use, medical diagnosis and guidance, education, informational resources, and general.

SUMMARY

Supportive services for hearing-impaired children and young adults are just beginning to be established in the schools and colleges of the nation. Legislative mandates, professional groups, and new models of delivery are causing rapid evolution and even revolutions in this heretofore neglected area. New breeds of specialists are emerging to provide audiological, clinical, and facilitative services for hearing-impaired individuals attending regular classes. Finally, a new specialization of educational audiology is playing an increasing role in this development.

REFERENCE

Berg F: Breakthrough for the Hard of Hearing Child. Smithfield, Utah, Ear Publication, 1971

Berg F: A model for a facilitative program for hearing impaired college students. Vol Rev 74:370–375, 1972

Berg F: Educational Audiology, Hard of Hearing. Final Report, Project No. 6, OEG 0 71 3681 (603). Logan, Utah State University, 1973

Berg F: Home study coursework in educational audiology. Vol Rev 77:461, 1975

Bitter G: Systems ONE (orientation to normal environment). Vol Rev 77:461, 1975

Dublinski S: The Hearing Clinician. Des Moines, Iowa Department of Public Instruction, 1971

Dyer D: Program Development Guidelines for Hard of Hearing Children in the Tulsa Public Schools. MS Thesis. Logan, Utah State University, 1969

Fellendorf G: An EDUHEALTH Delivery Service Index: A Profile of Education and Health Services to Young Hearing Impaired Children and Their Parents. Washington, DC, AG Bell Assn Deaf, 1975

Fox-Buckley J, Friedrich B, Clemis J, et al: Impedance Audiometry for Identification of Conductive Component in School Children. Las Vegas, Nevada, ASHA Convention, 1974

Fricke J: A Study of Current Practices in Education for Hard of Hearing Children. Washington, DC, Joint Committee on Audiology and Education of the Deaf, of the American Speech and Hearing Association, and the Conference of Executives of American Schools for the Deaf, 1969

Gengel R: Acceptable speech-to-noise ratios for aided speech discrimination by the hearing impaired. J Audiol Res 11:219–222, 1971

Guidelines for Oral Program. American Organization of Educators of the Hearing Impaired. Washington, DC, AG Bell Assn Deaf, 1971

Healey W: National Profile for the Hard of Hearing Child. Proceedings of Institute on Job Task in Educational Audiology. Supported by BEH, OE Project No. 6. Logan, Utah State University, 1971

Huddleston R: Job Tasks of the Hearing Clinician. Proceedings of Institute on Job Task in Educational Audiology. Supported by BEH, OE Project No. 6. Logan, Utah State University, 1971

Ivory R: Facilitative Program for the Hearing Impaired. Department of Communicative Disorders. Logan, Utah State University, 1975

Jerger J (ed): Handbook of Clinical Impedance Audiometry. Dobbs Ferry, New York, American Electromedics, 1975

Johnson F: Evaluation of Habilitative Endeavor in Auditory Remediation. Project H.E.A.R., by Berg F. Spencer, West Virginia, Roane County Schools, 1974a

Johnson F: Habilitative Endeavor in Auditory Remediation. ESEA III Project H.E.A.R. Spencer, West Virginia, Roane County Schools, 1974b

Jones R, Murphy H: The Northridge plan for higher education of the deaf. Am Ann Deaf 117:612–616, 1972

McCandless G: Future directions. In Jerger J (ed): Handbook of Clinical Impedance Audiometry. Dobbs Ferry, New York, American Electromedics, 1975

McCandless G, Thomas G: Impedance audiometry as a screening procedure for middle ear disease. Trans Am Acad Ophthalmol Otolaryngol 78:2, 1974

Northcott W: Introduction. In Northcott W (ed): The Hearing Impaired Child in a Regular Classroom. Washington, DC, AG Bell Assn Deaf, pp 1–10, 1973

Pauls L: Management Guide for the Hearing Impaired Child in the Regular Classroom. ESEA III Project. Pontiac, Michigan, Oakland Schools, 1974

Rawlings B, Trybus R, Delgado G, et al: A Guide to College/Career Programs for Deaf Students. Washington, DC, Gallaudet College, and Rochester, New York, National Technical Institute for the Deaf, 1975

Ross M: Model Educational Cascade for Hearing Impaired Children. In Nix G (ed): Mainstream Education for Hearing Impaired Children and Youth. New York and London, Grune & Stratton, p. 229, 1976

Sanders D: Noise conditions in normal school classrooms. Except Child 31:344–353, 1965

Shattuck P: Vision and Hearing Medicheck Activities. Springfield, Illinois Department of Public Health, October 26, 1973

Sommers R: Hearing services for school children: Retesting, referral and rehabilitation. Part II. Maico Audiological Library Series 6:No. 7, 1968

Standards and guidelines for comprehensive language, speech, and hearing programs in the schools. Washington, D.C., American Speech and Hearing Association, 1973–74

Stuckless R: A Notetaking Procedure for Deaf Students in Regular Classes. Rochester, New York, National Technical Institute for the Deaf, 1969

Thomas D: Suggestions for Regular Classroom Teachers. Regional Facility for the Deaf. Portland, Oregon, Public Schools, 1971

Willeford J: Personal communication. Fort Collins, Colorado State University, January 25, 1971

Yater V: The Hearing Clinician in St. Louis Special School District. Proceedings of the Institute on Job Task in Educational Audiology. Supported by BEH, OE, Project No. 6. Logan, Utah State University, 1971

Author Index

Subject Index